Mrs. Wud
from
Jill

CRUEL AS THE GRAVE

A NOVEL

BY
Mrs. EMMA D. E. N. SOUTHWORTH

Author of "Ishmael," "Self-Raised," "The Missing Bride," "A Beautiful Fiend,"
"How He Won Her," "A Noble Lord," "The Artist's Love," "Tried for
her Life," "Fatal Marriage," "The Bride's Fate," "The Widow's Son,"
"Family Doom," "The Prince of Darkness," "Victor's
Triumph," "The Curse of Clifton," "Spectre Lover,"
"Maiden Widow," "Fair Play," "Allworth
Abbey," "The Deserted Wife," "The
Changed Brides," "Mother-
in-Law," Etc., Etc.

NEW YORK
HURST AND COMPANY
PUBLISHERS

MRS. SOUTHWORTH SERIES

UNIFORM WITH THIS VOLUME
By MRS. E. D. E. N. SOUTHWORTH

Allworth Abbey.
Beautiful Fiend, A.
Bride's Fate, The.
Capitola, the Madcap.
Changed Brides.
Cruel as the Grave.
Curse of Clifton, The.
Deserted Wife.
Discarded Daughter.
Hidden Hand.
India.
Ishmael; or, In the Depths.

Lost Heiress, The.
Miriam, the Avenger.
Missing Bride, The.
Mother-in-Law, The.
Mystery of a Dark Hollow.
Retribution.
Self-Raised; or, From the Depths.
Three Beauties, The.
Tried for Her Life.
Victor's Triumph.
Vivia.

Price, postpaid, 50c. each, or any three books for $1.25

HURST & COMPANY
PUBLISHERS, NEW YORK

CONTENTS.

CHAPTER		PAGE
I.	The Berners of the Burning Hearts	5
II.	John Lyon Howe	9
III.	Sybil Berners	14
IV.	The Beautiful Stranger	26
V.	The Landlord's Story	28
VI.	Rosa Blondelle	38
VII.	Down in the Dark Vale	48
VIII.	Black Hall	52
IX.	The Guest-Chambers	59
X.	The Jealous Bride	66
XI.	Love and Jealousy	76
XII.	"Cruel as the Grave"	83
XIII.	More than the Bitterness of Death	95
XIV.	The First Fatal Hallow Eve	101
XV.	The Masquerade Ball	109
XVI.	On the Watch	114
XVII.	Driven to Desperation	119
XVIII.	Lying in Wait	137
XIX.	Swooping Down	144
XX.	The Search	151
XXI.	Sybil's Flight	157
XXII.	The Haunted Chapel	165
XXIII.	The Solitude is Invaded	174
XXIV.	The Verdict and the Visitor	180
XXV.	The Fall of the Dubarrys	192
XXVI.	The Specter	203
XXVII.	Fearful Waiting	214
XXVIII.	A Ghastly Procession	222
XXIX.	Ghostly and Mysterious	239
XXX.	Flight and Pursuit	250
XXXI.	The Arrest	265
XXXII.	A Desperate Venture	275
XXXIII.	A Fatal Crisis	284
XXXIV.	The Pursuit	292
XXXV.	The Fugitives	300

CRUEL AS THE GRAVE.

CHAPTER I.

THE BERNERS OF THE BURNING HEARTS.

"Their love was like the lava flood
That burns in Etna's breast of flame."

NEAR the end of a dark autumn-day, not many years ago, a young couple, returning from their bridal tour, arrived by steamer at the old city of Norfolk ; and, taking a hack, drove directly to the best inn.

They were attended by the gentleman's valet and the lady's maid, and encumbered besides with a great amount of baggage, so that altogether their appearance was so promising that the landlord of the "Anchor" came forward in person to receive them and bow them into the best parlor.

The gentleman registered himself and his party as Mr. and Mrs. Lyon Berners, of Black Hall, Virginia, and two servants.

"We shall need a private parlor and chamber communicating for our own use, and a couple of bedrooms for our servants," said Mr. Berners, as he handed his hat and cane to the bowing waiter.

"They shall be prepared immediately," answered the polite landlord.

"We shall remain here only for the night, and go on in the morning, and should like to have two inside and two outside places secured in the Staunton stage-coach for to-morrow."

"I will send and take them at once, sir."

"Thanks. We should also like tea got ready as soon as possible in our private parlor."

"Certainly, sir. What would you like for tea?"

"Oh, anything you please, so that it is nice and neatly served," said Mr. Berners, with a slightly impatient wave of his hand as if he would have been rid of his obsequious host.

"Ah-ha! anything I please! It is easy to see what ails him. He lives upon love just now; but he'll care more about his bill of fare a few weeks hence," chuckled the landlord, as he left the public parlor to execute his guest's orders.

The bridegroom was no sooner left alone with his bride than he seated her in the easiest arm-chair, and began with affectionate zeal to untie her bonnet-strings and unclasp her mantle.

"You make my maid a useless appendage, dear Lyon," said the little lady, smiling up in his eyes.

"Because I like to do everything for you myself, sweet Sybil; because I am jealous of every hand that touches your dear person, except my own," he murmured tenderly as he removed her bonnet, and with all his worshiping soul glowing through his eyes, gazed upon her beautiful and beaming face.

"You love me so much, dear Lyon! You love me so much! Yet not too much either! for oh! if you should ever cease to love me, or even if you were ever to love me *less*,—I—I dare not think what I should do!" she muttered in a long, deep, shuddering tone.

"Sweet Sybil," he breathed, drawing her to his bosom and pressing warm kisses on her crimson lips—"sweetest Sybil, it is not possible for the human heart to love *more* than I do, but I can never love you less!"

"I do believe you, dearest Lyon! With all my heart I do!—Yet—yet——"

"Yet what, sweet love?"

She lifted her face from his bosom and gazing intently in his eyes, said:

"Yet, Lyon, if you knew the prayer that I never fail to put up, day and night! What do you think it is for, dear Lyon?"

"I know; it is for Heaven's blessing to rest upon our wedded lives."

"Yes, my prayer is for that always, of course! but that is not what I mean now. That is not the stronger,

stronger prayer which I offer up from the deeps of my spirit in almost an agony of supplication!"

"And what is that prayer, so awful in its earnestness, dear love?"

"Oh, Lyon! it is *that you may never love me less than now, or if you should, that I may never live to know it,*" she breathed with an intensity of suppressed emotion that drew all the glowing color from her crimson cheeks and lips and left them pale as marble.

"Why, you beautiful mad creature! You are a true daughter of your house! A Berners of the burning heart! A Berners of the boiling blood! A Berners of whom it has been said, that it is almost as fatal to be loved, as to be hated, by one of them! Dear Sybil! never doubt my love; never be jealous of me, if you would not destroy us both," he earnestly implored.

"I do not doubt you, dearest Lyon; I am not jealous of you! What cause, indeed, have I to be so? But—but——"

"But what, my darling?"

"——Ever since I have been in this house, a darkness and coldness and weight has fallen upon my spirits, that I cannot shake off—a burden, as of some impending calamity! And as there is no calamity that can possibly affect me so much as the lessening of your love, I naturally think most of that," she answered, with a heavy sigh.

"Dear love! this depression is only reaction! fatigue! the effect of this damp, dull, dreary room! We will change all this!" said Lyon Berners, cheerfully, as he pulled the bell-cord and rang a peal that presently brought the waiter to his presence.

"Are our rooms ready?" shortly demanded Mr. Berners.

"Just this moment ready, sir," answered the man, with a bow.

"Gather up these articles, then, and show us to our rooms," said Mr. Berners, pointing to a collection of outer garments and traveling bags that occupied a center-table.

With another bow the man loaded himself with the personal effects of the guests and led the way up-stairs.

Mr. Berners, drawing his wife's arm through his own, followed the waiter to a cheerful little private parlor, where the bright red carpet on the floor, the bright red curtains at the windows, the bright red covers of the chairs and sofas, the glowing coal fire in the grate, and above all the neatly spread tea-table, with its snowy damask table-cloth, and its service of pure French china, invited the hungry and weary travelers to refreshment and repose.

Through a pair of partly drawn sliding doors a vista was opened to a clean and quiet chamber, furnished to match the parlor, with the same bright-red carpet, window curtains, and chair covers, but also with a white-draperied tent-bedstead, with bed-pillows and coverings white and soft as swan's-down. In the glow of the coal fire in the inner room sat and waited a pretty mulatto girl, Delia, or Dilly, the dressing maid of Mrs. Berners.

On seeing her mistress enter the parlor, Dilly quickly arose and met her, and handed a chair and relieved the waiter of his burden of portable personal property, which she hastened to carry into the chamber to put away.

"Bring in the tea immediately and send my own man Hannibal here to attend us," said the guest to the waiter, who promptly left the room to execute the orders.

"Come, my darling! Take this easy-chair in the corner and make yourself comfortable! Here is a scene to inspire the saddest heart with cheerfulness," said the bridegroom cordially, as he drew forward the easy arm-chair and led his bride to it.

She sank into the soft seat and smiled her satisfaction.

In a few moments the waiters of the inn entered and arranged a delicious little repast upon the table and then withdrew, leaving Hannibal, the faithful servant of the bridegroom, to attend his master and mistress at their tea.

The young pair sat down to the table. And in that quiet and cheerful scene of enjoyment, the young bride recovered her spirits. The transient shadow that had for a moment darkened the splendor of her joy, even as a passing cloud for an instant obscures the glory of the sun, had vanished, leaving her all smiles and gayety.

To say that these wedded lovers were very happy,

wo d scarcely express the delirium of pure joy in which they had dreamed away their days and nights for the last few weeks—joy that both were too young and untried to know could not last forever, could not indeed even last long—joy so elevated in its insanity as almost to tempt some thunderbolt of malignant fate to fall upon it with destroying force, even as the highly rarefied air sometimes draws on the whirlwind and the storm.

But then the story of their loves was rare and strange, and almost justified the intensity of their mutual devotion, and that story is briefly this:

CHAPTER II.

JOHN LYON HOWE.

"A brow half martial and half diplomatic,
An eye upsoaring like an eagle's wing."

JOHN LYON HOWE was the youngest son of a planter, residing in one of the wildest mountain regions in central Virginia. The elder Howe was blessed with a large family, and cursed with a heavily mortgaged estate—a combination of circumstances not unusual among the warmhearted, generous and extravagant people of the Old Dominion.

John Lyon Howe had been educated in the Law School of the University of Virginia, where, at the age of twenty-three, he graduated with the highest honors.

Then, instead of commencing his professional life in one of the great Eastern cities, or striking out for the broad fields of enterprise opened in the Far West, young Howe, to the astonishment of all who were acquainted with the talents and ambition of the new lawyer, returned to his native county and opened his law office in Blackville; a small hamlet lying at the foot of the Black Valley, and enjoying the honor and profit of being the county-seat.

But the young lawyer had strong motives for his actions. He had great talent, an intense passion for politics, and quite as much State pride as personal ambition. He

wished to distinguish himself; yes, but not in Massa..u-
setts or Minnesota, nor in any other place except in his
native State, his dear old Virginia.

Sometime to represent her in the National Congress,
and to do her service and credit there, was the highest
goal of his youthful aspirations.

For this cause, he settled in the obscure hamlet of
Blackville, and opened his law office in one of the base-
ment-rooms of the county court-house.

While the courts were in session he attended them
regularly, and did a good deal of business in the way of
gratuitous counseling and pleading; advocating and de-
fending with great ability and success the cause of the
poor and oppressed, and winning much honor and praise,
but very little money, not enough, indeed, to pay his
office rent, or renew his napless hat and threadbare
coat.

Besides his unprofitable professional labors, he engaged
in equally unprofitable political contests.

He took the liberal view of statecraft, and sought to
open the minds of his fellow-citizens to a just and wise
policy, or what he, in his young enthusiasm, conceived to
be such. He wrote stirring leaders for the local papers,
and made rousing speeches at the political meetings.

He was everywhere spoken of as a rising young man,
who was sure to reach a high position some day. Yes!
some day ; but that desired day seemed very far distant
to the desponding young lawyer.

And to make his probation still more painful, he was in
love! not as men are who are taken with a new face every
year of their lives, but as the heroes of old used to be—
for once and forever! profoundly, passionately, desperately in love, almost despairingly, in love, since she
whom he loved was at once the richest heiress, the
greatest beauty, and the proudest lady in the whole community—Sybil Berners! Miss Berners, of Black Hall!—
in social position as far above the briefless young lawyer
as the sun above the earth ; at least so said those who observed this presumptuous passion, and predicted for the
young lover, should he ever really aspire to her hand, the
fate of Phaeton, to be consumed in the splendor of her
sphere, and cast down blackened to his native earth.

Had they who cavilled at his high-placed love but known the truth; how she whom he so worshipped, on her part, adored him? But this he himself did not know, or even suspect. Had he possessed much less of a fine, high-toned sense of honor, he might, by wooing the lady, have found this out for himself; but he, an almost penniless young man, was much too proud to ask the hand of the wealthy heiress. Or had he possessed a little more personal vanity, he might have suspected the truth; for certainly there was not a handsomer man in the whole county than was this briefless young lawyer with the napless hat and the threadbare coat. His person was of that medium height and just proportions necessary to give perfect elegance of form and grace of motion. His features were classic, with the straight forehead, hooked nose, short upper lip, and pointed chin of the strong old Roman type. His complexion was fair, his eyes blue, and his hair and beard a golden auburn. Added to these attractions, there was an intense magnetic power in the gaze of his dark eyes, and in the tone of his deep voice, a power that few could resist, and certainly not Sybil Berners.

But who and what besides heiress and beauty was Sybil Berners? To tell you all she was, I must first tell you something about her family, the "Berners of Black Hall."

Theirs was an old family, and a historical name, interwoven with the destinies of the two hemispheres. Their house was older than the history of the new world, and almost as ancient as the fables of the old world.

They were among the first lords of the manor in Colonial Virginia, and they claimed descent from a ducal house whose patent of nobility dated back to the first months of the Norman Conquest of England.

They had been great in history and in story; great in the field and the forum; great in the old country and in the new. They had been a brave, fierce, cruel, and despotic race, and few ever loved as these Berners loved, or hated as they hated. In the intensity of their love or their hate they were capable of suffering or inflicting death; these Berners, whose friendship was almost as fatal as their enmity; these Berners, who "never spared man in their hate or woman in their love;" these Berners of the burning heart; these Berners of the boiling blood; these Berners of Black Hall! and whose sole representative now was Sybil, the last daughter of their line, who concentrated in her own ardent, intense nature all the most beautiful, all the most terrible attributes of her strong and fiery race.

I said that she was the richest heiress as well as the most beautiful girl of the country.

She was the inheritor of the famous Black Valley manor, holding besides its own home plantation, several of the most productive and valuable farms in the neighborhood.

There is not in all the mountain region of Virginia a wilder, darker, gloomier glade than that forming the home manor of the Berners family, and known as the Black Valley. It is a long, deep, narrow vale, lying between high, steep ridges of iron-gray rock, half covered with a growth of deep-green stunted cedars.

At the head or northern extremity of the vale springs a cascade, called, for the darkness of its color, the Black Torrent. It rushes, roaring, down the side of the precipice, now hiding under a heavy growth of evergreen, now bursting into light as it foams over the face of some rock, until at length it tumbles down to the foot of the mountain and flows along through the bottom of the Valley, until about half way down its length, it widens into a little lake, called from its hue, the Black Water, or the Black Pond; then narrowing again, it flows on down past the little hamlet of Blackville, situated at the foot or southern extremity of the Black Valley.

The ancient manor house, known as the Black Hall, stands on a rising ground on the west side of the Black Water with its old pleasure gardens running down to the very edge of the lake.

It is a large, rambling, irregularly-formed old house, built of the iron-gray rocks dug from the home quarries; and it is scarcely to be distinguished from the iron-gray precipices that tower all around it.

The manor had been in the possession of the same family from the time of King James the First, who made a grant of the land to Reginald Berners, the first Lord of the Manor.

Bertram Berners was the seventh in descent from Reginald. He married first a lady of high rank, the daughter of the colonial governor of Virginia. This union, which was neither fruitful nor happy, lasted more than thirty years, after which the high-born wife died.

Finding himself at the age of sixty a childless widower and the last of his name, he resolved to marry again in the hope of having heirs. He chose for his second wife a young lady of good but impoverished family, the orphan niece of a neighboring planter.

But the new wife only half fulfilled her husband's hopes, when, a year after their marriage, she presented him with one fair daughter, the Sybil of our story.

Even this gift cost the delicate mother her life; for although she did not die immediately, yet from the day of Sybil's birth, she fell into a long and lingering decline which finally terminated in death.

Old Bertram Berners was nearly seventy years of age, when he laid his young wife in her early grave. Although he had been grievously disappointed in his hopes of a male heir, yet he was not mad enough, at his advanced period of life, to try matrimony again. He wisely determined to devote the few remaining days of his life to the rearing of his little daughter, then a child seven years of age.

Old Bertram loved and spoiled the infant as none but an old man can love or spoil his only child, who is besides the offspring of his age. He would not part with her to send her to school; but he himself became her instructor until she was more than ten years old.

After that, as she began to approach womanhood, he engaged a succession of governesses, each one of whom excessively annoyed him by persistently trying to marry him for his money, and who consequently got herself politely dismissed.

Next he tried a succession of tutors, but this second plan worked even worse than the first; for each one of the tutors in his turn tried to marry the heiress for the fortune, and naturally enough, got himself kicked out of the house.

So the plan of home education prospered badly. Perhaps old Bertram had been singularly unfortunate in his selection of teachers. It must have been so indeed, since he had been accustomed to say that "they all were as bad as they could be, and each one was worse than all the rest."

Thus the literary training of the heiress had been carried on in the most capricious, fitful and irregular manner, the worst suited to her, who more than most girls required the discipline of a firm and steady rule.

The educational result to her was a very superficial knowledge of literature, arts, and sciences, and a very imperfect acquaintance with ancient and modern languages.

She was in the habit of saying sarcastically, that "she had an utter confusion of ideas on the subjects of algebra, astronomy, and all the other branches of a polite education;" that, for instance, she never could remember whether the "Pons Asinorum" were a plant or a problem, or if it was Napoleon Bonaparte that discovered America and Christopher Columbus who lost the battle of Waterloo, or *vice versa*.

And after all, this was but a trifling exaggeration of the neglected condition of her mind.

CHAPTER III.

SYBIL BERNERS.

"All that's best of dark and bright
Meet in her aspect and her eye."

SYBIL BERNERS was at this time about eighteen years of age—a beautiful, black-haired, bright-eyed little brunette, full of fire, spirit, strength, and self-will. She was a law to herself. No one, not even her aged father, had the slightest control over her except through her affections, when they could be gained, or her passions, when they could be aroused; but this last means was seldom tried, for no one cared to raise the storm that none could quell.

Her father was now nearly eighty years old. And fondly, jealously, selfishly as he loved this darling daughter of his age, he wished to see her safely married before he should be called from the earth.

And certainly the beautiful heiress had suitors enough to select from—suitors drawn no less by her personal charms than by her great fortune. But one and all were politely refused by the fastidious maiden, who every one said was so very hard to please.

But even if Sybil Berners had accepted any one among the numerous suitors for her hand, the conditions of her father's consent would have been made rather difficult. The husband of the heiress would have been required to assume the name and arms of Berners in order to perpetuate the family patronymic, and to live with his wife at the old manor house in order not to separate the only child from her aged father. And it was not every proud young Virginian who would have given up his own family name either for a fortune or a beauty. But none of her suitors were put to the test, for Sybil promptly and unconditionally refused all offers of marriage.

And the reason of all this was, that Miss Berners of Black Hall loved a poor, briefless young lawyer, who had nothing but his handsome person, his brilliant mind, and his noble heart to recommend him. When, or where, or how her love for him began, she herself could never have told. Since his return from the university she had seen him every Sunday at church, and had grown to look and to long for his appearance there, until it came to this pass with her soul, that the very house of God seemed empty until *his* place was filled. And beside this, she often saw him and heard him speak at political and other public meetings, which she always attended only to beam in the sunshine of his presence, only to drink in the music of his voice. She took in all the local papers only to read his leaders and dream over his thoughts.

Moreover, she felt by a sure instinct that he passionately adored her, even while ignorant of her love for him, and silent upon the subject of his own passion.

This state of affairs exasperated the fiery and self-willed little beauty almost to frenzy. She had never in her life been contradicted or opposed. No desire of her heart had ever been left for a moment unsatisfied. She never knew until now the meaning of suspense or disappointment. And now here was a man whom she wildly loved, and who worshiped her, but who, from some delicate pride in his poverty, *would* not speak, while she, of course, *could* not.

Yet Sybil Berners was no weak "Viola," who would

"Let concealment, like a worm i' the bud,
Feed on her damask cheek, and pine in thought."

She was rather a strong "Helena," who would dare all and bear all to gain her lover.

Sybil did all that a young lady of her rank could do in the premises. She made her doting father give dinner parties and invite her lover to them. But the briefless young lawyer in the napless hat and threadbare coat never accepted one of these invitations, for the very simple reason that he had no evening dress in which to appear.

Under these circumstances, where any other young girl might have grown languid and sorrowful, Sybil became excitable and violent. She had always had the fiery temper of her race, but it had very seldom been kindled by a breath of provocation. Now, however, it frequently broke out without the slightest apparent cause. No one in the house could account for this accession of ill-temper —not her anxious father, nor Miss Tabitha Winterose, the housekeeper, not Joseph Joy, the house steward, nor any of the maids or men-servants under them.

"She's possessed of the devil," said Miss Winterose, to her confidant, the house steward.

"That's nothing new. All the Berners is possessed of *that* possession. It's entailed family property, and can't be got rid of," grimly responded Joe.

"Something has crossed her; something has crossed her very much," muttered her old father to himself, as he sat alone in his arm-chair in the warm chimney-corner of his favorite sitting-room.

Yes, indeed, everything crossed her. She was unhappy for the first time in her life, and she thought it was clearly the duty of her father or some other one of her slaves to make her happy. She was kept waiting, and it was every-

body's fault, and everybody should be made to suffer for
it. It was no use to reason with Sybil Berners. One
might as well have reasoned with a conflagration.

It was about this time, too, that her aged father began
to feel symptoms that warned him of the approach of
that sudden death by congestion of the brain, which had
terminated the existence of so many of his ancestors.

More than ever he desired to see his motherless daughter
well married before he should be called away from her.
So, one evening, he sent for Sybil to come into his sitting-
room, and when she obeyed his summons, and came and
sat down on a low ottoman beside his arm-chair, he said,
laying his hand lovingly on her black, curly head:

"My darling, I am very old, and may be taken from
you any day, any hour, and I would like to see you well
married before I go."

"Dear father, don't talk so. You may live twenty
years yet," answered the daughter, with a blending of
affectionate solicitude and angry impatience in her tones
and looks, for Sybil was very fond of the old man, and
also very intolerant of unpleasant subjects.

"Well, well, my dear, since you prefer it, I will live
twenty years longer to please you—*if I can*. But
whether I live or die, my daughter, I wish to see you well
married."

"Ah, father, why can you not leave me free?"

"Because, my darling, if anything should happen to me,
you would be left utterly without protection; your hand
would become the aim of every adventurer in the county;
you would become the prey of some one among them who
would squander your fortune, abuse your person, and
break your heart."

"You know very well, father, that I should break such
a villain's head first. *I* a victim—*I* the prey of a fortune-
hunter, or the slave of a brute! I look as if I was likely
to be—do I not? Father, you insult your daughter by
the thought," exclaimed Sybil, with flushing cheeks and
flashing eyes.

"There, there, my dear! don't flame up!" said the old
man, lying his hand upon the fiery creature's head; "be
quiet as you can, Sybil—I cannot bear excitement now,
child."

"Forgive me, dear father, and forbear, if you love me, for such talk as this. I never could become an ill-used, suffering, sniveling wife. I *detest* the picture as I utterly despise all weak and whimpering women. I have no sympathy whatever for your abused wives—even for your dethroned or beheaded queens. Why should a wife permit herself to be abused, or a queen suffer herself to be dethroned or beheaded, without first having done something to redeem herself from the contemptible rule of a victim, even if it was to change it for the awful one of criminal——"

"—Hush, Sybil, hush! You know not what you say. The Saviour of the world——"

"—Was a divine martyr, father," said Sybil, reverently bowing her head—" was a divine martyr, not a victim. All who suffer and die in a great cause are martyrs; but those who suffer and die for nothing but of their own weakness are victims, with whom I have no sympathy. I never could be a *victim*, father."

"Heaven help you, Sybil!"

"You need not fear for me, father. I can take care of myself as well as if I were a son, instead of a daughter of the House of Berners," said Sybil, haughtily.

"You may be able to protect yourself from all others, but can you always protect yourself *from yourself?*" sighed the old man.

Sybil did not answer.

"But, to come back to the point from which you started, like the fiery young filly that you are—Sybil, I greatly desire to see you married to some worthy young gentleman whom you can love and I approve."

"Where can you find such an one, father?" murmured Sybil, with a quick, strange, wild hope springing up in her heart.

What if he should speak of the young lawyer? But that was not likely. He spoke of some one else.

"There is Ernest Godfree. No better match for you in the county. And I'm sure he worships the very ground you walk on."

Sybil made an angry gesture exclaiming:

"Then I wish he would have respect enough for the

ground he worships to keep himself off it altogether! I hate that man!"

"Well, well, hate is a poor return for love! But we'll say no more of him. But there's Captain Pendleton, a brave young officer."

"I wish his bravery were better employed in fighting the Indians on the frontier instead of besieging our house. I cannot endure that man!"

"Let him pass then! Next there is Charles Hanbury——"

"Ugh! the ugly little wretch."

"But he is so good, so wise, for so young a man. And he is your devoted slave."

"Then I wish my slave would obey his owner's orders, and keep out of her sight."

"Sybil, you are incorrigible," sighed the old man, but he did not yield his main point."

One after another he proposed for her consideration all the eligible young bachelors of the neighborhood, who, he knew, were ready upon the slightest encouragement to renew their once rejected suits for the hand of the beauty and heiress.

But one after another Sybil, with some sarcastic word, dismissed.

"Sybil, you are a strange, wayward girl! It seems to me that for any man to love you is to take a sure road to your hatred! And yet, oh, my dear! I wish to see you safely married. Is there not one among those whom you might prefer to all the rest?"

"No, my father, not one whom I could endure for an instant as a lover."

"And oh! when I feel this fatal rising of the heart and fulness of the head—this Wave of Death that is sure to bear me off sooner or later to the Ocean of Eternity—Oh, then, my Sybil, how my soul travails for you!" groaned the old man.

"Father! do you so much wish to see me married?"

"I wish it more than anything else in the world, my child."

"Father, you have named every young man in the neighborhood whom you would like as a son-in-law?"

"Every one, my daughter."

"Are you sure?"

"Quite sure, my love. Why do you ask?"

She slid down from her low ottoman to the floor, and laid her arms upon his knees and her beautiful black ringleted head upon her folded hands, and whispered:

"Because, dear father, there is one whom you have forgotten to name; one who loves me, and is altogether well worthy to be called your son."

"Ah!" cried the old man fiercely, under his breath—"a fortune-hunter, on my life! the danger is nearer than I had even apprehended!"

"No, father, no! He is as far as possible from being what you say!" fervently exclaimed Sybil.

"He is wealthy, then?"

"No, no, no! he is poor in everything but in goodness and wisdom!"

"Oh, no doubt you think him rich in these! But who is he, unhappy child? What is his name?"

Very subdued came the answer. Old Bertram was obliged to bend his gray head to his daughter's lips, and put his shriveled hand behind his ear to catch the sound of her low voice.

"He is the young lawyer newly settled in Blackville, whose praise is on everybody's lips."

JOHN LYON HOWE!" exclaimed the old man, throwing up his head in astonishment.

"Yes, father," breathed the girl.

"And he loves you?"

She nodded.

"And you love him?"

She nodded again.

"A briefless young lawyer, with a long list of impoverished brothers and sisters, aunts, uncles, and cousins! Bad enough; but not as it might have been. She can gain nothing by that connection! But then she need not lose anything either," murmured the old man to himself. After reflecting for a few moments, with his head upon his breast, he suddenly raised his eyes and exclaimed:

"But I have never seen the young man at this house!"

"No, father!"

"Nor at any other house where we visit."

"No, father; for although he receives many invitations to visit his friends, he accepts none. Father, I think he cannot afford to do so."

"Cannot afford to visit! Why?"

"Visiting requires dress, and dress money. And he does so much gratuitous work now in the beginning of his career that he has but little money; and his father will not help him at all, because they differ in politics."

"Yes, I know they do; but the young man is quite right I agree with his views perfectly. He will make his mark in the world some of these days, and then his father will be proud of him."

Sybil blushed with delight to hear her lover so praised by one in whose hands their happiness rested.

"But, my child, he was wrong and you were wrong to have entered into any engagement without my sanction," said the old man very gravely.

"There is no engagement, father," gently answered Sybil.

"Ah! no engagement? that is well! By my soul, though, it was not right for him even to have wooed you without my consent! Nor can I conceive what opportunity he has ever had to do so. He never comes here."

"He has never wooed me, dear father."

"Eh!"

"He has never sought my hand."

"But I thought you gave me to understand that you love each other!"

"So we do, father."

"Then, if he loves you, why don't he come and tell me so like an honorable man?"

"Father, he has never even told *me* so."

"Eh!"

"He has never breathed a word of love to me."

"Then how the deuce do you know that he loves you, girl?"

"Oh, by every glance of his eyes, by every tone of his voice, and by my own heart! Oh, father, do you think I would bear to tell you this, if I were not sure of it."

"Umph, umph! But why don't he speak?—that's what I want to know! Why don't he speak?"

"Dear father, can you not comprehend that he is too proud to do so?"

"Too proud! By my word! It is a new hearing that a Howe should be too proud to seek an alliance with a Berners!" exclaimed old Bertram hotly, rising from his chair.

"Old age ne'er cooled the Douglas blood,"

and it had not cooled his.

Sybil smiled to see how utterly he had misunderstood her, and making him sit down again, she said:

"You dear old darling, it is not that! It is the very opposite to that. It is because he is poor and we are rich, and he is too proud to be called a fortune-hunter."

"Oh! I understand! I understand!

' Among the rest young Edwin bowed,
But never told his love.
Wisdom and worth were all he had.'"

"Yes, dear father, that is just the truth. You wish me to marry; but, dear, dear father, I can never bring myself to marry any one but *him ;* and he loves me truly, but does not seek me!" she breathed in a low and tremulous tone, half smothered also by the hands with which she covered her blushing face.

"Now what am I to do in this case? I have nothing against the young man whatever, except his poverty and his long line of poor relations, that will be sure to be a burden to him!" grumbled old Bertram to himself.

"But, father, we are so rich! We have enough for so many people," pleaded Sybil.

"Not enough to enrich all the Howes, my dear! But I like the young man, I really do like him, and if he had more money, and less relations, I should prefer him to any young man in the neighborhood for a son-in-law."

"O father, dear father, thank you, thank you for saying that," exclaimed Sybil, fervently kissing his hands.

"And now that you have told me your mind, what do you want me to do, my darling?" he inquired, returning her caresses.

"Oh, dear father! an old man like you must know! I

do want you to give Lyon help and encouragement as you know best how to do it, without wounding his pride. You sympathize with his political principles; let him know that you do. You admire his character; let him feel that you do."

"What else?"

"This. Since old Mr. Godwin died you have had no agent for your large estate, and its accounts must be falling into disorder. Lyon is a lawyer, you know. Offer him the agency of your estate, with a liberal salary."

"Upon my word, I never thought of that before. Here for three months I have been thinking whom I could get as an agent, and m ;h as I esteemed that young man I never once thought of applying to him! But the fact is, I never looked upon him in the light of a business man, but only as a brilliant barrister, and eloquent pleader."

"Yet, father, you know he *must* be a good business man to have collected such great stores of statistics as he has always at command."

"Well, my love, I will go to-day and offer him the agency. Now what next?"

"He was too poor and too proud to come before, but as your agent, father, you must bring him often to the house on business."

"And then?"

"You must leave the rest to me."

Thus it was that the young lawyer became the agent for the great Black Valley Manor. This agency included not only the management of the revenues from several rich farms, but also those from the stone quarries, iron mines, and the water mill at the head of the valley, and also from the real estate in the village at the foot, all of which was included the Black Valley Manor.

The new agent was frequently called to Black Hall, where he was always received with the utmost courtesy. And as the acquaintance between the proprietor and the agent ripened into intimacy, a deep and strong attachment grew between them.

"Youth never showed itself wiser or better than in this young man," murmured Mr. Berners to himself.

"Age was never so venerable and beautiful as in this old man," thought John Lyon Howe to himself.

The old man loaded the young one with many marks of his esteem and affection. The young man returned these with the warmest gratitude and highest reverence.

When John Lyon Howe, with his heart filled with love for Sybil Berners, first entered Black Hall, it was without the slightest suspicion of her responsive love for him. But when they were thrown so much together, he was not very long in making the discovery so delightful to his soul, and yet—so trying too! for, as a man of good principles, there seemed to be but one course left open to him —the course of self-denial! He loved the great heiress, and had unintentionally won her love! Therefore he must fly from her presence, trying to forget her, hoping that she might forget him.

He summoned up courage for the sacrifice, and went into the study of his employer and in a few words told him that he had come to say good-by.

The astonished old man looked up for an explanation.

John Lyon Howe gave it to him.

"And so you wish to leave me, never to return to the Hall, because you love my daughter."

The young man bowed in silence; but could not conceal the misery it caused him to make this acknowledgment.

"But why should that oblige you to leave the house?" inquired Mr. Berners.

"Oh, sir! can you ask?" exclaimed Mr. Howe.

"Oh, I see! the little witch has refused you!" exclaimed old Bertram with a twinkle in his eye. "Come, is it not so?"

"Sir, I have never abused your confidence so far as to seek her hand I could not make so base a return for your kindness to me."

"Oh, you have never asked her to marry you! How in the world, then, can you know whether she will accept you or not? or, consequently, whether it will be necessary for you to leave or not?"

"Oh, sir! what is that you would say?" exclaimed the young man, in quick, broken tones, while his face turned pale with agitation.

"Nonsense, my boy! When I was young a youth didn't require so much encouragement to woo a maiden.

before you make up your mind to leave me, go and ask Sybil's consent to the step."

"Oh, sir! oh, Mr. Berners! do you mean this?" gasped the young man, catching at the back of the chair for support. He was inured to sorrow, but not to joy. And this joy was so sudden and overwhelming that he reeled under it.

"I mean what I say Mr. Howe. I esteem and respect you. I sanction your addresses to my daughter," said old Bertram, speaking with more gravity and dignity than he had before displayed.

John Lyon fervently kissed his old friend's hand, and went immediately in search of Sybil. And that same night, old Bertram had the pleasure of joining their hands together in solemn betrothal.

"And now I can die happy," said the old man, earnestly; "for it was not another great fortune, but a good husband that I coveted for my darling child."

Ten days from this night, old Bertram Berners dropped into his last sleep. He was well and happy up to the last hour of his life. The "Wave of Death," found him in his arm-chair, and bore him off without a struggle to the "Ocean of Eternity." So old Bertram Berners was gathered to his fathers.

The year of mourning was permitted to pass, and then John Lyon Howe, having, according to the conditions of the marriage contract, assumed the name and arms of Berners, was united in marriage to the beautiful Sybil. And they set out on their bridal tour as Mr. and Mrs. Lyon Berners.

And now we will again look in upon them as they linger over their tea-table in the old inn at Norfolk, where we first introduced them to our readers.

CHAPTER IV.

THE BEAUTIFUL STRANGER

"From the glance of her eye
Shun danger and fly,
For fatal's the glance."

VERY happy were the married lovers as they sat over their tea, even though the scene of their domestic joy was just now but an inn-parlor. Both the young people had good appetites: gratified love had not deprived them of that.

They talked of their homeward journey and how pleasant it would be in this glorious autumn weather, and of their home and how glad they would be to reach it—yes, how glad! For, paradoxical as it may seem to say so, there is no happiness so perfect as that which looks forward to something still more perfect, if such could be possible in the future. They talked of the Black Valley, and how beautiful even that would look in its gorgeous October livery.

Suddenly in the midst of their sweet converse they heard the sound of weeping—low, deep, heart-broken weeping.

Both paused, looked at each other and listened.

The sound seemed to come from a room on the opposite side of the passage to their own apartment.

"What is that?" inquired Sybil, looking up to her husband's face.

"It seems to be some woman in distress," answered Lyon.

"Oh! see what it is, dear, will you?" entreated Sybil.

She was herself so happy, that it was really dreadful to be reminded just then that sorrow should exist in this world at all.

"Oh, go and see what is the matter. Do, dear," she insisted, seeing that he hesitated.

"I would do so, dear, in a moment, but it might be indiscreet on my part. The lady may be a party to some

THE BEAUTIFUL STRANGER. 27

little domestic misunderstanding, with which it would be impertinent in any stranger to interfere," answered the more thoughtful husband.

"A domestic misunderstanding! O, dear Lyon, that such things should be. Fancy you and I having a misunderstanding!" exclaimed Sybil, with a shiver.

"I cannot fancy anything of the sort, my darling; Heaven forbid that I could!" said Lyon, fervently.

"Amen to that! But listen! Ah! how she weeps and wails! Oh, Lyon, how I pity her! Oh, how I wish I could do something for her! Oh, Lyon, are you sure it would be improper for me to go and see if I can relieve her in any way?" pleaded Sybil.

"Quite sure, my darling; I am quite sure that you must not interfere, at least at this stage. If this should be a case in which we can be of service, we shall be likely to know it when the waiter answers the bell that I rung some five minutes since," said Lyon, soothingly.

But Sybil could not rest with the sound of that weeping and wailing in her ears. She left her chair and began to walk up and down the floor, and to pause occasionally at her door to listen.

Suddenly a door on the opposite side of the passage opened, and the voice of the landlord was heard, apparently speaking to the weeping woman.

"I beg you won't distress yourself, ma'am; I am sure I wouldn't do anything to distress you for the world. Keep up your spirits, ma'am. Something may turn up yet, you know," he said as he closed the opposite door again; and then crossing the passage, he knocked at the door of the Berners' apartments.

"Come in," said Lyon Berners eagerly, while Sybil paused in her restless walk and gazed breathlessly at the door.

Both were so interested, they could not have told why, in that weeping woman.

The landlord entered and closed the door behind him, and advanced with a bow and an apology.

"I am afraid that you and your good lady have been disturbed by the noise in the other room; but really I could not help it. I have done all I could to comfort the poor creature; but really you know, 'Rachel weeping for her children' was nothing to this woman. She's been going on in this way for the last three days, sir. I did hope she would be quiet this evening. I told her that I had guests in these rooms. But, Lord, sir! I might just as well try to reason with a thunderstorm as with her. I wish I had quieter rooms to put you in, sir."

"Pray do not think of us. It is not the disturbance we mind on our own account; it is to hear a fellow-creature in so much distress. A guest of the house?" inquired Mr. Berners.

"Yes, sir; worse luck."

"She has lost friends or—fortune?" continued Berners delicately investigating the case, while Sybil looked and listened with the deepest interest.

"Both, sir! Both, sir! All, sir! Everything, sir! It is really a case of atrocious villainy, sir! And I may say, a case of extreme difficulty as well! A case in which I need counsel myself, sir," said the landlord, with every appearance of being as willing to give information as to take advice.

CHAPTER V.

THE LANDLORD'S STORY.

> "What wit so sharp is found in youth or age
> That can distinguish truth from treachery?
> Falsehood puts on the face of simple truth,
> And masks i' th' habit of plain honesty,
> When she in heart intends most villainy."

"Sit down, Mr. Judson; sit down, and tell us all about this matter; and if we can aid either you or your distressed lodger in any way, we shall be glad to do so," said Mr. Berners, earnestly.

"Yes, indeed," added Sybil, throwing herself down in her easy-chair, with a deep breath of relief and anticipation.

"Well, sir, and madam," commenced the landlord, frankly accepting the offered seat, "the case is this: About ten days ago there arrived in this city, by the ship Banshee, from Cork, a lady, gentleman, and child, with two

THE LANDLORD'S STORY. 29

servants, who came directly to this house. The gentleman registered his party as Mr. and Mrs. Horace Blondelle, child, nurse, and valet, and he engaged the very best rooms in the house—the rooms corresponding to these on the opposite side of the passage, you know, madam."

"Yes," assented Mrs. Berners.

"Well, sir, and Mr. Horace Blondelle ordered, besides the best rooms, everything else that was best in the house, and, indeed, better than the house contained; for, for his supper that very night, I had to send by his directions, and procure Johannesberg, Moselle, and other rare and costly wines, such as are seldom or never called for here. But then you know, sir, he was a foreign gentleman."

"Certainly," agreed Lyon, with a smile.

"Next day, the finest horses and carriages from the livery stables. And so on in the highest scale of expense, until his week's bill ran up to seven hundred dollars. As a good deal of this was money paid out of my pocket for costly wines and costly horses, I sent in my account on the Saturday night. It is the usual thing, however, madam."

"I know," answered Mrs. Berners.

"Well, Mr. Horace Blondelle very promptly settled it by handing me a check on the local bank for the amount. It was too late then to cash my check, as the bank had been for some hours closed. But I resolved to take it to the bank the first thing on Monday morning to get the money; and I left Mr. Horace Blondelle's apartments with a secret feeling of commendation for his prudence in putting his ready money in the local bank, instead of keeping it about him in a crowded hotel like this. For, you know, sir, that the recent daring robbery at the Monroe House has proved to us that even the office safe is not *always* ' safe.' "

"Not always," echoed Mr. Berners.

"Well, sir, and madam, I was so well pleased with my guest's promptitude in settling his bill, that I redoubled my attentions to his comfort and that of his party. On the Sunday he commenced the week's account by giving a large dinner-party, for he had made acquaintances in the town. And again the most expensive delicacies and the most costly wines were ordered, with the most lavish extravagance. And they kept up the festivities in rather a noisy manner through the whole night, which was painful to me, I being a Churchman. But then, you know, madam, a landlord cannot interfere with his guests to that extent."

"Certainly not," admitted Mrs. Berners.

"Well, sir, the next morning after such a carousal, I naturally expected my guests to sleep late, so I was not surprised that the stillness of their rooms remained unbroken by any sound even up to ten o'clock. At that hour, however, the bank opened, and I went myself to get my check cashed. There, sir, I got another check. Judge of my astonishment when the cashier, after examining Mr. Horace Blondelle's paper, declared that he knew no such person, and that there was no money deposited in that bank to the credit of that name."

"It was a swindle!" exclaimed Mr. Berners, impulsively.

"It was a swindle," admitted the landlord. "Yes, sir, a swindle of the basest sort, though I did not know it even then. I was inclined to be angry with the cashier, but I reflected that there was probably a mistake of some sort; so I hurried back home and inquired if Mr. Horace Blondelle had shown himself yet. I was told that he had not yet even rung his bell. Then I went to his private parlor, which had been the scene of last night's dinner giving and Sabbath breaking. The servants of the house had removed all signs of the carousal, and were moving noiselessly about the room while restoring it to order, so as not to disturb the rest of Mr. and Mrs. Horace Blondelle in the bedroom adjoining. I told my people that, as soon as Mr. Blondelle should awake, they must tell him that I begged leave to wait on him on a matter of business. It is as well to say, that while I lingered in the room, the nurse came in with the child, a pretty, fair-haired boy of five years old. They occupied a little chamber at the end of the passage, in easy reach of the child's mother. The nurse came in, hushing and cautioning the child not to make a noise, lest he should wake up poor mamma and papa, who were so tired. I mention this little domestic incident because, in some strange way that I cannot begin to understand, it quieted my misgivings, so that I went below and waited patiently for

THE LANDLORD'S STORY.

the rising of Mr. Horace Blondelle. Madam, I might have waited till this time!" said the landlord, pausing solemely.

"Why? go on and tell me!" impulsively exclaimed Mrs. Berners.

"Why? I will soon let you know. I waited until long after noon. And still no sound from the bedroom. I walked in and out of the sitting-room, where the table was set for breakfast, and still no sound from the bedroom. And in the sitting-room no sound of occupation but the waiting breakfast-table in the middle of the floor, and the nurse seated at one of the windows with the impatient child at her knee.

"'Your master and mistress sleep late,' I said.

"'Yes, sir, they were up late last night,' she replied while twisting the child's golden ringlets around her fingers, in pure idleness, for they did not need curling.

"I went away and stayed away for about an hour, and then returned to the sitting-room. No sound from the bedroom yet. No change in the sitting-room, except that the nurse had taken a seat at the corner of the table with the child on her lap, and was feeding him from a bowl of milk and bread.

"'Your master and mistress not up yet?' I ventured to say.

"'No, sir, and no sign of them; I am giving little Crowy his supper, and am going to put him to bed. And if the bell don't ring by that time, I shall make bold to knock at the door and wake them up. Because, sir, I'm getting uneasy. Something might be the matter, though I don't know what,' said the girl, anxiously.

"'So am I, I wish you would. And when your master has breakfasted, tell him I wish to be permitted to wait on him,' I said to the girl, and I left the room for the tenth time, I suppose, that day,"

"Well!" eagerly exclaimed Sybil.

"Well, madam, in less than an hour from that time, one of the waiters came to me with looks of alarm, and said that something must have happened in number 90, for that the lady's maid had been knocking and calling loudly at the door for the last ten minutes without being able to make herself heard within."

"Oh!" breathed Sybil, clasping her hands.

"Madam, I hurried to the spot. I joined my efforts to those of the terrified maid to arouse the sleepers within the chamber, but with no effect. The maid was almost crazy by this time, ma'am.

"'Oh, sir, are they murdered in their bed?' she cried to me.

"'Murdered? No, but something has happened, and we must force open the door, my good girl,' I said by way of calming her. You may well judge, sir, that I did not send for a locksmith; but with a crowbar, hastily procured from below, I hoisted the door from its hangings and effected an entrance."

"And then? And then?" breathlessly inquired Sybil, perceiving that the landlord paused for a moment.

"We found the room in the utmost confusion. Chests of drawers, clothes-presses, boxes, and so forth, stood wide open, with their contents scattered over the floor. We glanced at the bed, and the maid uttered a wild scream, and even I felt my blood run cold; for there lay the form of the lady, still, cold, pallid, livid, like that of a corpse many hours dead. No sign of Blondelle was to be seen about the chamber."

"Oh! had he murdered her and fled?" gasped Sybil, with a half-suppressed hysterical sob.

Mr. Berners passed his arm around her shoulders and drew her head down upon his breast, and signed for the landlord to proceed with his story.

"Sir," continued Mr. Judson, "I went up to that bedside in the worst panic I ever felt in all my life. My heart was hammering at my ribs like a trip-hammer First I took up the white hand that was hanging helplessly down by the side of the bed; and I was glad to find that it was limber, though cold as ice. Life might not be extinct. I ran down and dispatched several servants in different directions for physicians, being determined to insure the attendance of one, even at the risk of bringing a dozen, and having all their fees to pay."

"You never thought of fees, I'll guarantee," said Mr Berners.

"Indeed I did not. I thought only of the lady. I sent my old mother to her bedside, with a request that

THE LANDLORD'S STORY. 33

she would keep everybody else out of the room until the arrival of the physician, and to let nothing be touched; for you see, sir, I did not know but what the attendance of a coroner would be called for as well."

"Oh, how terrible!" murmured Sybil, from her shelter on her husband's breast.

"Yes, madam, but not so terrible as we feared. Not to tire you with too long an account of this bad business, I will tell you at once the result of the physician's examination. It was, that this death-like sleep or coma of the lady was produced by some powerful narcotic, but by what or for what purpose administered, he could not discover. The maid was questioned as to whether her mistress was in the habit of using any form of opium, and answered that she certainly was not. Well, madam, the doctor left the lady under the care of my mother, with directions to watch her pulse, and on any indication of its failure, to summon him immediately."

" She was in danger, then?"

"Apparently. My mother watched beside her bed all that night; the lady did not awake until the next morning—that was the Tuesday; and the poor soul thought it was Monday! You see twenty-four hours had been lost to her consciousness."

"And her infamous husband?" inquired Mr. Berners.

"Neither he nor his valet were to be found. I had the police upon his track, you may be sure; though I did not, at the time of the lady's awakening, know of the full extent of his atrocious villainy. I knew he had swindled me, but I did not know that he had robbed and forsaken his lovely young wife."

"Robbed and forsaken his wife?" echoed Sybil, piteously.

"Yes, madam, incredible as it seems. But I did not know this until the lady came to her senses. When she first awoke and found my mother seated by her bed, she expressed much surprise, at *her* presence and at her own husband's absence. My mother, a plain spoken old lady, blurted out the truth—how Mr. Horace Blondelle, after imposing a worthless check upon me, in payment of my bill, had absconded with his valet, and been missing ever since the night of the dinner-party, and that she,

Mrs. Blondelle, had slept profoundly through all these events.

"Oh, what a dreadful tale for the poor young wife to hear!" sighed Sybil.

"It was worse than anything I ever saw in my life, madam—her grief and shame and despair! She arose from her bed and began to examine her effects, to see what she might have left, and how far they would go towards settling my bill. She possessed some invaluable jewelry in diamonds, rubies, and emeralds. I know she did, for I had seen her wear them. She alluded to these, and said that they were worth many thousand dollars, and that she would sell some of them to satisfy my claims. She began to look for them, and then it was only by her broken exclamations of dismay that I came to know that he had robbed her."

"The unnatural monster!" indignantly exclaimed Mr. Berners, while Sybil gazed in almost incredulous consternation.

"Yes, sir, and madam, the truth was now apparent, even to the poor lady; and it was this—that on the night of the dinner-party he had heavily drugged her wine, so that when she retired to bed she fell into that deep, death-like sleep. Then he took advantage of her state to get possession of her keys, and to rifle her boxes and caskets, and make off with her money and jewels."

"Poor, poor woman!" sighed Sybil.

"This, madam," continued the landlord, turning to Mrs. Berners, "occurred four days ago. Since that time her base husband has been traced to New York, and there lost sight of."

"And she?" inquired Sybil.

"She, madam, has given herself up to the wildest grief and despair. She is as simple and as helpless as her own child. She has not the faintest notion of self-reliance. And here is where the trouble is with me. I have already lost several hundred dollars through this swindling villain. The wife and child he has left behind him are still occupying my best suit of apartments, for which, during their stay here, I shall not receive one penny of remuneration; therefore you see I cannot afford to keep this lady and her suite here, and neither can I find it in my heart

THE LANDLORD'S STORY.

to tell her to leave the house. For where, indeed, can she go? She has no friends or acquaintances in this country, no money, and no property that she can effectually turn into money."

"Has she no one to pity her among the ladies in the house?" inquired Sybil.

"There are no ladies staying in the house at present, madam. Our patrons are usually travelers, who seldom remain over one night."

"But—the women of your family?" suggested Sybil.

"There are no women in this family, except my old mother, who keeps house for me, and the female servants under her. I am a widower, madam, with half a dozen sons, but no daughters," returned the landlord.

Sybil lifted her head from her husband's shoulder, where it had rested so long, and looked wistfully in her husband's eyes. He smiled, and nodded assent to what seemed to have been a silent interrogation. Then she took from her pocket a little gold-enameled card-case, drew from it a card and a pencil, and wrote a few lines and handed it to the landlord, saying:

"Mr. Judson, will you do me the favor to take this in to the unhappy lady at once, and see if she will receive me this evening? I feel as if I would like to try to comfort and serve her."

"I will with pleasure, madam; and I have no doubt that the mere expression of sympathy from another lady will be to her like a drop of water to a feverish palate," said the landlord, as he left the room.

"Dear Lyon, I have a favor to ask of you," said Sybil, as soon as she was alone with her husband.

"A favor! a right, my beloved! There is nothing that you can ask of me that is not your right to receive!"

"No, no; a favor. I like to ask and receive favors from you, dear Lyon."

"Call my service what you will, dear love! a right or a favor, it is always yours! What, then, is this favor, sweet Sybil?"

"That you will give me a perfect *carte blanche* in my manner of dealing with this poor little lady, even though my manner should seem foolish or extravagant."

At these words from his ardent, generous, romantic

wife, Lyon Berners looked very grave. What, indeed might Sybil, with her magnanimity and munificence *not* think proper to do for this utter stranger—this possible adventuress? Lyon looked very solemn over this proposal from his wife. He hesitated for a moment; but her large, clear, honest eyes were fixed full upon him, waiting for his reply. Could he refuse her request? Did *he* not owe everything to her, and to that very highflown spirit of generosity which was not only a fault (if it were a fault) of Sybil, but a trait common to all her race.

"As you will, my darling wife! I should be a cur, and worse than a cur—a thankless wretch—to wish to restrain you in anything!" he answered, sealing his agreement on her velvet lips.

In another minute the landlord re-entered the room.

"Mrs. Blondelle's thanks and compliments, and she will be very grateful for Mrs. Berners' visit, as soon as Mrs. Berners pleases to come," was the message that Mr. Judson brought.

Sybil arose with a smile, kissed her hand playfully to her husband, and passed out of the room.

The landlord went before her, rapped at the opposite door, then opened it, announced the visitor, and closed it behind her.

Sybil advanced a step into the stranger's apartment, and then paused in involuntary admiration.

She had heard and read of celebrated beauties, whose charms had conquered the wisest statesmen and the bravest warriors, who had governed monarchs and ministers, and raised or ruined kingdoms and empires. And often in poetic fancy she had tried to figure to herself one of these fairy forms and faces. But never, in her most romantic moods, had she imagined a creature so perfectly beautiful as this one that she saw before her.

The stranger had a form of the just medium size, and of the most perfect proportions; a head of stately grace; features small, delicate, and clearly cut; a complexion at once fair and rosy, like the inside of an apple blossom; lips like opening rosebuds; eyes of dark azure blue, fringed with long dark eyelashes, and overarched by slender, dark eyebrows and hair of a pale, glistening, golden hue that fell in soft, bright ringlets, like a halo

THE LANDLORD'S STORY. 37

around her angelic face. She wore a robe of soft, pale, blue silk, that opened over a white silk skirt.

She arose with an exquisite grace to welcome her visitor.

"It is very good of you, madam, to come to see me in my misery," she murmured, in a sweet, pathetic tone that went to her visitor'sheart, as she set a chair, and, by a graceful gesture invited her to be seated.

Sybil was herself impulsive and confiding, as well as romantic and generous. She immediately drew her chair up to the side of the strange lady, took her hand affectionately, and tried to look up in her eyes, as she said:

"We are personal strangers to each other; but we are the children of one Father, and sisters who should care for each other."

"Ah! who would care to claim sisterhood with such a wretch as I am?" sighed the unhappy young creature.

"*I* would; but you must not call yourself ill-names. Misfortunes are not sins. I came here to comfort and help you—to comfort and help you not in words merely, but in deeds; and I have both the power and the will to do it, if you will please to let me try," said Sybil, gently.

The young creature looked up, her lovely, tearful, blue eyes expanded with astonishment.

"You offer to comfort and help me! *Me*—a perfect stranger, with a cloud of dishonor hanging over me! Oh, madam, if you knew *all*, you would certainly withdraw your kind offer," she said.

"I will not withdraw it in any event. I *do* know all that your landlord could tell me, and that awakens my deepest sympathy for you. But I do not know all that *you* could tell me. Now, dear, I want you to confide in me as you could not confide either in your landlord, or even in his mother."

"Oh, no, no! I could not tell either of them. They were kind; but—oh, so hard!"

"Now, dear, then, look in my face, look well, and tell me whether you can confide in me," said Sybil, gently.

"If I had never seen your heavenly countenance—if I had only heard your heavenly voice, I could confide in you, as in the holy mother of Christ," said the stranger fervently.

"Tell me then, dear; tell me all you wish to tell; relieve your heart; lay all your burdens on my bosom; and then you shall feel how well I can comfort and help you," said Sybil, putting her hand around the fair neck and drawing the little golden-haired head upon her breast.

Then and there the friendless young stranger—friendless now, no more—told her piteous story.

CHAPTER VI.

ROSA BLONDELLE.

Her form had all the softness of her sex,
Her face had all the sweetness of the devil
When he put on the cherub to perplex
Eve, and to pave, Heaven knows how, the road to evil.
—BYRON.

She had been the penniless orphan daughter of a noble, but impoverished Scotch family. She had been left, by the death of her parents, dependent upon harsh and cruel relatives. She had been given in marriage, at the age of fifteen, to a wealthy old gentleman, whose years quadrupled hers. But he had used her very kindly, and she had performed her simple duty of love and obedience as well as she knew how to do it. After two years of tranquil domestic happiness, the old man died, leaving her a young widow seventeen years of age, sole guardian to their infant son, between whom and herself he had divided his whole estate.

After the death of her old husband, the youthful widow lived in strict seclusion for nearly two years, devoting herself exclusively to the care of her child.

But in the third year the health of the little child required a change, and his mother, by her physician's advice, took the boy to Scarborough. That fashionable watering place was then at the height of its season, and filled with visitors.

Thus it was impossible but that the wealthy young widow should attract much attention. She was inevitably drawn into the maelstrom of society, into which she rushed with all the impetuosity of a novice or an inexperienced recluse, to which all the scenes of the gay world were as delightful as they were novel.

She had many suitors for her hand; but none found favor in her eyes but Mr. Horace Blondelle, a very handsome and attractive young gentleman, whose principal passport into good society seemed to be his distant relationship to the Duke of Marchmonte. *How* he lived no one knew. *Where* he lived every one might see, for he always occupied the best suite of apartments in the best hotel of any town or city in which he might be for the time sojourning.

We, every one of us know, or know *of*, Mr. Horace Blondelle. There are scores of him scattered about the great hotels of all the large cities in Europe and America. But the simplest maiden or the silliest widow in society, is seldom taken in by him.

There, however, at Scarborough, was an inexperienced poor little creature from the Highlands, who had never in her life seen any one more attractive than the red-headed heroes of her native hills, and who, having aurific tresses of her own, was particularly prejudiced against that splendid hue, and fatally ensnared by the raven ringlets and dark eyes of this professional lady-killer.

And thus it followed of course, that this beast of prey devoured the pretty little widow and all her substance with less hesitation or remorse than a cobra might have felt in swallowing a canary bird.

So complete was her hallucination, so perfect her trust in him, that she took no precaution of having any part of her property settled upon herself; and, in marrying this man she gave him an absolute control over her own fortune, and a dangerous, if limited, influence over that of her infant son.

This very imprudent marriage was followed by a few months of delusive happiness on the part of the bride; for the little fair beauty adored her dark-haired Apollo, who graciously accepted her adoration.

But then came satiety and weariness and inconstancy on the part of the husband, who soon commenced the pleasing pastime of breaking the wife's heart.

Yet still, for some little time longer, she, with a deplorable fatuity, believed in and loved him. After he had squandered her own fortune on gaming-tables and race-courses, he wished to get possession of the fortune of her son. To do this he persuaded her to sell out certain stock and entrust him with the proceeds, to be invested, as he convinced her, in railway shares in America, that would pay at least two hundred per cent. dividends, and in a few months double that money.

Acting as her son's guardian and trustee, acting also, as she thought, in his best interests, the deluded mother did as her husband directed. She sold out the stocks, and confided the proceeds to him.

Then it was that they made the voyage to America, ostensibly to purchase the railway shares in question. His real motive in bringing her to this country was, doubtless, to take her as far as possible from her native place and her old acquaintances, so as to prosecute the more safely and effectually his fraudulent designs.

How they had arrived at Norfolk and taken rooms at the Anchor, and how he had robbed and deserted her there, has already been told.

Sybil Berners listened to this sad and revolting story of woman's weakness and man's criminality with mingled emotions of pity and indignation.

"Believe me," she said, tenderly taking the hand of the injured wife, "I feel the deepest sympathy with your misfortunes. I will do everything in my power to comfort and help you—not in words only but in deeds; and I only grieve, dear, that I cannot give you back your husband in his honor and integrity as you once regarded him," added this loving and confiding wife, to whom no misery seemed so great as that caused by the default and desertion of a husband.

"Oh, do not name him to me!" burst forth in pain from the lips of Rosa Blondelle; "oh, I hope, as long as I may live in this world, never to be wounded by the sound of his base name, or blasted with the sight of his false face again."

Sybil Berners shrank in dismay from the excited woman, who continued, vehemently:

"Do you wonder at this? I tell you madam, it is possible for love to die a sudden and violent death, for mine has done so within the last three days."

"I am deeply grieved to hear you say so, for it proves how much you must have suffered—how much more than even I had imagined. But try to take a little comfort. I and my own dear husband will be your friends, will be a sister and a brother to you," said Sybil earnestly, with all the impulsive, unlimited generosity of her youth and her race, awakened by her sympathy with the sorrows of this young stranger.

"Oh, madam, you—" began Rosa, but her voice broke down in sobs.

"Take comfort," continued Sybil, laying her little brown hand on that fair golden head, "take comfort. Think, you have not lost all. You have your child left."

"Ah, my child!" said Rosa, in tone like a shriek of anguish, "my child, my wronged and ruined babe! The sight of him is a sword through my bosom! my child that *he* robbed and made *me* an accomplice in robbing—it is maddening to think of it."

"Then do not think of it," said Sybil, gently, and still caressing the bowed head; "think of anything else—think of what I am going to say to you. Listen. While you remain in this crowded and noisy hotel, you can never recover calmness enough to act with any good effect. So I wish you to come home with me and my dear husband to our quiet country house, and be our cherished guest until you can communicate with your friends, or come to some satisfactory decision concerning your future course."

Why Sybil spoke these words, the young stranger raised her head and looked up with gradually dilating eyes.

"Come, now; what say you.? Will you be our dear and welcome guest this autumn?" smiled Sybil.

"Oh, *do* you mean this? *can* you mean it?" exclaimed Rosa, in something like an ecstasy of surprise and gratitude.

"In our secluded country house, with sympathizing friends around you," continued Sybil, still caressing Rosa's little golden-haired head, and speaking all the more calmly because of Rosa's excitement, "you will have repose and leisure to collect your thoughts and to write to your friends in the old country, and to wait without hurry or anxiety to hear from them."

"Oh, angels in Heaven, do you hear what this angel on earth is saying to me! Oh, was ever such divine goodness seen under the sun before! Oh, dear lady, you amaze, you confound me with your heavenly goodness!" exclaimed the young stranger, in strong emotion.

Sybil took her hand, and still all the more gently for the increasing agitation of Rosa, she continued:

"We are daughters of the Divine Father, sisters in one suffering humanity, and so we should care for each other. At present you are suffering, and I have some power to comfort you. In the future our positions may be reversed, and *I* may be the sufferer and you the comforter. Who can tell?"

"O, dear lady, Heaven forbid that great heart of yours should ever be called to suffer, or that you should ever need such poor help as mine. But this I know: so penetrated am I by your goodness, that, if ever you should lose your present happiness and my death would restore it, I would die to give it back to you," fervently exclaimed the stranger.

And for the moment she felt as she had spoken, for she was most profoundly moved by a magnanimity she had never seen equaled.

Sybil blushed like a child, and found nothing to say in reply to this excessive praise. She only left her hand in the clasp of the stranger, who covered it with kisses, and then continued:

"When I first saw your little white card and the delicate tracery of your name and your kind words, I seemed to know it was a friend's writing. And when I first saw your sweet face and heard your tender tones, both so full of heavenly pity, I felt that the good Lord had not forsaken me, for He had sent one of his holy angels to visit me. Ah, lady, if you had only come and looked at me so and spoken to me so, and then passed out and away forever, still, still, that look and that tone would have remained with me, a comfort and a blessing for all time. But now—but now to hold out your hands to lead me to a place in your own home, by your own side—oh, it is too much! too much!"

And tears of many mingled emotions flowed down the speaker's cheeks.

"There, there!" said Sybil, utterly confused by this excessive, but most sincere adulation, yet still caressing the stranger's fair head, "there, dear, dry your eyes, and tell me if you can be ready to leave this place with us to-morrow morning."

Again the foreign lady seized and kissed the hands of her new friend, exclaiming fervently :

"Yes, dear lady, yes! I am too deeply touched by your heavenly goodness not to be anxious to profit by it as soon as possible."

"Then I will leave you to your preparations for the journey," said Sybil, rising.

Rosa also stood up.

"There will be much to be done in a short time. Will you let me send my maid to help yours?" inquired Sybil, with a hesitating smile.

"Thanks, dear madam. I shall be much obliged," replied Rosa, with a bow.

"And there is yet another request I have to make," added Mrs. Berners, pausing with her hand upon the latch of the door—"Will you kindly meet us at breakfast at eight o'clock to-morrow morning in our private sitting-room, so that I may make you acquainted with my husband before we all start on our journey together?"

"With pleasure, dear lady! It is your will to load me with benefits, and you must be gratified," replied Rosa, with a faint smile.

"Then I will come myself and fetch you, a little before the hour," added Sybil, playfully throwing a kiss as she darted through the door.

When she re-entered her own apartment, she found her husband impatiently pacing up and down the floor.

"How very long you have been, my darling Sybil," he said, with all the fondness of a newly-wedded lover, as he went to meet her.

"Oh, I am so glad you thought it long!" she answered mischievously, as she took his hand and pulled him to the big easy-chair and pushed him down into it.

"Sit down there, and listen to me," she said, with a pretty little air of authority. Then she drew an ottoman to his side and sunk down upon it, and leaned her arms upon his knees, and lifted her beautiful dark face, now all aglow with the delight of benevolence, and told him all that had passed in the interview between herself and Mrs. Blondelle.

And Lyon Berners, with his arm over her graceful shoulders, his fingers stringing her silken black ringlets, and his eyes gazing with infinite tenderness and admiration down on her eloquent face, listened with attentive interest to the story. But at its close, great was his astonishment.

"My dear, impulsive Sybil, what have you done!" he exclaimed.

"What!" echoed Sybil, her crimson lips breathlessly apart—her dark eyes dilated.

"Love, you have invited a perfect stranger, casually met at a hotel—a gambler's wife, even by her own showing, an adventuress by all other appearances, to come and take up her abode with us for an indefinite length of time!"

Sybil's mouth opened, and her eyes dilated with an almost comical expression of dismay. She had not a word to say in self-defence!

"Do not think I blame you, dear, warm, imprudent heart! I only wonder at you, and—adore you!" he said, earnestly pressing her to his bosom.

"Oh, but you would have done as I did, if you had seen her distress!" pleaded Sybil, recovering her powers of speech.

"But could you not have helped her without inviting her home with us?"

"But how?" inquired Sybil.

"Could you not have paid her board? or lent her money?"

"Oh, Lyon! Lyon!" said Sybil, slowly shaking her head and looking up in his face with a heavenly benevolence beaming through her own. "Oh, Lyon! it was not a boarding-house she wanted, it was a *refuge*, a home with friends! But I am very sorry if this displeases you."

"Dear, impetuous, self-forgetting child! I am not so impious as to find fault with you."

"But you do not like the lady's coming."

"I should not like any visitor coming to stay with us and prevent our *tête-à-têtes*," said Lyon, gravely.

"I thought of that too, dear, and with a pang of selfish regret; for of course I would much rather that you and I should have our dear old home to ourselves, than that any stranger should share it with us. But then, oh, dearest Lyon, I reflected that we are so rich and happy in our home and our love, and she is so poor and sorrowful in her exile and desertion, that we might afford to comfort her from the abundance of our blessings," said Sybil, earnestly.

"My angel wife! you are worthier than I, and your will shall be done," he gravely replied.

"Not so, dear Lyon! But when you see this lady in her beauty and her sorrow, you also will admire and pity her, and you will be glad that she is coming to the refuge of our home."

"I may be so," replied Mr. Berners with an arch smile, "but how will your proud neighhors receive this questionable stranger?"

The stately little head was lifted in an instant, and—

"My 'proud neighbors' well know that whom Sybil Berners protects with her friendship is peer with the proudest among them!" she said, with a hauteur not to be surpassed by the haughtiest in the Old Dominion.

"Well said, my little wife. And now, as this matter is decided, I must see about taking additional places in the stage-coach. How many will be wanted? What retinue has this foreign princess in distress," inquired Lyon, rather sarcastically.

"There will be three places required, for the lady, child, and nurse."

"Whe-ew! My dear Sybil, we are collecting a ready-made family! Does the child squall? or the nurse drink?" inquired Lyon, with a laugh, as without waiting for a reply he rang the bell, and gave the order for three more places to be taken inside the Staunton coach for the morning.

And soon after this the young pair retired to rest.

Very early the next morning Sybil Berners came out of her chamber, looking fresh and bright as the new day itself. She wore a close-fitting traveling dress of crimson merino, that well became her elegant little figure and rich, dark complexion.

She glanced around the room to see that everything was in order. Yes; the fire was bright, the hearth clean, the breakfast-table neatly set, and the morning sun shining through the red-curtained windows and glancing upon the silver tea-service.

With a smile of satisfaction, she tossed back her raven-black ringlets, and passed from the room and through the hall, and rapped at the door of her new acquaintance.

Mrs. Blondelle herself opened it, and stood there quite ready to accompany her friend to breakfast.

Radiantly beautiful looked the fair young stranger this morning, in the dark, bright-blue cloth habit that so highly enhanced the dazzling splendor of her blooming complexion and the golden glory of her hair.

An instant Sybil paused in involuntary admiration, and then recovered herself and greeted the lady with affectionate warmth.

"It is nearly eight o'clock, dear, and breakfast is quite ready. Will you come now?" inquired Sybil, when these salutations were passed.

Rosa assented with a sweet smile, and Sybil led the way to her own sitting-room.

Mr. Berners had come in during his wife's short absence, and he now stood before the fire with the morning paper in his hand. He put it down on the table, and came forward to meet his wife, and to welcome her guest.

"Mrs. Blondelle, Mr. Berners," said Sybil, introducing the parties to each other by the simplest formula.

And while they were bowing together, Sybil was watching mischievously to see what effect the dazzling beauty of Rosa Blondelle would have upon Lyon Berners.

She saw it!

After bowing, they lifted their heads and looked at each other—he, at first, with the courtesy of a host—but she with a radiant and enchanting smile.

Sybil was prepared to see Lyon's surprise at the first view of this peerless creature; but she was by no means prepared to witness the involuntary gaze of intense and breathless admiration and wonder that he fixed for a moment on her beautiful face. That gaze said as eloquently as words could have spoken:

"This is the most wondrous, perfect creature that the world ever saw! This is the masterpiece of nature."

With the sunlight of her smile still shining on him, Rosa held out her hand, and said in the sweetest tones:

"Sir, I have no words good enough to tell you how deeply I feel your kindness and that of your dear wife to me."

"Dear lady, Mrs. Berners and myself do but gratify our own tastes in *trying* to serve you; for it will be a great happiness to us if we succeed in doing so," replied Lyon Berners, with a look and tone that proved his perfect sincerity and earnestness.

As thus they smiled and glanced, and spoke to each other, Sybil also glanced from the one to the other; a sudden pang shot through her heart, exciting a nameless dread in her mind. "*Even so quickly may one catch the plague.*"

"Let me lead you to the table," said Mr. Berners, offering his arm to Mrs. Blondelle, and conducting her to her place.

Above all, Sybil was a lady; for she was a Berners. So, with this strange wound in her heart, this vague warning in her mind, she took her seat at the head of her table and did its honors with her usual courtesy and grace.

Mr. Berners seconded his wife in all hospitable attentions to their beautiful young guest.

While they were all still seated at the table, a groom rapped at the door and reported the stage-coach ready.

They all arose in a hurry, and began to make the last hasty preparations for departure.

Mrs. Blondelle hurried into her own room, to have her luggage taken down-stairs to be put on the coach, and also to summon her nurse with the child.

When Sybil Berners found herself for a moment alone with her husband, she laid her hand upon his coat sleeve to stay him, in his haste, and she inquired:

"What do you think of her now?"

"I think, my darling Sybil, that you were right in your judgment of this lady. And I agree with you perfectly

I think, my only love, that in what you have done for this stranger, you have acted not only with the goodness, but with the wisdom of an angel," replied Lyon Berners, snatching her suddenly to his heart, and holding her closely there while he pressed kiss after kiss upon her crimson lips, and murmured:

"I must steal a kiss from these sweet lips when and wherever I can, my own one, since we are not to be much alone together now."

And then he released her, and hurried off to put on his overcoat.

Sybil stood for a minute, smiling, where he had left her, and so happy that she forgot she had to get ready to go. The pain was gone from her heart, and the cloud from her brain.

And as yet, so little did she know of herself or others, that she could not have told why the pain and the cloud ever came, or why they ever went away.

As yet she did not know that her husband's admiring smiles given to a rival beauty had really caused her nameless suffering; or that it was his loving caresses, bestowed upon herself, that had soothed it.

In a word, Sybil Berners, the young bride, did not dream that the bitter, bitter seed of JEALOUSY was germinating in her heart, to grow and spread perhaps into a deadly upas of the soul, destroying all moral life around it.

CHAPTER VII.

DOWN IN THE DARK VALE.

Where rose the mountains, there for her were friends,
　Where fell the valley, therein was her home;
Where the steep rock and dizzy peak ascends,
　She had the passion and the power to roam.
The crag, the forest, cavern, torrent's foam,
　Were unto her companions, and they spake
A natural language clearer than the tone
　Of her best books, which she would oft forsake
For Nature's pages, lit by moonbeams on the lake.—BYRON.

JEALOUSY, once called to life in any human heart, is not easily to be destroyed. Sybil Berners' almost unconscious jealousy suddenly called into existence, and as suddenly soothed to sleep, was awakened again by something that occurred just as the travelers were about to start.

It was the merest trifle, yet one of those trifles which turn the course of fate just as surely as the little switch of the railroad controls the direction of the train.

The travelers were just entering the stage-coach. Mr. Berners handed in first Mrs. Blondelle, then Mrs. Berners, and then he himself endered.

"You sit down here in this right-hand corner, Lyon, dear, and I will sit in the middle next to you, and Mrs. Blondelle shall sit in the left-hand corner next to me," said Sybil, still standing while she pointed out their several places on the back seat; and she spoke perhaps under the influence of a latent jealousy, that instigated her to place herself between her husband and her guest, for that long journey.

"No, no, my dear, not so; but if you will change places with me and take the right-hand corner-seat, while our fair friend occupies the left-hand one, I will sit between you two ladies, the proverbial 'thorn between two roses,'" replied Lyon Berners, gaily and gallantly, with perhaps on his side a latent desire to sit next the beautiful blonde, but also quite unconscious of how these words had disappointed and wounded her whom he would not have willingly wronged for the world.

Sybil silently took her seat, leaving the others to follow her example. Mr. Berners politely put Mrs. Blondelle in the left-hand corner, and then seated himself in the middle seat, between his wife and her guest.

In front of them, on the movable central seat, sat Mrs. Blondelle's child and nurse. Facing them on the front seat, with their backs to the horses, were the two negro servants, Mr. Berners' valet and Mrs. Berners' maid.

Though the morning was a very fine one for traveling, there were no other passengers inside, or out. Mr. Berners and his party had the whole coach to themself, at least, at starting.

Sybil thought she had never seen her husband in gayer spirits. As the horses started and the coach rattled along over the stony streets of the city, Mr. Berners turned smilingly to Mrs. Blondelle, and said:

"I know of few pleasanter things in this pleasant world than a journey through our native State of Virginia, taken at this delightful season of the year; and of all routes I know of none affording such a variety of beautiful and sublime scenery as this we are now starting upon."

"How long will it take you to reach your beautiful home?" sweetly inquired Rosa Blondelle.

"We might reach it in two days, if we were to travel day and night; but we shall be four days on the road, as we propose to put up at some roadside inn or village each night," answered Lyon Berners.

Meanwhile the coach rattled out of the city and into the open country, where the landscape was fair, well-wooded, well-watered, but not striking.

"You must not judge the scenery of our State by this flat country around our seaport," said Mr. Berners to his guest, with the air of a man making an apology.

"Yet this is very pleasant to look upon," answered Rosa, sincerely.

"Yes, very pleasant, as you say; but you will use stronger language when you see our vast forests, our high mountains, and deep valleys," answered Lyon Berners with a smile.

Sybil did not join in the conversation. She had not spoken since she had unwillingly taken that corner seat. And worse than all, to her apprehension, neither her husband nor her guest had noticed her silence. They were apparently quite absorbed in each other.

Some hours of jolting over bad turnpike roads brought the coach to the interior of an old forest, where, at a wayside inn, the horses were changed, and the travelers dined. Here, on resuming their seats in the coach, they were joined by two other travelers, elderly country gentlemen, who took the two vacent places inside, and who would have made themselves very confidential with Mr. Berners on any subject within their knowledge, from crops to Congress, if he had not been too engaged with his fair guest to pay them much attention. Sybil continued silent, except when occasionally her husband would ask her if she was comfortable, or if he could do anything for her, when she would thank him and answer that she was quite comfortable, and that he could do nothing. And as far as bodily ease went, she spoke the truth. For the rest, Sybil could not then and there ask him to leave off devoting himself to their guest, and show *her* more attention.

A few more hours of more jolting over worse turnpike roads brought the coach to the foot of the Blue Ridge, and to the picturesque village of Underhill, where our party passed the night. Here, in the village inn, Sybil Berners, feeling that Rosa Blondelle, as her guest, was entitled to her courtesy, made an effort to forget the pain in her heart, the shadow on her mind, and to do the honors of the table with her usual affability and grace.

After supper, which was pleasantly prolonged, the travelers separated, and were shown to their several bed-chambers.

And now after twelve hours, Sybil found herself once more alone with her husband. He had not perceived her silence and dejection during the journey, or if he had, he certainly had not ascribed it to the right cause. He was equally unconscious of having done a wrong, or inflicted a wound. And now his manner to his wife was as tender, loving, and devoted as it had ever been since their marriage. His very first words showed this. On entering the room and closing the door, he suddenly threw his arms around her, and clasped her to his bosom as a recovered treasure, exclaiming:

"Now, my darling, we are alone together once more, with no one to divide us."

"Thank Heaven!" breathed Sybil with all her heart; and her jealousy was lulled to rest again by the kisses that he pressed on her lips. She said to herself that all his devotion to Rosa Blondelle in the stage-coach was but the proper courtesy of a gentleman to a lady guest, who was, besides, a stranger in the country; and that she, his wife, ought to admire, rather than to blame him for it—ought to be pleased, rather than pained by it.

Very early the next morning the travelers arose, in order to take the earliest coach, which, having left Norfolk at sunset, would reach Underhill at sunrise.

Poor, ardent, impulsive Sybil! She had passed a very happy night; and this morning she met her guest with a gush of genuine affection, embracing and kissing her and her child, and making them even more welcome than she had done before, and feeling that to-day she could not deal too kindly by Rosa, to atone for having yesterday thought so hardly of her.

Under these pleasant auspices the travelers sat down to an excellent breakfast.

But the warning horn blew, and they prepared to resume their journey.

On entering the coach, they found the other passengers, three in number, already on the back seat. But they were gentlemen, who voluntarily and promptly gave up their seats to the two ladies and their escort. The coach started.

Their route now lay through some of the wildest passes of the Blue Ridge. And here the enthusiasm of Rosa Blondelle burst forth. She said that she had seen grand mountains in Scotland, but nothing—no, nothing to equal these in grandeur and beauty!

And Lyon Berners smiled to hear her speak so, as one might smile at the extravagant delight of a child, for as a child this lovely stranger often seemed to him and to others. And she, with her sweet, blue eyes, smiled back to him.

And Sybil looked and listened, and felt again that strange wound deepening in her heart—that strange cloud darkening over her mind.

CHAPTER VIII.

BLACK HALL.

Seest thou our home? 'tis where the woods are waving
  In their dark richness to the autumn air;
Where yon blue stream its rocky banks are laving,
  Leads down the hills a vein of light—'tis there.—HEMANS.

At the close of that second day, they stopped at a hamlet on the summit of Blue Ridge, from which they could view five counties. At the little hotel they were entertained very much in the same manner as at the inn o Underhill. Again Sybil's unspoken and unsuspected jealously was soothed by the caresses of her husband.

In the morning they resumed their journey in the early coach, that took them across the beautiful valley that lies between the Blue Ridge and the Alleghany Mountains. And again Lyon Berners' devotion to Rosa Blondelle deeply distressed Sybil. At nightfall they reached Staunton, where they slept.

On the morning of the fourth and last day of their journey, they took the cross-country coach and changed their route, which now led them towards the wildest, dreariest, and loneliest passes of the Alleghanies.

About mid-day the coach entered the dark defile known as the "Devil's Descent." And, in fact, it needed all the noon sunshine to light up the gloom of that fearful pass. Here the delight of the impressible young foreigner deepened into awe.

"I have never seen anythiug like this in the old country," she breathed in a low, hushed tone.

And again Lyon Berners smiled most kindly and indulgently on her, and again Sybil Berners sickened at heart. Every time Lyon so smiled on Rosa, Sybil so sickened. She strove against this feeling, but she could not overcome it.

As the day declined and the coach went on, wilder, drearier, and lonelier became the road, until, at nightfall, it entered a pass so gloomy, so savage, so terrific in its aspect, that the young stranger involuntarily caught her breath and clung for protection to the arm of Lyon Berners.

"I have never *dreamed* of a place like this," she gasped.

"You think," he said indulgently, "that if the other pass was called the 'Devil's Descent,' this should be the 'Gates of Hell.' Yet to us, it is the 'Gates of Heaven;' since it is the entrance to our Valley Home."

And this affectionate mention of their mutual home almost consoled the wife for the smile he bestowed on their beautiful guest while speaking.

Then all the women except Sybil held their breath in awe.

It was indeed an awful pass! a road roughly hewn through the bottom of a deep, narrow, tortuous cleft in the mountains where, at some remote period, by some tremendous convulsions of nature, the solid rocks had been rent apart, leaving the ragged edges of the wound hanging at a dizzy height between heaven and earth! The dark iron-gray precipices that towered on each side were clothed in every cleft, from base to summit, with clumps of dark stunted evergreens as somber as themselves. So tortuous, besides, was the pass, that the travelers could see but a few yards before them at any time. There was but one cheering sight in earth or sky, and that was the young crescent moon straight before them in the west, and shining down in tender light upon the rudest precipice of all.

"It does remind one of Dante's descriptions of the 'Entrance into the Infernal Regions,' does it not?" inquired Lyon Berners.

"All except the little moon! Without that, its gloom would be perfectly horrible! and it is horrible enough now," answered Rosa with a shudder.

"But I love it! Even its gloom and horror have a weird fascination for me. It is my abode. I only seem to live my own life in my own Black Valley," said Sybil, in a low, deep voice that thrilled with emotion.

They were suddenly silenced, for they were at the sharpest, steepest, most difficult and dangerous turn in that most dangerous pass; and to go down with any chance of safety required the utmost care and skill on the part of the coachman, whose anxiety was shared by all within the coach. Each passenger clung for support to what was nearest at hand, and might reasonably have expected every instant to be dashed to pieces on the rocks by the coach pitching over the horses' heads, as it tossed and tumbled and thundered down the falling road, more like a descending avalanche than a well-conducted four-wheeled vehicle.

Our travelers only let go their holdings and loosed their tongues again at the foot of the precipice.

"That was—that was—Oh, there is no word to express what it was. It was more than terrible! more than awful! And it is just a miracle that we have escaped with our lives!" gasped Rosa Blondelle, aghast with horror.

"There has never yet been an accident on this road," observed Lyon Berners, soothingly.

"Then there is a miracle performed every time a vehicle passes down it," replied Rosa, with a shudder.

"But look now, there is a very fine scene," said Mr. Berners, pointing through the window as the coach rolled on. Sybil was already gazing through the right-hand window, and so Rosa stretched her fair neck to look from the left-hand one.

Yes, it was a fine scene. The young crescent moon with its tender beam had gone down; but the great stars were out in all their glory, and by their shining the travelers saw before them a beautiful little river, whose rippling surface reflected in fitful glimmers the cheerful lights of a village on its opposite bank.

"This is the Black River. It rises in those distant mountains, which are called the Black Rocks, and which shut in our Black Valley. The village here is called Blackville," explained Lyon Berners.

"What a deal of blackness!" replied Rosa Blondelle.

"If you think so, I must tell you in the first place that we are not responsible for having named these places; and in the second, that the names are really appropriate. The stupendous height and dark iron-gray hue of the rocks that overshadow and darken the valley and the river, and also the situation of the village at the entrance of the dark valley, justify these names. And even if they did not, still we are not so irreverent as to interfere with the arrangements of those who have gone before us," laughed Lyon Berners.

And as he spoke the stage-coach reached the banks of the river, and drew up before the little ferry-house. Here the travelers alighted, and had their baggage taken off. And the coach, waiting only long enough to change horses and to pick up passengers, all of whom, both man and beast, had been brought over from the village by the ferry-boat, went on its way, which lay along the east bank of the river.

Mr. Berners had his luggage and that of his party put upon the ferry-boat, and then he led the ladies on board. He saw them comfortably seated, and the nurse and child in a safe place, and then he turned to the aged ferry-man with hearty good will, and inquired:

"Well, old Charon! all right with you?"

"Yes, sir, thank Heaven!" replied the old man, whose occupation, combined with his great age and flowing gray locks, yet stalwart form and unbroken strength, had conferred upon him the name of his infernal predecessor—the navigator of the River Styx.

"All right in the village, and in the valley?" further inquired Mr. Berners.

"All right in the willage, sir. And Joe, who has just arrove at the tavern, do report all right in the walley," was the satisfactory answer of the ferryman.

"Oh! then our carriage is waiting for us there?"

"Yes, sir, which it arrove just about twenty minutes ago, punk-too-well to time!" replied the old man.

The passage across the Black River is very short, and just as the ferryman spoke, the boat touched the wharf immediately under the lighted windows of the hotel, before the doors of which they saw the Black Hall carriage and horses standing.

Mr. Berners assisted the ladies of his party to land, and proposed that they should stop at the hotel and take supper before going on to Black Hall.

"Oh, no! please don't, on any account! I feel sure that Miss Tabby has laid out all her talent on the supper that is awaiting us at home. And she would weep with disappointment and mortification if we should stop to supper here," eagerly objected Sybil.

"Miss Tabby is our housekeeper; the best creature, but the greatest whimperer in existence. She is, in turn, Sybil's tyrant and Sybil's slave; for she is both despotic and devoted, and scolds and pets her alternately and unreasonably as a foolish mother does an only child," explained Mr. Berners, turning to Mrs. Blondelle.

"And her lady?" inquired Rose, with an admiring glance toward Mrs. Berners.

"Oh! Sybil turns the tables, you may be sure, and indulges or rebukes her housekeeper as the occasion may demand," laughed Lyon.

"Come here, Joe!" called Mrs. Berners to her coachman, who was seen coming out of the tap-room.

"Bress my two eyes, Miss Sybil! how glad dey is to see you, and you too, Marse Lyon!" exclaimed a very black, short, squarely built, good-humored looking negro coachman, as he came and bowed to his master and mistress.

"Joe! you have been at your old tricks again. Joe! Why can't you let bar-rooms alone? Joe where *do* you expect to go when you die?" solemnly inquired Sybil, shaking her finger at the delinquent.

"I do 'spect to go straight to de debbil, miss, for sure! Dat's de reason why I wants to take a drap of comfort in dis worl', 'cause I nebber shall get none dere. But bress my two eyes, miss, how glad dey is to look on your putty face again."

"My 'putty' face? I want to know if *that's* a compliment? But, Joe, what has Miss Tabby got for supper?"

"Lor' bress your putty little mouf, Miss Sybil; it's easier to tell you what she hasn't got," exclaimed Joe, stretching his eyes. "Why, Miss Sybil, there an't a man nor a maid about the house, what ha'n't been on their feet all dis day a getting up of that there supper," he added.

"There! I told you so!" said Sybil, turning to her husband.

"Then let's go on and eat it, my love. We can leave our two servants here to follow in the wagon with the baggage," said Lyon Berners, leading his wife and his guest to the carriage, and placing them inside with the child and nurse, while he himself mounted to the box beside the coachman.

"Oh! I am very sorry Mr. Berners has been crowded out," regretfully exclaimed Rosa Blondelle, looking after him in surprise as he climbed to his roost.

"Oh, he has not been crowded out! He has gone up there to drive; for the road is not very safe at night, and our coachman is rather too much exhilarated to be trusted," answered Sybil, touching very tenderly upon the weakness of her old servant.

Their road lay along the bank of the river up the valley between the two high mountain ridges; but it was so dark that nothing but these grander features of the landscape could be discerned.

As the carriage rolled slowly and carefully along this rough road, the music of distant waters fell upon the listening ear, and from the faintest hum that could hardly be heard, it gradually swelled into a deafening roar that filled the valley.

"What is that?" fearfully inquired Rosa.

"What is what?" echoed Sybil.

"That horrid noise!"

"Oh! that is the Black Torrent, the head of our Black River," answered Sybil in a low, pleased tone; for the sound of her native waters, however dreadful it might be to strange ears, was delightful to hers.

"Oh! more blackness!" shivered Rosa.

"But it is a beautiful cascade! All beautiful things are not necessarily light, you know."

"No, indeed," answered Rosa, " for the most beautiful woman I have ever seen in my life is very dark." And she raised and pressed the hand of her hostess, to give point to her words.

Sybil did not like the implied flattery, delicately as it was conveyed. She drew her hand away; and then, to heal the little hurt she might have made in doing so, she opened the window and said, pleasantly:

"Look, Mrs. Blondelle! You see the lights of our home now."

Rosa leaned across Sybil to look in the direction indicated, and she saw scattered lights that seemed to be set in the side of the mountain. She saw no house, and she said so.

"That is because the house is built of the very same dark iron-gray rocks that form the mountain; and being immediately at the foot of the mountain, and closely surrounded with trees, cannot at night be distinguished from the mountain itself."

Here the carriage road curved round an expansion of the river that might have been taken either for a very small lake, or a very large pond. And about midway of this curve, or semicircle, the carriage drew up.

On the left-hand was dimly seen the lake; on the right-hand the gate letting into the elm-tree avenue that led straight up to the house.

"That is the Black Pond, and there is Black Hall. More 'blackness,' Mrs. Blondelle," smiled Sybil, who was so delighted to get home that she forgot her jealousy.

The carriage waited only until the gates could be opened by the slow old porter, whom Sybil laughingly greeted as "Cerberus," although the name given him in baptism was that of the keeper of the keys of heaven, and not that of the guardian of the entrance to the other place.

"Cerberus," or rather Peter, warmly welcomed his

young mistress back, and widely stretched the gate for her carriage to pass.

As the carriage rolled easily along the avenue, now thickly carpeted with forest leaves, and as it approached the house, the fine old building, with its many gable ends and curiously twisted chimneys, its steep roofs and latticed windows—all monuments of the old colonial days—came more and more distinctly into view from its background of mountains. Lights were gleaming from upper and lower and all sorts of windows, and the whole aspect of the grand old hospitable mansion proclaimed, "WELCOME."

CHAPTER IX.

THE GUEST-CHAMBERS.

> Deserted rooms of luxury and state,
> Which old magnificence had rudely furnished
> With pictures, cabinets of ancient date,
> And carvings, gilt and burnished.—HOOD.

THE carriage drew up at the foot of a flight of stone steps, leading to the front entrance of the house. The double oak doors stood wide open, showing the lighted hall and a group of people waiting.

Sybil looked eagerly from the carriage window.

"I do declare," she exclaimed, "if there is not, not only Miss Tabby, but Miss Libby and Mrs. Winterose besides; Mrs. Winterose," she explained, turning to her guest, "is the widow of our late land steward. She is also my foster-mother, and the mother of the two maiden ladies, Miss Tabby, who is our housekeeper, and Miss Libby who lives with the widowed parent at home. They have come to welcome us back. Heaven bless them!"

As Sybil spoke, Mr. Berners dropped down from his perch on the coachman's box, and opened the carriage door.

He assisted first his wife, and then their guest, to alight. And then he took the sleeping child from the nurse's arms, while she herself got out.

"You know the way, dearest Sybil! Run on before,

and I will take charge of our fair friend," said Mr. Berners, as he gave his arm to Mrs. Blondelle to lead her up the steps.

But Sybil had not waited for his permission. Too eager to meet the dear old friends of her childhood to care for any one else just then, or even to feel a twinge of jealousy at the words and actions of her husband, she flew past him up the stairs and into the arms of her foster-mother, who folded the beautiful, impetuous creature to her bosom, and welcomed her home with heartfelt emotion.

Miss Tabby and Miss Libby next took their turns to be embraced and kissed.

And then the old servants crowded around to welcome their beloved young mistress; to every one of them she gave a cordial grasp of her hand, and loving words.

"It is very delightful," she said, with tears of joy in her eyes, "it is very, very delightful to be so warmly welcomed home."

"Everything as well as everybody welcomes you home, Miss Sybil! Even the Black Torrent! I never heard the cascade sing so loud and merry as it does to-night!" said Old Abe, or Father Abraham, as he was called, for being a full centenarian and the oldest negro, by twenty years, of any on the estate.

"Thank you, dear Uncle Abe! I *know* you all welcome me home! And I love to think that my torrent does too! And now, Miss Tabby, you got the letter I wrote from Underhill, asking you to have the spare rooms prepared for the visitors we were to bring with us?" inquired Sybil, turning to her housekeeper.

"Yes, ma'am, and your orders is obeyed, and the rooms is all ready, as well as yourn and Mr. Berners', even to the kindling of the fires, which has been burning in the chimneys to air them rooms all this blessed day," answered Miss Tabby.

"That is right, and I thank you; and now here comes our visitor," said Sybil, as her guest approached leaning on her husband's arm. They had certainly lingered a little on the way; but Sybil was too happy to notice that circumstance now. The jealous wife was for the time subdued within her, and all the hospitable hostess was in the ascendant.

"You are welcome to Black Hall, my dear Mrs. Blondelle," she said, advancing to receive her guest. "And now, will you walk into our sitting parlor and rest awhile before taking off your wraps; or shall I show you at once to your rooms, which are quite ready for you?"

"At once to my rooms, if you please, Mrs. Berners; for, you see, my poor little Cromartie is already fast asleep."

"Come, then; you will not have far to go. It is on this floor," said Sybil, with a smile, as she led the way down the wide hall, past the great staircase, and then turned to the right and went down a long passage, until she came to a door, which she opened.

"Here is your bedchamber," said Sybil, inviting her guest to enter a large and richly furnished room; "and beyond this, and connected with it, is another and a smaller apartment, which is properly the dressing-room, but which I have had fitted up as a nursery for your child and his nurse."

"Many thanks," replied Rosa Blondelle, as she followed her hostess into the room, and glanced around with the natural curiosity we all feel in entering a strange place.

The room was very spacious, and had many doors and windows. Its furniture was all green, which would have seemed rather gloomy, but for the bright wood fire on the hearth, that lighted up all the scene with cheerfulness.

Sybil drew an easy-chair to the chimney corner, and invited her guest to sit down.

But Rosa was too curious about her surroundings to yield herself immediately to rest.

"What an interesting old place," she said, walking about the chamber and examining everything.

Meanwhile the nurse-maid, more practical than her mistress, had found the door of the adjoining nursery and passed into it to put her infant charge to bed.

"Oh!" exclaimed Rosa, who had drawn aside one of the green moreen window curtains and was looking out—"Oh! what a wild, beautiful place! But these windows open right upon the grounds, and there are no outside shutters! Is there no danger?"

"No danger whatever, my dear Mrs. Blondelle. These windows open at the back of the house, upon the grounds, which run quite back to the foot of the mountain. These grounds are *very* private, being quite inaccessible, except through the front grounds of the house," said Sybil, soothingly.

"But oh!" whispered Mrs. Blondelle, nowise tranquilized by the answer of her hostess—"Oh! what are those white things that I see standing among the bushes at the foot of the mountain? They look like—tombstones!" she added, with a shudder.

"They *are* tombstones," replied Sybil in a low, grave voice; "that is our family burial-ground, and all the Berners, for seven generations, lie buried there."

"Oh, good gracious!" gasped Rosa Blondelle, dropping the curtain and turning away.

"Don't be alarmed," smiled Sybil. "The place is much farther off than it seems. And now, my dear Mrs. Blondelle, let me make you acquainted with the bearings of this green bedroom, and then you will like it better. You see it is in the right wing of the house, and that accounts for its having windows on three sides, back, front, and end, and doors that connect with the house and doors that lead to the grounds. *This* door," she said, opening one on the left-hand side of the fireplace—"this door leads up this little narrow stair-case directly into my chamber, which is immediately above this, as my dressing-room is immediately above your nursery. So, my dear, if ever you should feel nervous or alarmed, all you have to do is to open this little door, and run up these stairs and knock loudly at the upper door, which is near the head of my bed. I shall hear you, and fly to your assistance."

"Yes," laughed Rosa. "But suppose some robber were to get into these windows, and be right upon me before I could run, what should I do then?"

"Call for assistance, and Mr. Berners and myself will run down to your rescue. But in order to make that practicable, you must always leave that lower stair door unfastened: and you may do it with perfect safety, as it leads nowhere but into my bedroom."

"I will remember always to leave it unfastened," replied Rose.

"But, my dear, I assure you there it not the least shadow of a shade of danger. Our faithful negroes are all around us on the outside, and our faithful dumb guard-

THE GUEST-CHAMBERS. 63

lans sleep on the mats in the large hall and the smaller passages. However, if you still feel nervous, I will have one of the maids sleep in your room, and one of the men sleep in the passage outside," said Sybil.

"Oh, no, not for the world would I disturb the arrangements of the family. I am not at all nervous *now*," said Rosa Blondelle.

"Then, dear, get ready for supper; for it has been ready for us for an hour past, and I am sure you must need it. I will, with your permission, go up to my own room by these stairs; and when I have changed my dress, I will come down the same way and take you in to supper," said Sybil, as, with a smile and a bow, she opened the door and slipped away up to her own room.

Rosa Blondelle passed into the little adjoining nursery to see after her child.

The room, small as it was, had two windows, one west and one south, and a little fireplace north. The east side was only broken by the door that communicated with the bedroom. There were green curtains to the two windows, green carpet on the floor, and green covers to the rocking-chair and the child's chairs, which were the only ones in the room. There was a cot-bed for the nurse and a crib for the child. A well-supplied wash-stand completed the furniture. The child lay sleeping soundly in his crib and the nurse sat by him, occupying herself with some white embroidery that she habitually carried in her pocket, to fill up spare moments profitably.

"Crow is quite well, Janet?" inquired the young mother, approaching and looking at her rosy boy.

"Yes, me leddy, and sleeping like an angel," answered the woman.

"These are very comfortable quarters, Janet."

"Yes, me leddy, though the roaring of yon Black Torrent, as they ca' it, gars me grew. I wonder does it always roar sae loud."

"Oh no, Janet. Mr. Berners says that it only sounds so when very much swollen by the rains. And Mr. Berners should know."

"Aye, ma'am, and sae he suld! And a very fine gentleman is the laird!"

"He is not a laird, Janet! There are no lairds in America."

"And what will he be then, ma'am?"

"Simply a gentleman—Mr. Berners."

"It is a pity he is na a laird, ma'am, and a duke to the back of that! a princely gentleman he is, me leddy."

"I quite agree with you, Janet. Well, leave your charge for a moment, and come and arrange my hair for me. Unluckily I cannot change my dress, for my luggage was left behind at Blackville, and I don't suppose it has arrived here yet," said Rosa Blondelle, as she returned to her room attended by her maid. But there an agreeable surprise met her. She found her trunks set in order, ready for her.

"I declare, there they are! And I suppose the servants who brought them, finding the door wide open and no one in the room, just put them in here and retired. Janet, open that trunk and get out my black velvet, and point lace set. I must not wear anything very light and gay on this first evening, after a fatiguing journey, when we all feel so tired as to be fit for nothing but bed," said Rosa Blondelle, throwing herself languidly into the green-covered easy-chair before the dressing-table.

"And, 'deed, me leddy, there's nae dress ye look say weell in as that bonny black velvet," said the maid.

Rosa knew this well, and for this reason, perhaps, selected the dress.

The maid quickly and skilfully arranged her mistress's hair in its natural golden ringlets, that needed no ornament whatever. And when her toilet was complete, Rosa Blondelle's fair beauty was even more resplendent than usual, from its contrast with the rich blackness of her dress.

"'A star upon the brow of night!'" quoted Sybil, as she entered the room and stood for a moment in involuntary admiration. Then, with a smile, she drew the arm of her guest within her own and led her off to the supper-table, where they were joined by Mr. Berners.

It was a warm wainscotted little room, with crimson carpet and crimson curtains, a good open fire of hickory wood, and a small, but luxuriously spread supper-table.

Mr. Berners led their guest to her place at the board.

THE GUEST-CHAMBERS. 65

and left his wife to follow. These courtesies were no doubt due the visitor, yet they made the wife's heart ache. She hated to miss the attentions her husband had always hitherto bestowed on her alone ; and she hated more to see them lavished on another, and that other a beautiful, fascinating, and, as she half suspected, most dangerous woman. It was in vain she said to herself that these attentions were no more than any gentleman should show to the invited visitor of his wife. She could not argue away her heartache. She could not endure to see her husband touch the beauty's hand. It drove her almost out of her self-possession to see their eyes meet in that provoking mutual smile. Oh! how she repented ever having invited this fatal beauty to her house! And yet she pitied the friendless stranger too, and she struggled bravely against those feelings of jealousy and hatred that were creeping into her heart. And, in fact, from this time the whole inner life of Sybil Berners became one hard struggle between her passions and her reason. And this struggle soon manifested itself in a series of inconsistencies of conduct that were perfectly incomprehensible to both Lyon Berners and Rosa Blondelle.

For instance, on this first night at home, while they sat at the supper-table. Sybil was silent, abstracted, and depressed. Her companions mentally ascribed her condition to fatigue ; but Sybil then scarcely knew what fatigue meant. After supper she aroused herself by an effort, and offered to attend Mrs. Blondelle back again to that lady's chamber ; and when they got there, even lingered a little while, and very kindly repeated her request that if Rosa should be frightened in the night, she should run up the communicating stairs and rap at Sybil's bedroom door for assistance. And then Sybil bade her visitor good-night, and vanished up the stairs.

The travelers were all very tired, and so, notwithstanding Rosa's fears and Sybil's jealousy, they were all soon fast asleep.

CHAPTER X.

THE JEALOUS BRIDE.

Yes, she was jealous, though she did not show it,
For jealousy dislikes the world to know it.—BYRON.

Rosa was the last to wake up in the morning. The nurse had already dressed the child and taken him from the room; so Rosa rang her bell to bring the truants back.

Janet came alone.

"Where is little Crow?" inquired Crow's mamma.

"In the breakfast-room, me leddy, on the laird's knee," answered the girl.

"I tell you there are no lairds in America, Janet!" said the lady, impatiently.

"Well, on the gentleman's knee, ma'am."

"Very well, now come help me to dress."

Janet hastened to obey, and in half an hour Rosa Blondelle issued from her chamber, looking if possible even more beautiful than she had looked on the previous evening; for she wore an elegant morning robe of white cashmere, embroidered down the front and around the bodice, sleeves and skirt with a border of blue bells, and she had her splendid hair dressed in the simple natural ringlets that were the most becoming to her.

Janet walked before her mistress, to show the way. Far up the great hall, she opened a door on the left-hand side, admitting the lady to a delightful front room, whose front windows looked out upon the lake, the valley, and the opposite range of mountains.

It was a golden October morning, and from a cloudless deep-blue sky the sun shone down in dazzling splendor upon the valley, kindling up into a conflagration of living light all the variegated foliage of the trees, upon the mountain sides and the river's banks, where the glowing crimson of the oak and the flaming orange of the elm mingled with the royal purple of the dogwood and the deep green of the cedar. And all this gorgeousness of coloring was reflected in the lake, whose waters seemed dyed with all the prismatic hues of the rainbow.

"' Black Valley,' indeed ! " said Rosa Blondelle, with a smile, as she entered the breakfast-room and glanced through the windows upon the magnificent scene; "' Black Valley,' call you this ?—I should rather call it 'Bright Valley.' Oh, what a glorious day, and oh, what a glorious scene ! Good-morning, Mrs. Berners. Good-morning, Mr. Berners. Little Crow, this kind gentleman is spoiling you," she said, as she advanced with smiling eyes and outstretched hands to greet her host and hostess, who had risen from their chairs to meet her.

They both received her very kindly, even affectionately; and as they had waited only for her presence to have breakfast, Sybil now rang and ordered it to be brought in.

Sybil's own little " high chair " had been rummaged out from its corner in the lumber-room and dusted, and brought in for the use of the baby-boy; who, in honor of his mother, was permitted to sit up to the table with the grown people.

" But why, I repeat, should you call this glorious vale the ' Black Valley ' ? " inquired Rosa, as they all gathered around the board.

" It was black enough last night, was it not?" asked Mr. Berners, with a smile.

" Oh, it was black everywhere last night; but no blacker here than elsewhere, so I don't see the justice of calling this the Black Valley. I should call it rather the ' Valley of the Sun.' "

" Would not the ' Valley of the Pyrotechnics' do as well ? " inquired Lyon Berners, with dry humor.

"I think it would," replied Rosa, quite seriously, " for certainly this morning, with this glorious sunshine and these glowing, sparkling woods and waters, the place is a perfect spectacle of fireworks ! "

" You view the scenery at its best and brightest. It is never so beautiful and brilliant as on a clear sunny autumn noonday. At all other seasons, and at all other hours, it is gloomy enough. In a very few hours from this, when the sun gets behind the mountain, it will be quite black enough to justify its name," said Mr. Berners very gravely

The conversation had been carried on between Mr. Berners and Mrs. Blondelle exclusively. Sybil had not volunteered a word; and it happened also that neither of her companions had addressed a word to her. She felt as if she were dropped out of their talk, and though bodily present, dropped out of their company as well. She felt that this was very hard; and once more she experienced the wild and vain regret that she had ever invited this too-alluring stranger to become an inmate of her house.

Before now, when they had been together, Lyon Berners had been accustomed to think of, smile on, talk to, only her, his wife! Now his thoughts, smiles, conversation were all divided with another!—Oh no! Oh no! *not divided*, but almost entirely absorbed by that other! At least so suspected the jealous wife.

"Is it possible, oh! is it possible that he loves me less than formerly? that he loves me not at all? that he loves this stranger?" thought Sybil, as she watched her husband and her friend, entirely taken up with each other, and entirely oblivious of her! And at this thought a sensation of sickness and faintness came over her, and she saved herself from falling, only by a great effort of self-command. They, talking to each other, smiling at each other, enjoying each other's exclusive attention, did not observe her emotion, although almost any casual spectator must have seen it in the deadly pallor of her face.

In all this there was little to arouse her jealousy; and perhaps there was nothing at all. Her heart pang may have come of a false fear, or a true one; who could then tell?

For my own part, looking towards this situation of affairs through the light of after knowledge, I think that her fears were, even, then well-founded; that even then it was a true instinct which warned her that her adored husband, he to whom her whole heart, soul, and spirit were entirely given, he for whom only she "lived and moved and had her being," he was becoming fascinated, for the time being at least, by this beautiful stranger, who was evidently also flattered by his attentions. And this in the very honeymoon of the bride to whom he owed so much!

And yet indeed, I say, still speaking in the light of after knowledge, that at this time he was equally unconscious of his wife's jealousy, or of any wrong-doing on his own part, calculated to arouse it. Had Lyon Berners suspected that his attentions to their fair guest gave such deep pain to his high-spirited wife, he would at least have modified them to retain her confidence. But he suspected nothing. Sybil revealed nothing; her pride was even greater than her jealousy; for this last daughter of the House of Berners inherited all the pride of all her line. At this time, this pride quite enabled her to keep her pain to herself.

At length the severe ordeal was, for the moment, over. She perceived that her companions had finished breakfast, and so she arose from the table, leaving her example to be followed by them.

"Let me lead you to our pleasant morning parlor. It is just across the hall, and commands the same view of the lake and mountains that this room does—from the front windows I mean; but from the end windows you get a view *up* the valley, and may catch glimpses of the Black Torrent as it rushes roaring down the side of the mountain," said Mr. Berners, as he offered his hand to Mrs. Blondelle and led her from the breakfast parlor.

Sybil looked after them with pallid cheeks and darkening brows; then she rushed up into her own chamber, locked her door, threw herself upon her bed and gave way to a storm of sobs and tears. While she was still weeping vehemently, there came a knock at the door. She lifted up her head and listened; controlling her voice as well as she could, she inquired:

"Who is there, and what is wanted?"

"It is I, my dear, and I want to come in," answered the voice of her husband.

"I have not even the privilege of shutting myself up to weep alone! for I belong to one who can invade my privacy or command my presence at his pleasure!" exclaimed Sybil in bitterness of spirit; and yet bitterness that was mingled with a strange, deep sweetness too! for she loved to feel that *she did* belong to Lyon Berners; that *he had* the privilege of invading her privacy, or commanding her presence at his pleasure. And ah! *that* was a happiness Rosa Blondelle would not share!

"Well, well my darling! are you going to let me in?" inquired Mr. Berners, after a moment of patient waiting.

"Yes, in an instant, dear!" exclaimed Sybil, hastily wiping her eyes and trying to efface all signs of weeping from her countenance.

Then she opened the door.

Her husband entered, closed the door, and then turned around with some light, gay word; but at the sight of his wife's pale and agitated face, he started in surprise and distress, exclaiming:

"Why, Sybil! Why, my darling! What on earth is the matter? What has happened?"

At the sound of his anxious voice, at the sight of his troubled face, Sybil turned aside, sank upon the corner of the sofa, dropped her head upon its cushions, and yielded to a tempest of sobs and tears.

He hurried to her side, sat down and drew her head upon his bosom, and in much alarm exclaimed again:

"In the name of Heaven, Sybil! what is all this about? what has happened to distress you so deeply? Have you heard any bad news?" he inquired as he caressed and tried to soothe her.

She did not repel his caresses; for, jealous as she was, she felt no anger towards him then. She laid her head upon his bosom, and sobbed aloud.

"What bad news have you heard, dear Sybil?" repeated Mr. Berners.

"Oh, none at all! What bad news *could* I hear to make *me* weep? I do not care as much as that for anything on earth, or anybody except you!" she answered, lifting her head from his bosom as she spoke, and then dropping it again when she had finished.

"Then what is it that troubles you, my own dear wife? What cause can you have for weeping?" he inquired, tenderly caressing the beautiful, wayward creature.

She lifted her head, and smiled through her tears as she answered:

"None at all, I believe. What does Kotzebue say? 'To laugh or cry without a reason, is one of the few privileges women have.' I have no good reason to weep, dear Lyon! I know that I have not. But I am nervous and hysterical, I believe," she added; for, as before, his tender caresses dispelled her jealousy and restored her trust. With her head resting on his bosom; with his arms around her; with his eye smiling down upon hers, she could not look in his face and retain her jealous doubts.

"I have no reason in the world for weeping. I am just a nervous, hysterical woman—*like the rest!* It is no wonder men, who see the weakness of our sex, refuse to trust us with any power," she added, with a light laugh

"But I utterly deny this alleged 'weakness of your sex.' You bewray yourself and sex by repeating the the slander, though even in jest, as I see you are. *You* are not weak, my Sybil. Nor do you weep without a cause. You have some good and sufficient reason for your tears."

"Indeed, no; I have none. I am only nervous and hysterical, and thoroughly ashamed of myself for being so," she answered, very sincerely, for she was really thoroughly ashamed of her late jealousy, and anxious to conceal it from her husband.

He looked at her so inquisitively, not to say so incredulously, that she hastened to add:

"This is really nothing but nervous irritability, dear Lyon. Do not distress yourself about my moods."

"But I must, my darling. Whether their cause is mental or physical, real or imaginary, I must trouble myself about your tears," answered Lyon Berners, with grave tenderness.

"Then let it be about my *next* ones; not these that are past and gone. And now to a pleasant topic. The ball that we are expected to give."

"Yes, dear, that is *your* affair. But I am ready to give you any assistance in my power. Your cards, I believe, are all printed?"

"Yes; that was a happy idea to get the cards printed while we stopped in New York."

"Now they only need filling up with names and dates.

"And the addition of one little word, Lyon."

"Well and what is that?"

"*Masks.*"

"MASKS!" echoed Mr. Berners, in surprise.

"MASKS," reiterated Mrs. Berners with a smile.

"Why, my dear Sybil, what on earth do you mean?"

"Why, that our party shall be a masked, fancy-dress ball. That will be something new in this old-fashioned neighborhood."

"Yes, and something startling to our old-fashioned neighbors," said Mr. Berners, with a dubious shake of his head.

"So much the better. They need startling, and I intend to startle them."

"As you please, my dear, wayward Sybil. But when do you propose this affair to come off?"

"On All-Hallow Eve."

"Good. All-Hallow Eve is the proper sort of an eld ritch night for such a piece of diablerie as a mask ball to be held," laughed Mr. Berners.

"But, now, seriously, Lyon; do you really dislike or disapprove this plan? If you do I will willingly modify it according to your judgment; or even, if you wish it, I will willingly drop it altogether," she said, very earnestly.

"My dear, impetuous Sybil, you should make no such sacrifices, even if I *did* dislike or disapprove your plan; but I do neither. I dare say I shall enjoy the masquerade as much as any one; and that it will be very popular and quite a success. But now, near Sybil, let me hear what fantastic shape you will assume at this witches' dance?"

"I will tell *you*, Lyon; but mind, you must keep the secret."

"Oh! inviolably," said Mr. Berners, with a laugh.

"Oh! I mean only that you must not speak of it outside the family, because, you see, it is such a perfectly original character that if it was known it would be taken by half a dozen people at least."

"I will never breathe its name," laughed Lyon.

"Then the character I shall take is——"

"What?"

"Fire!"

"Fire?"

"Fire."

"Ha! ha! ha! it will suit you admirably, my little Berners of the Burning Heart. But how on earth will you contrive to costume and impersonate the consuming element?"

"It would take me a week to tell you, and then you, would not understand. But you shall see."

"I hope you will not set all your company in a flame; that is all, my dear."

"But I shall *try* to do so. And now, dear Lyon, if you wish to help me, sit down at my writing-table, there, and fill out and direct the invitations, you will find the visiting list, printed cards, aud blank envelopes all in a parcel in the desk."

"But is it not early to send them?" inquired Mr. Berners, as he seated himself at the table.

"No; not for a mask ball. This is the tenth. The ball is to come off on the thirty-first. If the cards are sent to-day, our friends will have just three weeks to get ready, which will not be too long to select their characters and contrive their costumes."

"I suppose you know best, my dear," said Mr. Berners, as he referred to the visiting list and began to prepare for his task.

Sybil went to her dressing-glass and began to arrange her somewhat disordered hair. While she stood there, she suddenly inquired:

"Where did you leave Mrs. Blondelle?"

"I did not leave her anywhere. She left me. She excused herself, and went—to her room, I suppose."

"Ah!" sighed Sybil. She did not like this answer. She was sorry to know that her husband had remained with the beauty until the beauty had left him. She tortured herself with the thought that, if Mrs. Blondelle had remained in the morning room, Mr. Berners would have been there at her side.

So morbid was now the condition of Sybil that a word was enough to arouse her jealousy, a caress sufficient to allay it. *She* would not leave Lyon to himself, she thought. He should know the difference between his wife and his guest in that particular. So the guest, being now in her own room, where her hostess heartily wished she might spend the greater portion of the day, Sybil felt free from the pressing duties of hospitality, at least for the time being; and so she drew a chair to the corner of the same table occupied by her husband, and she began to help him in his task by directing the envelopes, while he filled out the cards. Thus sitting together, working in unison, and conversing occasionally, they passed the morning—a happier morning than Sybil had seen for several days.

But of course they met their guest again at dinner, where Rosa Blondelle was as fascinating and Lyon Berners as much fascinated as before, and where Sybil's mental malady returned in full force.

Oh, these transcient fascinations, what eternal miseries they sometimes bring!

But a greater trial awaited the jealous wife in the evening, when they were all gathered in the drawing-room, and Rosa Blondelle, beautifully dressed, seated herself at the grand piano, and began to sing and play some of the impassioned songs from the Italian operas; and Lyon Berners, a very great enthusiast in music, hung over the siren, doubly entranced by her beauty and her voice. Sybil, too, stood with the little group at the piano; but she stood back in the shade, where the expression of her agonized face could not be seen by the other two, even if they had been at leisure to observe her. She was suffering the fiercest tortures of jealousy.

Sybil's education had been neglected, as I have told you. She had a fine contralto voice and a perfect ear, but these were both uncultivated; and so she could only sing and play the simplest ballads in the language. She had often regretted her want of power to please the fastidious musical taste of her husband; but never so bitterly as now, when she saw that power in the possession of another, and that other a beauty, a rival, and an inmate of her house. Oh, how deeply she now deplored her short-sightedness in bringing this siren to her home!

At the most impassioned, most expressive passages of the music, Rosa Blondelle would lift her eloquent blue eyes to those of Lyon Berners, who responded to their language.

And Sybil stood in the shadow near them, with pallid cheeks, compressed lips, and glittering eyes—mute, still, full of repressed anguish and restrained fury.

Ah, Rosa Blondelle, take heed! Better that you should

come between the lioness and her young than between Sybil Berners and her love!

Yet again, on this evening, this jealous wife, this strange young creature, so full of contradictions and inconsistencies; so strong, yet so weak; so confiding, yet so suspicious; so magnanimous, yet so vindictive; once again, I say, successfully exerted her wonderful powers of self-control, and endured the ordeal of that evening in silence, and at its close bade her guest good-night without betraying the anguish of her heart.

When she found herself alone with her husband in their chamber, her fortitude nearly forsook her, especially as he himself immediately opened the subject of their beautiful guest.

"She is perfectly charming," said Mr. Berners. "Every day develops some new gift or grace of hers! My dear Sybil, you never did a better deed than in asking this lovely lady to our house. She will be an invaluable acquisition to our lonely fireside this winter."

"You did not use to think our fireside was lonely! You used to be very jealous of our domestic privacy!" Sybil *thought* to herself; but she gave no expression to this thought. On the contrary, controlling herself, and steadying her voice with an effort, she said smilingly:

"If you had met this 'lovely lady' before you married me, and had found her also free, you would have made her your wife."

"I! No, indeed!" impulsively and most sincerely answered Lyon Berners, as he raised his eyes in astonishment to the face of Sybil. But he could see nothing there. Her face was in deep shadow, where she purposely kept it to conceal its pallor and its tremor.

"But why, if you had met her before you married me, and found her free, why should you not have made her your wife?" persisted Sybil.

"'Why?'—what a question! Because, in the first place, dear Sybil, I loved *you, you only*, long before I ever married you!" said Lyon Berners in increasing surprise.

"But—if you had met her before you had ever seen me, you would have loved and married her."

"No! On my honor, Sybil!"

"Yet you admire her so much!"

"Dear Sybil! I admire all things beautiful in nature and art, but I don't want to marry all!"

"And are you sure that this beautiful Rosa Blondelle would not make you a more suitable companion than I do?" she inquired.

His whole manner now changed. Turning towards her he took both her hands in his own, and looking gravely and sweetly in her face, he answered:

"My wife! such questions between you and me ought never to arise, even in jest. I hold the marriage relation always too sacred for such trifling! And *our* relations towards each other seem to me dearer, sweeter, more sacred even, than those of most other married couples! No, my own Sybil! Soul of my soul! there is no woman that I ever did, or ever could prefer to you!" And he drew her to his bosom, and pressed her there in all good faith and true love. And his grave and tender rebuke did even more to tranquilize her jealousy than all his caresses had done.

"I know it! I know it, my dear husband! But it is only when I feel how imperfect, how unworthy of you, I am, that I ever have doubts!" she murmured with a sigh of infinite relief.

CHAPTER XI.

LOVE AND JEALOUSY.

There was a time when bliss
Shone o'er her heart from every look of his;
When but to see him, hear him, breathe the air
In which he dwelt, was her soul's fondest prayer;
When round him hung such a perpetual spell,
Whate'er he did none ever did so well;
Yet now he comes, brighter than ever, far,—
He beamed before; but ah! not bright for her.—MOORE.

FORTUNATELY for the fascinated husband and the jealous wife, the Circuit Court was now sitting at Blackville, and the lawyer's professional duties demanded all Mr. Berners' time.

Only one year before this, when the struggling young lawyer depended upon his work for his bread, he could

LOVE AND JEALOUSY. 77

hardly get a paying client; now that he was entirely independent of his profession, he was overwhelmed with business. As the wealthy master of the Black Valley manor with its rich dependencies of farms, quarries, mills, and hamlets, he might have led the easy life of a country gentleman. But in Lyon Berners' apprehension, work was duty; and so to work he went, as if he had had to get his living by it.

Every day he left home at nine o'clock in the morning in order to be present at the opening of the court at ten. He reached home again at four in the afternoon, and dined with Sybil and Rosa. After dinner he retired to his study, and spent the evening in working up his briefs and preparing for the next day's business.

Thus he was entirely separated from his guest, who never saw him except at the table, with the breadth of the board between them, and almost entirely from his wife, who only had his company to herself at night.

Yet Sybil was content. Her love, if, in some of its phases, it was a jealous and exacting passion, in others was a noble and generous principle. She would not spare a glance, a smile, a caress of his, to any other woman; yet she would give him wholly up to his duty, his profession, his country, or to any grand *impersonal* object. And the few hours out of the twenty-four when she could enjoy his society apart from her dreaded rival, compensated her for the many when he was absent or engaged upon his professional duties.

But ah! this could not last!

It happened, very naturally, that while Mr. Lyon Berners spent his mornings in the court-house, Mrs. Lyon Berners spent hers in receiving the calls and congratulations of her friends, to whom she always presented her permanent visitor, Mrs. Blondelle.

At length two unconnected events happened at the same time. The court adjourned, and the last visit of ceremony was paid.

Sybil, at the instance of Mr. Berners, gave a dinner-party, and they entertained the judges and barristers of the court. And upon that occasion, Mrs. Blondelle of course was introduced, and equally of course, her beauty made a very great sensation. And Sybil was well pleased.

She was perfectly willing that her protégée should outshine her in every company, if only she did not outrival her in her husband's admiration.

But ah! whether it was that the long interruption of his conversations with the beautiful blonde had given a new zest to the pleasure he enjoyed in her society, or whether his admiration for her had been ever, under all circumstances, on the increase, or whether both these causes combined to influence his conduct, is not known; but it is certain that from this time, Lyon Berners became more and more blindly devoted to Rosa Blondelle. And yet, under and over and through all this, the husband loved his wife as he never did or could love any other woman. But Rosa Blondelle was one of those vain and shallow women who must and will have a sentimental flirtation or a platonic friendship with some man or boy, always on hand. She, like those of her mischievous class, really meant no harm, while doing a great deal of wrong. Such a woman will engage a husband's affections and break a wife's heart from mere vanity, and for mere pastime, without the slightest regard for either of her victims. And yet, because they have not been grossly guilty, as well as deeply sinful, they retain their positions in society.

Rosa Blondelle's whole life lay in these sentimental flirtations and platonic friendships. Without a lover, she did not care to live at all. Yet hers was a sham love, though her victims were not often sham lovers. With her fair and most innocent face, Rosa Blondelle was false and shallow. And Lyon Berners knew this; and even while yielding himself to the fascination of her smiles, he could not help comparing her, to her great disadvantage, with his own true, earnest, deep-hearted wife.

But every morning, while Sybil was engaged in her domestic duties, which were now greatly increased by the preparations that were going on for the masquerade ball, Lyon Berners would be walking with Rosa Blondelle, exploring the romantic glens of the Black Valley, or wandering along the picturesque banks of the Black River. Or if the weather happened to be inclement, Mr. Berners and Mrs. Blondelle would sit in the library together, deep in German mysticism or French sentiment.

Every evening Rosa sat at the grand piano, singing for him the most impassioned songs from the German and Italian operas; and Lyon hung over her chair turning her music, and enraptured with her beauty.

Ah! Rosa Blondelle! vain and selfish and shallow coquette! Trifle, if you must, with any other man's love, with any other woman's peace; but you had better invade the lair of the lioness, and seize her cubs—you had better walk blindfold upon the abyss of Hades, than come between Sybil Berners and her husband!

For Sybil saw it all! and not only as any other woman might have seen it, just as it was, but as the jealous wife did—with vast exaggerations and awful forebodings.

They did not suspect how much she knew, or how much more she imagined. Before them the refined instinct of the lady still kept down the angry passions of the woman.

Whenever her emotions were about to overcome her, she slipped away, not to her own room, where she was liable to interruption, but far up into the empty attics of the old house, where, in some corresponding chamber of desolation, she gave way to such storms of anguish and despair as leave the deepest

"Traces on heart and brain."

And after an hour or two she would return to the drawing-room, whence she had never been missed by the pair of sentimentalists, who had been too much absorbed in each other, and in Mozart or Beethoven, to notice her absence.

And while all unconscious of her, they continued their musical flirtation, she would sit with her back to the light, toying with her crochet-work and listening to Rosa's songs.

She was still as a volcano before it bursts forth to bury cities under its burning lava flood!

Why did she not, in the sacred privacy of their mutual apartment appeal to the better nature of her husband by telling him how much his flirtation with their guest pained her, his wife? Or else, why had she not spoken plainly with her guest?

Why? Because Sybil Berners had too much pride and too little faith to do the one or the other. She could not stoop to plead with her husband for the love that she thought he had withdrawn from her; still less could she bend to tell her guest how much his defection troubled her. Nor did she believe her interference would do any good. For, to Sybil Berners' earnest nature, all things seemed earnest, and this vain and shallow flirtation wore the aspect of a deep, impassioned attachment. And in her forbearance she acted from instinct rather than from reason, for she never even thought of interfering between these platonists. So, outwardly at least, she was calm. But this calmness could not last. Her heart was bleeding, burning, breaking! and its prisoned flood of fire and blood must burst forth at length. The volcano seems quiet; but the pent up lava in its bosom must at last give forth mutterings of its impending irruption, and swiftly upon these mutterings must follow flames and ruin!

It happened thus with Sybil.

One morning, when the weather was too threatening to permit any one to indulge in an outdoor walk, it chanced that Lyon and Sybil Berners were sitting together at a center-table in the parlor—Lyon reading the morning paper; Sybil *trying* to read a new magazine—when Rosa Blondelle, with her flowing, azure-hued robes and her floating golden locks, and her beaming smiles, entered the room and seated herself at the table, saying sweetly:

"My dear Mrs. Berners, is it to-morrow that you and I have arranged to drive out and return the calls that were made upon us?"

"Yes, madam," politely replied Sybil.

"Then, dear Mr. Berners, I shall have to ask you to write a few visiting-cards for me. I have not an engraved one in the world. But you write such a beautiful hand, that your writing will look like copper-plate. You will oblige me?" she inquired, smiling, and placing a pack of blank cards before him.

"With the greatest pleasure," answered **Lyon Berners**, promptly putting aside his paper.

Rosa turned to leave the room.

"Will you not remain with us?" courteously inquired Sybil.

"No, dear; much as I should like to do so," replied Rosa.

"But why?" inquired Lyon Berners, looking disappointed

"Oh! because I have my dress to see about. We are far from all fashionable modistes here; but I must try to do honor to madam's masquerade for all that," laughed Rosa, as she passed gracefully out of the room.

With a sigh that seemed to his sorrowing wife to betray his regret for the beauty's departure, Lyon Berners drew the packet of blank cards before him, scattered them in a loose heap on his left hand, and then selecting one at a time began to write. As he carefully wrote upon and finished each card, he as carefully laid it on his right hand, until a little heap grew there.

Sybil, who glorified in all her husband's accomplishments, from the grandest to the least, admired very much his skill in ornamental chirography. She drew her chair closer to the table, and took up the topmost card, and began to decipher rather than to read, the name in the beautiful old English characters, so tangled in a thicket of rosebuds and forget-me-nots as to be scarcely legible. She looked closely and more closely at the name on the card.

What was there in it to drive all the color from her cheeks?

She snatched up and scrutinized a second card, a third, a fourth; then, springing to her feet, she seized the whole mass, hurled them into the fire, and turned, and confronted her husband.

Her teeth were clenched upon her bloodless lips, her face seemed marble, her eyes lambent flames.

He rose to his feet in surprise and dismay.

"SYBIL! what is all this? Why have you destroyed the cards?"

"Why?" she gasped, pressing both hands upon her heart, as if to keep down its horrible throbbing. "Why? Because they are lies! *lies!* LIES!"

"SYBIL! have you gone suddenly mad?" he cried gazing at the "embodied storm" before him with increasing astonishment and consternation.

"No! I have suddenly come to my senses!" she gasped between the catches of her breath, for she could scarcely speak.

"You must calm yourself, and tell me what this means, my wife," said Lyon Berners exerting a great control over himself, and pushing aside the last card he had written.

But she snatched up that card, glanced at it fiercely tore it in two, and threw the fragments far, apart exclaiming in bitter triumph:

"Not yet! oh! not yet! I am not dead yet! Nor have the halls and acres of my fathers passed quite away from their daughter to the possession of a traitor and an ingrate."

He gazed upon her now in amazement and alarm. *Had* she gone suddenly mad?

She stood there before him the incarnation of the fiercest and intensest passion he had ever seen or imagined.

He went and took her in his arms, saying more gently than before:

"Sybil, what is it?"

She tried, harshly and cruelly, to break from him. But he held her in a fast, loving embrace, murmuring still:

"Sybil, you must tell me what troubles you?"

"What troubles me!" she furiously exclaimed. "Let me go, man! Your touch is a dishonor to me! Let me go!"

"But, dearest Sybil."

"Let me go, I say! What! will you use your *brute strength to hold me?*"

He dropped his arms, and left her free.

"No; I beg your pardon, Sybil. I thought you were my loving wife," he said.

"You were mistaken. I am not Rosa Blondelle!" she cried.

"Hush! hush! my dearest Sybil!" he muttered earnestly, as he went and closed and locked the parlor door, to save her from being seen by the servants in her present insane passion.

But she swept past him like a storm, and laid her hand on the lock. She found it fast.

"Open, and let me pass," she cried.

"No, no, my dear Sybil. Remain here until you are calmer, and then tell me—"

"Let me out, I say!"

"But, dearest Sybil."

"What! would you *keep me a prisoner—by force ?* " she cried, with a cruel sneer.

He unlocked the door and set it wide open.

"No, even though you are a lunatic, as I do believe. Go, and expose your condition, if you must. I cannot restrain you by fair means, and I will not by foul."

And Sybil swept from the room, but she did not expose herself. She fled away to that "chamber of desolation," where she had passed so many agonizing hours, and threw herself, face downwards, upon the floor, and lay there in the collapse of utter despair.

Meanwhile Lyon Berners paced up and down the parlor-floor.

CHAPTER XII.

"CRUEL AS THE GRAVE."

Go, when the hunter's hand hath wrung
From forest cave her shrieking young,
And calm the raging lioness;
But soothe not—mock not my distress.—BYRON.

LYON BERNERS was utterly perplexed and troubled He could not in any way explain to himself the sudden and furious passion of his wife.

Suddenly it occurred to him that it was in some way connected with the cards she had thrown into the fire. They were not all burned up. Some few had fallen scorched upon the hearth. These he gathered up and examined; and as he looked at one after another, his face expressed, in turn, surprise, dismay, and amusement. Then he burst out laughing. He really could not help doing so, serious as the subject was; for upon every single card, instead of Rosa Blondelle, he had written:

Mrs. ROSA BERNERS.

"Was there ever such a mischief of a mistake?" he exclaimed, as he ceased laughing and sat down by his table to consider what was to be done next.

"Poor Sybil! poor, dear, fiery-hearted child, it is no wonder! And yet, Heaven truly knows it was because I was thinking of *you*, and not of the owner of the cards, that I wrote that name upon them unconsciously," he said to himself, as he sat with his fine head bowed upon his hand, gravely reviewing the history of the last few days.

His eyes were opened now—not only to his wife's jealousy, but to his own thoughtless conduct in doing anything to arouse it.

In the innermost of his own soul he was so sure of the perfect integrity of his love for his wife, that it had never before occurred to him that *she* could doubt it—that any unconscious act or thoughtless gallantry on his part could cause her to doubt it.

"Now, however, he remembered with remorse that, of late, since the rising of the court, all his mornings and evenings had been spent exclusively in the company of the beautiful blonde. Any wife under such circumstances might have been jealous; but few could have suffered such agonies of wounded love as wrung the bosom of Sybil Berners,—of Sybil Berners, the last of a race in whose nature more of the divine and more of the infernal met than in almost any other race that ever lived on earth.

Her husband thought of all this now. He remembered what lovers and what haters the men and women of her house had been.

He recalled how, in one generation, a certain Reginald Berners, who was engaged to be married to a very lovely young lady, on one occasion found his betrothed and an imaginary rival sitting side by side, amusing themselves with what they might have considered a very harmless flirtation, when, transported with jealous fury, he slew the man before the very eyes of the girl. For this crime Reginald was tried, but for some inexplicable reason, acquitted; and he lived to marry the girl for whose sake he had imbrued his hands in a fellow-man's blood

He recalled how, in another generation, one Agatha Berners, in a frenzy of jealousy, had stabbed her rival, and then thrown herself into the Black Lake. Fortunately neither of the attempted crimes had been consummated, for the wounded woman recovered, and the would-be suicide lived to wear out her days in a convent.

Reflecting upon these terrible outbursts of the family passion, Lyon Berners became very much alarmed for Sybil.

He started up and went in search of her. He looked successively through the drawing-room, and dining-room, and library. Not finding her in any of these rooms, he ascended to the second floor and sought her in their own apartment. Still not finding her, his alarm became agony.

"I will search every square yard within these walls," he said as he hurried through all the empty chambers of that floor, and then went up into the attic.

There, in the lumber-room—the chamber of desolation—he found his wife, lying with her face downwards on the floor. He hastened towards her, fearing that she was in a swoon. But no; she was only exhausted by the violence of her emotions.

Without saying a word, he lifted her in his arms as if she had been a child. She was too faint now to resist him. He carried her downstairs to her own chamber and laid her on the sofa, and while he gently smoothed the damp dark hair from her pale brow, he whispered softly:

"My wife, I know now what has troubled you. It was a great error, my own dear Sybil. You have no cause to doubt me, or to distress yourself."

"She did not reply, but with a tearless sob, turned her face to the wall."

"It was of *you* that I was thinking, my beloved, when I wrote that name on the cards," he continued, as he still smoothed her hair with his light mesmeric touch. She did not repel his caresses, but neither did she reply to his words. And he saw, by the heaving of her bosom and the quivering of her lips, that the storm had not yet subsided.

He assayed once more to reassure her.

"Dear wife," he earnestly commenced, "you believe that my affections are inconstant, and that they have wandered from you?"

She answered by a nod and another tearless sob, but she did not look around or speak to him.

"Yet withal you believe me to be a man of truthful words?"

Again she nodded acquiescence.

"Then, dear Sybil, you must believe my words when I assure you, on my sacred trust and honor, that your suspicions of me are utterly erroneous."

Now she turned her head, opened her large dark eyes in astonishment, and gazed into his earnest face.

"As Heaven hears me, my own dear wife, I love no other woman in the world but you."

"But—you are almost always with *her!*" at length replied Sybil, with another dry sob.

"I confess that, dear; but it was because you were almost always absent on your domestic affairs."

"You hang enraptured over her, when she sings and plays!"

"Enraptured with her music, darling, not with her. To me she is a prima donna, whose performances I must admire and applaud—nothing more.'

"Then I wish I was a prima donna too," said Sybil, bitterly.

"My wife!" he exclaimed.

"Yes, I do! I would be all in all to you, Lyon, as you are everything to me," she cried, her face quivering, her bosom heaving with emotion.

"My own dear Sybil, you *are* all in all to me. Do you not know dear, that you are unique? that there is not another like you in the world; and that I value you and love you accordingly? What is this shallow-hearted blonde beauty to me? This woman, who, in a week, could forget the man who had robbed and deserted her, and give herself up to amusement! No, dear wife. I may be pleased with her good-natured efforts to please me; I may admire her beauty and delight in her music; but I care so little for herself, that were she to die today, I should only say, 'Poor thing,' and immediately forget her, while if *you* were to die, dear wife, life would be a living death and the world a sepulchre to me!"

"Is this true? Oh! is this indeed true?" exclaimed Sybil, in deep emotion.

"As I am a man of truth, it is as true as Heaven!" answered Lyon Berners, earnestly.

And Sybil turned and threw herself in his arms, weeping for joy.

"You shall have no more cause for distress, dear, warm-hearted wife. This lady must find other audience for her music. For, as to me, I shall not indulge in her society at such a cost to your feelings," said Lyon Berners earnestly, as he returned her warm caress.

"No, no, no, no," exclaimed Sybil, generously. "You shall deny yourself no pleasure, for my sake, dear, dear Lyon! I am not such a churl as to require such a sacrifice. Only let me feel sure of your love, and then you may read with her all the morning, and play and sing with her all the evening, and I shall not care. I shall even be pleased, because you are so. But only let me feel sure of your love. For, oh! dear Lyon! I live only in your heart, and if any woman were to thrust me thence, I should die!"

"Nor man, nor woman, nor angel, nor devil, shall ever do that, dear Sybil," he earnestly answered.

The reconciliation between the husband and the wife was perfect. And Sybil was so happy that, in the lightness of her heart, she became kinder to Mrs Blondelle than she had been for many days past.

But as for Mr. Berners, from this time he carefully avoided Mrs. Blondelle. He was as courteous to her as ever, even more courteous than ever when his wife was present, but as soon as Sybil would leave the room, Lyon would make some excuse and follow her. This went on for some days, during which Mrs. Blondelle, being cut short in her platonic flirtation, first wondered and then moped, and then resolved to win back her fancied slave. So she whitened her face with bismuth, to make it look pale and interesting, and she arranged her golden locks and flowing robes with the most studied air of graceful neglect, and she affected silence, pensiveness, and abstraction; and thus she utterly imposed on Lyon Berners, whose sympathies were awakened by her.

"Is it possible that this pretty little fool can really be pleased with me, and pained by my neglect?" he inquired of himself. And then, human being like, he flattered himself and pitied her.

When this course of conduct had been kept up for a

week, it happened one day that Sybil went alone to Blackville to purchase some articles for her approaching mask ball.

Lyon Berners was reclining on the sofa in the drawing-room, with the last number of the "North American Review" in his hands.

Suddenly a soft hand stole into his, and a soft voice murmured in his ear:

"Mr Berners, how have I been so unhappy as to offend you?"

He looked up in surprise to see Rosa Blondelle standing by him. Her lovely face was very pale, her beautiful hair in disorder, her blue eyes full of tears, her tender voice tremulous with emotion.

As Lyon Berners met her appealing gaze his heart smote him for his late coldness to her.

"In what manner have I been so unhappy as to offend you, Mr. Berners?" she repeated, tearfully.

"In no manner at all, dear. How could one so gentle as yourself offend any one?" exclaimed Lyon Berners, rising, and taking both her unresisting hands in his own; and feeling for the first time a sentiment of *tenderness*, as well as of admiration, for her.

"But I thought I had offended you. You have been so changed to me of late," murmured Rosa, with her blue eyes full of tears.

"No, no, dear, not really changed, indeed. Only—absorbed by other engagements," answered Lyon Berners, evasively.

"You are the only friend I have in the whole world. And if *you* should desert me, I should perish," murmured Rosa, pathetically.

"But I will never desert you, dear. Nor am I the only friend you have in the world. My wife is surely your friend," said Lyon Berners, earnestly.

Slowly and sorrowfully Rosa Blondelle shook her head, murmuring sadly:

"No woman ever was my friend. I know not why."

"*I* can easily imagine why. But in regard to my dear wife, you are mistaken. Surely she has proved herself your friend."

"She is a noble lady, and I honor her. She is my

benefactress, and I thank her. But she is not my friend, and so I do not love her."

"I am sorry to hear you say so, dear."

"And I am sorry to be obliged to say so. But it is true. *You* are my only friend, Mr. Berners. The only friend I have in the wide, wide world."

"And do you love me?" inquired Lyon Berners, taking the siren's hand, and utterly yielding to her allurements; "say, fair one, do you love me?"

"Hush! hush!" breathed Rosa, drawing away her hand and covering her face—"hush! that is a question you must not ask, nor I answer."

"But—as a *brother*, I mean?" whispered Lyon.

"Oh! yes, yes, yes! as a dear brother, I love you dearly," fervently exclaimed Rosa.

"And as a dear sister you shall share my love and care always," earnestly answered Mr. Berners.

"And you will not be cold to me any longer?"

"No, dear."

"And you will come and listen to my poor little songs this evening, and let me do my best to amuse you?"

"Yes, dear, I will throw over all other engagements, and delight myself in your heavenly strains to-night," answered Lyon Berners.

"Oh! I am so happy to hear you promise that! Of late I have had no heart to open the piano. But to-night I will awaken for you its most glorious chords!"

He raised her hand to his lips, and thanked her warmly.

And just at that very instant Miss Tabitha Winterose appeared in the doorway, her tall, thin form drawn up to its utmost height, her pale, pinched face lengthened, and her dim blue eyes and skinny hands lifted up in surprise and disapprobation.

"Well!" simultaneously exclaimed Mr. Berners and Mrs. Blondelle, as they instinctively drew away from each other.

But Miss Tabitha could not easily recover her composure. She was shocked and scandalized to see a gentleman and lady, who were not related to each other, sitting so close together, while the gentleman kissed the lady's hand!

"Did you want anything?" inquired Mr. Berners, rather impatiently.

"No, I didn't. Yes, I did," answered Miss Winterose, crossly and confusedly. "I came after that lady there to tell her that I think her child is going to be very sick, and I want her to come and look after him. That is, if she an't more pleasanter engaged!" added Miss Tabitha, scornfully.

"Please excuse me, Mr. Berners," murmured Rosa, sweetly, as she got up to go out with the housekeeper. "*Oid Cat!*" she muttered, under her breath, as soon as she was out of Lyon's hearing.

When Mr. Berners was left alone, he did not resume the reading of his review. His heart became the prey of bitter-sweet reflections, made up of gratified self-love and of severe self-reproach.

"That beautiful creature *does* care for me, and is pained by my coldness! Ah! but I hope and trust she loves me *only* as a sister loves a brother! She has no brother, poor child! And her heart must have some one to lean on. I must be that one, for she has chosen me, and I will not be so recreant to humanity as to reject her trust."

Then his conscience smote him. And he felt he had shown more tenderness for this lady than the occasion called for, or than his duty warranted. He had called her "dear"; he had kissed her hand; he had asked her if she loved him! And this in the face of all his late protestations to his wife!

Lyon Berners was an honorable man and devotedly attached to his wife, and he was shocked now at the recollection of how far he had been drawn away from the strict line of duty by this lovely blonde!

But then he said to himself that he had only caressed and soothed Rosa in a brotherly way; and that it was a great pity Sybil should be of such a jealous and exacting nature, as to wish to prevent him from showing a little brotherly love to this lovely and lonely lady.

And worried by these opposing thoughts and feelings, Lyon Berners left his sofa and began to pace up and down the length of the drawing-room floor.

In truth now, for the first time, the mischief was done!

"CRUEL AS THE GRAVE."

The siren had at last ensnared him, in her distress and dishabille, with her tears and tenderness, as she never had done in the full blaze of her adorned beauty, or by the most entrancing strains of divine melody.

While Lyon Berners paced up and down the drawing-room floor, he seemed to see again the tender, tearful gaze of her soft blue eyes upon him; seemed to hear again the melting tones of her melodious voice pleading with him: "How have I been so unhappy as to offend you, Mr. Berners?" What a contrast this sweet humility of friendship with the fiery pride of Sybil's love!

While he was almost involuntarily drawing this comparison, he heard the wheels of the carriage that brought Sybil home roll up to the door and stop.

From her morning drive through the bright and frosty air, Sybil entered the drawing-room blooming, and glowing with health and happiness. For since that full explanation with her husband, she had been very happy.

Lyon Berners hastened to meet her. And perhaps it was his secret and painful consciousness of that little episode with Rosa, that caused him to throw into his manner even more than his usual show of affection, as he drew her to his bosom and kissed her fondly.

"Why!" exclaimed Sybil, laughing and pleased, "you meet me as if I had been gone a month, instead of a morning!"

"Your absence always seems long to me, dear wife, however, short it may really be," he answered earnestly. And he spoke the truth; for notwithstanding his admiration of Rosa, and the invidious comparison he had just drawn between her and Sybil, in his heart of hearts he still loved his wife truly.

She threw off her bonnet and shawl, and sat down beside him and began to rattle away like a happy girl, telling him all the little incidents of her morning's drive—whom she had seen, what she had purchased, and how excited everybody was on the subject of her approaching fancy ball.

"The first one ever given in this neighborhood, you know, Lyon," she added.

And having told him all the news, she snatched up her bonnet and shawl and ran up-stairs to her own room, where she found her thin housekeeper engaged in sorting out laces and sniveling

"Why, what's the matter now, Miss Tabby?" cheerfully inquired Sybil.

"Well, then, to tell you the truth, ma'am, I am dreadfully exercised into my own mind," answered Miss Winterose, wiping a tear from the tip of her nose.

"What about, now?" gayly demanded Sybil, who felt not the slightest degree of alarm on account of Miss Tabby, knowing that lady to be a constitutional and habitual whimperer.

"Then, it's all along of the wickedness and artfulness and deceitfulness of this here world."

"Well, never mind, Miss Tabby; you'll not have to answer for it all. But what particular instance of wickedness frets your soul now?" laughed Sybil.

"Why, now, there's where it is! I don't know whether I ought to tell, or whether I ought'n to; nor whether, if I was to tell, I would be looked upon into the light of a mischief-maker, or into the light of a true friend!" whimpered Miss Winterose.

"I can soon settle that question of ethics for you," laughed Sybil, all unsuspicious of what was coming. "Do just as your conscious directs you, Miss Tabby, no matter how people may look upon you."

"Very well, then, ma'am; for my conscience do order me to speak! Oh, Miss Sybil! I have knowed you ever since you was a baby in my arms, and I can't bear to have you so deceived and imposed upon by that there treacherous ungrateful White Cat!"

"White Cat?" echoed Sybil, in perplexity.

"Yes, Miss Sybil, that red-headed, false-hearted White Cat, as you took into your house and home, for to beguile and corrupt your own true husband!"

With a gasp and a suppressed cry, Sybil sank into her seat.

Miss Tabby, too full of her subject to notice Sybil's agitation, continued:

"No sooner had your carriage left the door this morning, Miss Sybil, than that there White Cat comes tipping on her tiptoes out of her room, in a long loose dressing-gown, with her hair all down, in a way as no real lady would ever be seen out of her own chamber, and she tips, tips, tips into the drawing-room, where she knows Mr. Berners is alone, and lying on the sofa!"

With a powerful effort Sybil controlled her violent emotion, held herself still, and listened.

"And that was bad enough, Miss Sybil! but that was nothing to what followed!" sighed Miss Tabby, wiping another tear from the end of her nose.

"What followed?" echoed Sybil, in an expiring voice.

"What followed, ma'am, was this: but to make you understand, I must tell you what I ought to a told you at the start, which is how it happened as I seen her tip, tip, tip, on her tiptoes to the drawing-room, just for all the world like a cat after cream. Well, I was up here, in this very room where I am now, a sorting out of your fine things as come up from the wash, and I found one o' *her* lace handkerchers among yourn, fotch up by mistake. So I jest took it and went down them back stairs as leads from this room down to hern, to give her back her handkercher; when jes as I got into her room, I seen her slip outen the other door leading into the hall. So after her I goes, to give her her handkercher—which I thought it was best to give it into her own hands, than to put it anywhere in her room, because I didn't know nothing about this forring nuss o' hern; and you know yourself, ma'am, as we ought to be cautious in dealing with strangers."

"Yes, yes! Go on! go on!" gasped Sybil.

"Well, ma'am, she flitted through them passages too fast for me, jes as if she was afraid o' being caught afore she got out o' sight!"

"Oh, why didn't you follow her in?" groaned Sybil.

"Yes, why didn't I, ma'am; which I wish I had, and would a done if it hadn't a been for that forring nuss a coming outen *her* room, and a screeching after me:

"'Missus Winterblossom! Missus Winterblossom!' which I allus told that huzzy as I wasn't a 'missus,' but a 'miss,' nor likewise a 'blossom,' but a 'rose.' Howsever, there she was, a yelling at the top of her voice, 'Missus Winterblossom! Missus Winterblossom! until I had to run to her only to stop her mouth!"

"Ah! the wretch! she was the accomplice of her mistress, and wished to bring you away," breathed Sybil more to herself than to her housekeeper, and in a tone too low to reach the ears of Miss Tabby, who continued:

"It was the baby, as had been eating of new chestnuts, and got the cramp. So the forring nuss, as wasn't worth her salt, comes screaming after me to come and do something for the baby. Of course I went and did what was right and proper for the poor little suffering creetur; and when I had put him to sleep, I thinks about his neglectful mother, and so I ups and goes after her. And when I opens the drawing-room door, ma'am—well, I sees a sight as strikes me intor a statty o' stone, or a pillar o' salt, like Lot's wife."

"What? what?" panted Sybil.

"I seen 'em both, him and her, a sitting close together and a going on jes like two lovyers as was going to be married to-morrow, or a bride and groom as was married yesterday."

"How? how?"

"Well, ma'am, if her head wasn't a leaning on his shoulder, it was so nigh it as it made no difference! And her hand was squeezed inter hizzen, and her eyes was rolled up inter hizzen in the most be-devilling way as ever I see in my life—for all the world as if she was a loving of him, and a worshiping of him, and a praising of him, and a praying to him, all in one gaze!"

"And he!—and he!"

"Oh, my dear honey! what can you expect of a poor, weak, *he-man?* He looks down on her as if he enjoyed being loved and worshiped and praised and prayed to, and he squeezes of her hand up to his mouth as if he'd like to have eaten it!"

"*Oh, my heart! my heart!*" moaned Sybil, turning deadly pale.

Still, Miss Tabby, full of her own subject, scarcely noticed the pain she was inflicting, so she continued:

"And jes that minute they happened either to see or to hear me, I don't know which. Anyways, they looks up, and—whew! they jumps apart as if a fire-cracker had gone off between 'em! Well, I tells my lady as her child is sick, and she jumps up, impatient like, to go and look after him. And I comes away too. And that was just about ten minutes before you got home yourself."

"Deceived! Betrayed! Scorned! Laughed at!" bitterly exclaimed Sybil.

"And that's all. And now look here, honey! Don't you go to taking on about this here piece o' business! And don't you get mad long o' your husband on any woman's account, whatever you do! Come down on the woman! That's what you do. It is all *her* fault, not hizzen! *He* couldn't help himself, poor innocent creetur! Lor! honey, I don't know much about married life, bein' of a single woman myself; but I have heard my mother say as men are mons'rous weak-minded poor creeturs, and need to be guided by their wives; and if they an't ruled by their wives, they are sure to be by some other woman! And it stands to reason it is more respectable to be ruled by their wives! And so, honey, my advice to you is, to send that bad woman about her business, and take that innocent man firmly in hand."

And so Miss Tabby babbled on, no longer heeded by Sybil, who soon slipped away and hid herself in one of the empty spare rooms.

CHAPTER XIII.

MORE THAN THE BITTERNESS OF DEATH.

> He to whom
> I gave my heart with all its wealth of love,
> Forsakes me for another.—MEDEA.

"OH my heart! my heart!" moaned Sybil, as she sank down upon the floor of that spare-room, the door of which she had bolted, to secure herself from intrusion.

"Oh, my heart! my heart!" she wailed, pressing her hand to her side like one who had just received a mortal wound.

"Oh, my heart! my heart!" she groaned, as one who complains of an unsupportable agony. And for some moments she could do no more than this. Then at length the stream of utterance flowed forth, and—

"He loves me no longer! my husband loves me no longer!" she cried in more than the bitterness of death. "He loves that false siren in place of me, his true wife. He gives her all the tender words, all the warm caresses he used to lavish on me. His heart is won from me. I am desolate! I am desolate, and I shall die! I shall die! But oh, how much I must suffer before I can die, for I am so strong to suffer! Ah, how I wish I might die at once, or that suicide were no sin!"

But suddenly, out of this deep abasement of grief, blazed up a fierce and fiery anger. She started from her recumbent position, and began to walk wildly up and down the floor, beating her hands together, and exclaiming distractedly:

"But why should I die in my youth, and go down to the dark grave, to make room for *her*, the traitress! to make room in the heart of my husband and the home of my fathers for her, the—! Oh! there is no word bad enough to express what she is! And shall *she* live to bloom and smile and brighten in the sunshine of his love, while I moulder away in the earth? Oh!" she cried, striking her hands violently together, "there is madness and more than madness in the thought! I will not die alone; no, no, no, no, so help me, just Heaven! I will not die alone. Oh, Samson was a brave man as well as a strong one when he lifted the pillars of the temple, and willingly fell beneath its crumbling ruins, crushing all his foes. I will be another sort of Samson; and when I fall, I too will pull down destruction upon the heads of all who have wronged me!"

These and many more wild and wicked words she uttered as she walked fiercely up and down the room, her eyes blazing, her cheeks burning, her whole aspect full of frenzy.

At length, again her mood changed; the fire died out of her eyes, the color faded from her cheeks; her frenzy subsided, and gave place to a stillness more awful than any excitement could possibly be. She sank down upon a low ottoman, and rested her elbows upon her knees and her chin upon the palms of her hands, and gazed straight before her into vacancy. Her face was deadly pale; her **lips** bloodless and compressed; her eyes contracted and glittering with a cold, black, baleful light; her hair unloosed in her agitation, streamed down each side, and fell upon her bosom like the ends of a long black scarf. At times she muttered to herself like any maniac:

"And oh, how deeply deceitful they have both been with me, affecting a mutual indifference while I was by; falling to caressing each other just as soon as my back was turned! She—she only acted out her false and treacherous nature. But he—oh, he! in whose pure truth I had such pride. Ah, Heaven! how low she must have drawn him before he could have gained his own consent to deceive me so! before he could come fresh from her side and her caresses, and meet and embrace me! What stupendous duplicity! Well, well!" she continued, nodding grimly; "well, well, since deceit is the fashion of the day, I too will be in the fashion; I too will wear a mask of smiles! But behind that mask I will watch!—Oh, how I will watch! Not at my fancy-ball alone will I play a part, but before it, and perhaps *after it!* None shall ever know how I watch, what I see, until I descend with the fell swoop of the eagle. And henceforth let me remember that I am a daughter of the house of Berners, who never failed a friend or spared a foe. And oh, let the spirit of my fathers support me, for I must ENDURE until I can AVENGE!" she said, as she got up with a grim calmness and paced up and down the floor to recover full self-command.

At length, when she felt sufficiently composed, she went to her own chamber, where she made a more elaborate and beautiful toilet than usual, preparatory to joining her husband and their guest at the dinner-table.

"Now smile, eyes! smile, lips! flatter, tongue! Be a siren among the sirens, Sybil! Be a serpent among the serpents!" she hissed, as she glided down the stairs and entered the dining-room.

They were there! They were standing close together, in the recess of the west window, gazing out at the sun, which was just setting behind the mountain. They started, and turned towards her as she advanced. But Sybil, true to her tactics, spoke pleasantly, saying:

"You get a beautiful view of the sunset from that window, Mrs. Blondelle."

"Yes, dear," answered Rosa, sweetly. "I was just drawing Mr. Berner's attention to it, and telling him that I really believe use has blinded him to its beauty."

"Possession is a great disenchanter," answered Sybil.

Both the others looked up to see if she had any hidden meaning under her words. But apparently she had not. She was smiling very gayly as she took her place at the head of the table and invited her companions to take their seats.

Throughout the dinner-hour Sybil seemed in very high spirits; she was full of anecdote and wit; she talked and laughed freely. Her companions noticed her unusual gaiety; but they ascribed it to the exhilarating effects of her morning drive, and to the anticipations of her mask ball, which now formed the principal subject of conversation at the table.

After dinner, they went into the drawing-room, where Sybil soon left her husband and her guest alone together; or rather, she pretended to leave them so; but really, with that insanity of jealousy which made her forget her womanhood, she merely went out and around the hall into the library, and placed herself behind the folding doors communicating with the drawing-room, where she could hear and see all that might be going on between her husband and her rival.

It is proverbial that "listeners never hear any good of themselves."

Sybil's case was no exception to this rule. This is what she heard of *herself*.

"What ever could have ailed Mrs. Berners," inquired Mrs. Blondelle, with a pretty lisp.

"What could have ailed Sybil? Why, nothing, that I noticed. What *should* have ailed her?" on his side inquired Mr. Berners.

"She was very much excited!" exclaimed Mrs. Blondelle, with a significant shrug of her shoulders.

"Oh! that was from her exhilarating morning ride, which raised her spirits."

"Which excited her excessively, *I* should say, if it really *was* the ride."

"Of course it was the ride. And I admit that she was very gay," laughed Mr. Berners.

"Gay?" echoed Rosa, raising her eyebrows—"Gay? Why, she was almost delirious, my friend!"

"Oh! well; Sybil gives full vent to her feelings; always did, always will. My little wife is in many respects a mere child, you know," said Mr. Berners, tenderly.

"Ah! what a happy child, to have her faults so kindly indulged! I wish I were that child!" sighed Rosa.

"But why should you wish to be anything else but yourself, being so charming as you are?" he softly inquired.

"Do you really like me, just as I am, Mr. Berners?" she meekly inquired, dropping her eyes.

"I really do. I have told you so, Rosa," he answered, approaching her, and taking her hand.

She sighed and turned away her head; but she left her hand in his clasp.

"Dear Rosa! dear child!" he murmured. "You are not happy."

"No, not happy," she echoed, in a broken voice.

"Dear Rosa! what can I do to make you happy?" he tenderly inquired.

"You? What can you do? Oh!—But I forget myself! I know not what I say! I must leave you, Mr. Berners!" she exclaimed, in well-acted alarm, as she snatched her hand from his grasp and fled from the room.

Mr. Berners looked after her, sighed heavily, and then began to walk thoughtfully up and down the room.

Sybil, from her covert, watched him, and grimly nodded her head. Then she also slipped away.

An hour later than this, the three, Mr. and Mrs. Berners and Mrs. Blondelle, were in the drawing-room together.

"You promised me some music," whispered Lyon to Rosa.

"Oh yes; and I will give you some. I am so glad you like my poor songs. I am so happy when I can do anything at all to please you," she murmured in reply, lifting her humid blue eyes to his face.

"Everything you do pleases me," he answered, in a very low voice.

Sybil was not standing very near them, yet with ears

sharpened by jealousy, she overheard the whole of that short colloquy, and—treasured it up.

Lyon Berners led Rosa Blondelle to the piano, arranged her music-stool, and placed the music sheets before her. She turned to one of Byron's impassioned songs, and while he hung enraptured over her, she sang the words, and ever she raised her eyes to his, to give eloquent expression and point to the sentiment. And then *his* eyes answered, if his voice and his heart did not.

That song was finished, and many more songs were sung, each more impassioned than the other, until at last, Rosa, growing weary and becoming slightly hoarse, arose from the piano, and with a half-suppressed sigh sank into an easy-chair.

Then Sybil—who had watched them through the evening, and noted every look and word and smile and sigh that passed between them, and who now found her powers of self-command waning—Sybil, I say, rang for the bedroom candles. And when they were brought, the little party separated and retired for the night.

From this time forth, in the insanity of her jealousy, and with a secretiveness only possible to the morally insane, Sybil completely concealed her suspicions and her sufferings from her husband and her guest. She was affectionate with Lyon, pleasant with Rosa, and confiding in her manners towards both.

And they were completely deceived, and never more fatally so than when they imagined themselves alone together.

They were never alone.

There was never a tender glance, a fluttering sigh, a soft smile, a low toned, thrilling word passed between the false flirt and the fascinated husband, that was not seen and heard by the heart-broken, brain-crazed young wife!

And oh! could these triflers with sacred love—these wanderers on the brink of a fearful abyss—have seen the look of her face then, they would have fled from each other forever, rather than to have dared the desperation of her roused soul.

But they saw nothing, knew nothing, suspected nothing! They were, like children playing with deadly poisons, with edge tools, or with fire, ignorant of the fatal toys they handled.

And, moreover they meant nothing. Theirs was the shallowest pretence of love that ever went by the name of a flirtation. On the woman's side, it was but a love of admiration and an affectation of sentiment. On the man's side, it was pity and gratified self-love. So little did Rosa Blondelle really care for Lyon Berners, and so truly did she estimate the value of her very luxurious home at Black Hall, that had she known the state of Sybil's mind, she would very quickly have put an end to her flirtation with the husband, and done all that she could to recover the confidence of the wife, and then—looked out among the attractive young men of the neighborhood for another party to that sentimental meaningless love-making which was yet a necessity to her shallow life.

And as for Mr. Berners, had he dreamed of the real depth of anguish this trifling with the blonde beauty caused his true-hearted wife, he would have been the first to propose the immediate departure of their guest.

Had Sybil been frank with either or both the offenders, much misery might have been saved. But the young wife, wounded to the quick in her pride and in her love, hid her sufferings and kept her secret.

And thus the three drifted towards the awful brink of ruin.

CHAPTER XIV.

THE FIRST FATAL HALLOW EVE.

AMBROSE—Where be these maskers, fool?
COLLIN—Everywhere, sage! But chiefly there
Where least they seem to mask!
JONSON—THE CARNIVAL.

IT was All-Hallow Eve, a night long anticipated with delight by the whole neighborhood, and much longer still remembered with horror by the whole country.

It was the occasion of Sybil Berners' mask ball; and Black Hall, the Black Valley, and the town of Blackville were all in a state of unprecedented excitement; for this was the first entertainment of the kind that had ever been given in the locality, and the gentry of three contiguous counties had been invited to assist at it.

Far distant from large cities and professional costumers as the rural belles and beaux of the neighborhood were, you will wonder what they did for fancy dresses.

They did very well. They ransacked the old cedar chests of their great-grandparents, and exhumed the rich brocades, cloths of gold and silver, lute-strings, lamas, fardingdales, hair-cushions, and all the gorgeous paraphernalia and regalia of the ante-revolutionary queens of fashion. And they referred to old family portraits, and to pictures in old plays and novels, and upon the whole they got up their dresses with more fidelity to fact than most costumers do.

Some also went to the trouble and expense of a journey to New York to procure outfits, and these were commissioned to buy masks for all their friends and acquaintances who were invited to the ball.

These preparations had occupied nearly the whole month of October. And now the eventful day had come, and the whole community was on tiptoe with expectation.

First, at Black Hall all was in readiness, not only for the ball and the supper, but for the accommodation of those lady friends of the hostess who, coming from a great distance, would expect to take a bed there.

And all was in readiness at the village hotel at Blackville, where gentlemen, coming from a distance to attend the ball, had engaged rooms in advance.

Nevertheless the landlord of the hotel was in a "stew," for there were more people already arrived, on horseback and in carriages of every description, from the heavy family coach crammed with young ladies and gentlemen, to the one-horse gig with a pair of college chums. And the distracted landlord had neither beds for human beings nor stalls for the horses. But he sent out among his neighbors, and tried to get "accommodations for man and beast" in private houses and stables.

"And the coach be come in, sir, and what be we to do with the passengers?" inquired the head waiter.

"Blast the coach! I wish it had tumbled down the 'Devil's Descent' into the bottomless pit!" exclaime

THE FIRST FATAL HALLOW EVE. 103

the frantic host, seizing his gray locks with both hands, and running away from before the face of his tormentor —and jumping from the frying-pan into the fire, when he came full upon his daughter Bessie, who stopped him with :

"Pop, you must come right into the parlor. There's a gentleman there as come by the coach, and says he *must* have a bed here to-night, no matter how full you may be, or how much it may cost."

"Impossible, Bessie! Clean impossible! Don't drive me stark mad!" cried the landlord, jerking at his gray hair.

"Well, but, Pop, you must come and tell the gentleman so, or he'll sit there all night," remonstrated the girl.

"Blow the fellow to blazes! Where is he!"

"In the parlor, Pop."

The landlord trotted into the parlor and gave a little start, for, at first sight, he thought the gentleman's head was on fire! But a second glance showed him that the gentleman only had the reddest hair he had ever seen in his life, and that the level rays of the setting sun, shining through the western window, and falling full upon this head, set this red hair in a harmless blaze of light.

Recovering from his little shock, he advanced to the gentleman, bowed, and said:

"Well, sir, I am the landlord, and I understand you wish to see me."

"Yes; I wish to engage a room here to-night."

"Very sorry, sir; but it is out of the question. Every room in the house is engaged; even my room and my daughters' room, and the servants' rooms. And not only that, sir, but every sofa is engaged, and every rug; so you see it is clean impossible."

"Impossible is it?" inquired the stranger.

"Clean impossible, sir! utterly impossible!" returned the host.

"All right; then it shall be done."

"Sir!"

"I say, because it is impossible, it shall be done."

"Eh!"

"Here is a hundred dollars," said the stranger, laying down two bank-notes of fifty dollars each. "I will give you this money if you can induce any of your guests to give up a room for me to-night."

"Why, really, sir, I should be delighted to accommodate such a very liberal gentleman but,—"

"You must decide at once. Now, or never," said the stranger, firmly, for he saw the game was now in his own hands.

"Well, yes, sir; I will find you a room. The two young college gents who took a room between them may be induced to give it up."

"*Must* give it up, you mean," amended the stranger.

"Well, yes, sir; just as you say, sir."

"And I must have it in fifteen minutes."

"Yes, sir."

"And supper served there in half an hour."

"Yes, sir."

"And your company at supper, as I want to have a little talk with you."

"All right, sir."

"And now, you can go and see about the room."

"Just so, sir," said the landlord, gathering up the two fifty-dollar bills that had bought him, body and soul, and then bowing himself out of the room.

"'Money makes the mare go,' and the horse too. I wonder what he'll think when he finds out his bank bills are not worth the paper they are printed on, mused the stranger, as he paced thoughtfully up and down the room.

Fortunately for the landlord's speculation, bad as it ultimately proved, the two collegians who had engaged his best front bedroom had not yet arrived to take possession of it. Therefore the business of turning it over to a more profitable party was the more immediately practicable. All the landlord had to do was to see that a fire was kindled in the fireplace, and the table was set for supper.

Then he returned to the parlor, to conduct, in person, such a wealthy and munificent patron to his apartment.

"Ah! this is cosy!" said the stranger, sinking into an arm-chair, and spreading his hands over the blazing fire, whose beams were caught and reflected by his red hair, until it shone like a rival conflagration.

THE FIRST FATAL HALLOW EVE.

"Glad you like your quarters, sir," said the landlord, putting hand upon the pocket that contained the purse with the two fifty-dollar bills to see that they were safe.

"Ah! here comes the supper. Now, landlord, I want you to join me, that we may have that little chat I spoke of," said the stranger, wheeling his arm-chair around to the table, while the waiter arranged the dishes, and stared at the flaming red head of the guest.

"What name might I have the honor of entering on my books, sir, if you please?" inquired the host, as he obligingly took his seat opposite his guest.

"What name might you have the honor of entering on your books?" repeated the stranger, helping himself to a huge slice of ham. "Well, you *might* have the honor of entering quite a variety of names on your books, as I dare say you do; but for the sake of brevity, which is the soul of wit, you may put down Smith—John Smith of New York city. Common name, eh, landlord, and from a big city? Can't help that—fault of my forefathers and godfathers. Whenever I have to sign a check the bankers make me write myself down as 'John Smith of John.' Can't do any better than that if it were to avert a financial crisis. All my ancestors have been John Smiths, from the days of William Rufus, when his chief armorer John, surnamed the 'Smiter,' for his lusty blows, founded the family. So you may set me down as 'John Smith of John, New York city.' And now send the waiter away, and fall to and tell me some of your neighborhood news."

Nothing but the consciousness of the possession of those two big bills would have given the landlord courage to have left his business below stairs to take care of itself even for the half hour to which he mentally resolved to limit his interview with the stranger. However, he dismissed the waiter with some extra charges, and then placed himself at the service of his guest, and even took the initiative of the *tête-à-tête* by asking:

"You are quite a stranger in this neighborhood, sir?"

"Quite."

"Traveling on business, or for pleasure?"

"Pleasure."

A delightful season this, to travel in, sir; neither too

warm, nor too cold. And the country never looks so rich and beautiful as in its autumn foliage."

"True," answered the stranger, briefly, and then he added, "I didn't ask you to come here to catechize me, my good friend; but to submit to be catechized yourself, and to amuse me with the gossip of the neighborhood."

Again nothing but the consciousness of a heavy fee would have induced the host of the "Antlers" to put up with this traveler's "nonsense," as he termed his general assumption of superiority.

"What would you like to hear about, then, sir?" growled the landlord.

"First, what important families have you in this part of the country?"

"Well, sir, the most principlest is the Bernerses of Black Hall, which have returned from their bridal tour about a month ago and taken up their abode there in the old ancestral home."

"The Berners! Who are they?" inquired the traveler, carelessly trifling with the wing of a pheasant.

"You must be a stranger, indeed, sir, not to know the Bernerses of Black Hall," said the landlord, with an expression of strong disapprobation.

"Well, as I don't know them, and as they seem to be persons of the highest distinction, perhaps you will tell me all about them," said the traveler.

And the landlord not unwillingly gave the guest the full history of the Berners of Black Hall, down to the marriage of the last heiress, at which the bridegroom took the name of the bride's family. And then he described the situation of the Hall and the way in which it might be reached, and ended by saying;

"And if you think of making any stay in this neighborhood, sir, and will send your card to Mr. and Mrs. Berners, they will be sure to call on you and show you every attention in their power, sir; invite you to their house, introduce you to the neighbors, make parties for you, and make you generally welcome among us."

"They are very hospitable then?"

"Hospitable! Why, sir, even when they were on their bridal tour, they fell in with a lovely lady in distress, and what do they do but pay her bills at the hotel, and fetch

THE FIRST FATAL HALLOW EVE. 107

her and her child and her servant, all, bag and baggage, home with themselves, to stay at Black Hall as long as ever she likes?"

"Indeed! That was a very unusual stretch of hospitality. And this lady is still with them?" inquired the stranger.

"She is that, sir; although the word do go around that it would be well if she was to go away."

"Ah! why so?"

"Well, sir—but, lord, it is all servants' gossip, and there may be nothing in it: but they do say that the master of the house is too fond of the visitor, and likewise she of him; and that this do make the mistress of the house very unhappy."

"Ah!" exclaimed the stranger, in a half-suppressed voice.

"They do say, sir, that whenever the mistress turns her back, they two—the master and the guest—do go on like any pair of sweethearts, which is a great scandal, if it's true."

"Ah ha!" muttered the stranger, clenching and grinding his teeth.

"However, sir, if the master is in love with the visitor, and the mistress is made unhappy thereby, that is no reason why they should put off their mask ball and disappoint the whole community, I suppose they think; so they have not done so; but they have their ball this evening, just as if they were the happiest household in the country."

"Oh a mask ball have they, this evening! And what sort of an affair is it to be?"

"Well, sir, the ball is to be like other balls, I believe, only that the guests are to appear in fancy dresses, or in loose gowns called dominoes, and to wear false faces until supper-time, when they unmask and reveal themselves to each other."

"Yes, that is just like other mask balls," said the stranger, and then he seemed to fall into thought for a few minutes; and then, rousing himself, he said:

"Landlord, you told me that your house is very full to-night, and so you must have a great deal of business on your hands."

"I just have, sir," replied the impatient host.

"Then I will not detain you any longer from your other guests. Pray send the waiter to remove this service immediately. And then, I think, as I am very much fatigued by my stage-coach journey over your beastly roads, I will retire to bed," said the stranger.

And the landlord, glad to be relieved, got up and bowed himself out.

His exit was soon followed by the entrance of the waiter who quickly cleared the table and also retired.

The next proceedings of the stranger were rather singular.

As soon as he found himself quite alone, he locked his door, to secure himself from any possibility of interruption, and hung a towel over the keyhole, to guard his movements from observation, and then he unlocked his portmanteau, and took from it a strange and horrible disguise, that I will try to describe, so as to make it plain to the reader.

It was a tight-fitting suit, the pantaloons and jacket being made all in one piece, and of such elastic material as to fit close to the form. The ground of this dress was black; but upon it was painted, in strong relief of white, the blanched bones of a skeleton—thus: down the legs of the pantaloons were traced the long bare leg bones, with the large joints of the hips, knees, and ankles; across the body was traced the white ribs, breast-bone, and collar-bone; and down the sleeves were traced the long bones of the arms, with the large shoulder-blades, elbow-joints, and wrists; the bones of the hands were traced in white upon tight-fitting black gloves, and those of the feet upon tight-fitting black socks: around a skull-cap was to be drawn over the head; this was all white, to represent the skull, and had its skeleton features marked out with black.

The stranger having divested himself of his upper garment then put on this horrible dress. When he had finished his revolting toilet, even to the drawing on of the skull-cap, he surveyed himself in the mirror that reflected as ghastly a figure of "Death," as Milton, Dante, or even Gustav Doré, ever conceived.

He laughed sardonically, as he exclaimed:

"Ah ha! they will not expect 'Death' to be a guest at their ball!"

Then over this grim costume he threw a large traveling cloak, and upon his head he placed a broad-brimmed black felt hat. And now, being all ready, he prepared to leave the room.

First he put out the light, and then he cautiously unlocked the door, and, secure from observation himself, he looked out to see if the coast was clear.

The passage was dark, but soon he saw a door on the opposite side open, and two young men come out in masquerade dresses, and hasten, laughing and talking, down the stairs. They were evidently on their way to the mask ball.

The next instant, the door on the same side with his own opened, and a lady and gentleman, both in black dominoes and masks, came out and passed down-stairs.

"Good!" said the stranger to himself. "If I am met at all, I shall be mistaken for one of the invited guests of the ball, and pass out without being recognized." And so saying, he softly drew the key from the inside of the lock, and closed and locked the door, and taking the key with him, glided down the stairs and out of the house, and took the road to Black Hall.

CHAPTER XV.

THE MASQUERADE BALL.

Light up the mansion, spread the festive board;
  Welcome the gay, the noble, and the fair!
Through the bright hall in joyous concert poured,
  Let mirth and music sound the dirge of care!
But ask thou not if happiness be there,
  If the loud laugh disguise convulsive throe,
Or if the brow the heart's true livery wear;
  Lift not the festal mask!—enough to know
No scene of mortal life but teems with mortal woe!
—WALTER SCOTT.

THE whole front of Black Hall blazed with festive lights, and these lights were all reflected in the dark waters of the lake, and by the glowing foliage of the trees that clothed the mountains, and by the sparkling spray of the cascades that sprung from the rocks on the other side.

The space immediately before the house was crowded with carriages of every description, from the splendid open barouche to the comfortable family coach and the plain gig.

The portico and passages in front of the house were thronged with arriving guests and waiting attendants ready to show them to the dressing-rooms, which were lighted and warmed, and supplied with every convenience for the completion of the toilets.

The drawing-room and dancing saloon brilliantly lighted by chandeliers, and beautifully decorated with festoons of dark bright evergreens and wreaths of gorgeous autumn leaves and bouquets of splendid autumn flowers, stood ready with wide open doors to welcome the company.

At the hall door, at the head of the servants, stood Mr. Joseph Joy the house steward, and Miss Tabitha Winterrose the housekeeper, both disgusted with the heathenish costumes, distracted with the confusion, disapproving of the whole proceedings, yet determined to do their duty.

Their duty was to see that the men and maids did *theirs*, in showing the gentlemen and ladies to their dressing-rooms. They had both in turn been astonished, scandalized, and appalled by the grotesque figures that had passed them. But their manner of expressing their sentiments was quite different.

Joseph Joy stared, wondered, and shook his head.

Miss Tabby sighed, whimpered, and moralized.

"I feel as if I had been drinking for a week, and had a lively sort of a nightmare! Here comes another ghoul, in a false face and black gown and hood! Now, how is anybody to tell what it is? Whether it is a tall woman or a short man? Gentleman, or lady, if your honor pleases?" said Joseph Joy, addressing himself to a black domino that just then came up.

"Gentleman," answered the unknown.

"Pass to the right, then, if you please, sir! Here Alick, show this gentleman in the black shroud to the gentlemen's dressing-room."

A trembling darky came forward and took charge of this terrific personage.

THE MASQUERADE BALL. 111

"Ah, my goodness! no good will ever come of this!" sighed Miss Tabby.

"No good? Yes there will too!" answered Joseph Joy, who was fond of contradiction. "All these bare-necked, bare-armed, and bare-legged people will get the pleurisy and be laid on the flat of their backs for three months, when they will have the opportunity of meditating on the iniquity of their ways! And won't that be good?"

"Yes, it will; and I hope it will be sanctified to their souls," sighed Miss Tabitha.

"And now here comes another bogie! Gentleman, or lady, please?" politely inquired the usher, as a red domino approached.

"Lady," softly murmured the domino.

"Pass the lady on to your maids, Miss Winterose! And here's another that certainly belongs to your department too! And another, and another, and a whole dozen of them!" exclaimed Mr. Joy, as a troupe of bayaderes, gipsies, peasants, court ladies, et cætera, filed up.

All these Miss Winterose passed on to Delia, with directions to show them to the ladies' dressing-rooms. And then she turned to Mr. Joy with a deep sigh, whimpering:

"Ah! Joseph, where do all these people expect to die when they go to? I—I mean, to go to when they die?"

"They don't trouble themselves about that, I reckon," said contradictory Joe.

"Ah! but it is written that we shall not make to ourselves the likeness of anything that is in the heavens above, or in the earth beneath, or in the waters under the earth. And here are all these people making of themselves—" Miss Tabby stopped and sniveled, and then stopped again to wipe a tear from the tip of her nose.

"Well, what?" demanded antagonistic Joe. "What are these people making of themselves? Nothing that breaks the first commandment, for surely you don't mean to say that they make of themselves the image of anything in the heavens above, the earth below, or the waters under the earth, do you?"

"No, Joseph; but I was mistrusting as they had made themselves up into images of something in t'other place."

"With the Evil One for a pattern, eh? And here he

comes, sure enough. Talk of the d—— and you know what happens," muttered Joe Joy, as a most appalling apparition approached. It was a tall, thin figure, clad in a tight-fitting black suit, that clung close to the skin from the crown of the head to the soles of the feet and the palms of the hands; skull-cap, mask, jacket, sleeves, trousers, shoes and gloves seeming to be knit all of one piece, or else very artistically joined together. Crowning the black brows were two tall white horns; tipping the black fingers were long white talons; terminating the black feet were cloven white hoofs. Crimson glass goggles over the eyes gave the look of burning coals; and by some "devilish cantrip strange," some trick in chemistry, at least, little jets of flames appeared to issue from the mouth and nostrils of the mask.

"Heaven save us! There's no mistaking his sex, or identity either," gasped Mr. Joe, backing himself away from this diabolical figure until he was stopped by the wall, from which he cried out, "Here, Jerry, show the— Enemy—into the gentlemen's dressing-room."

The shuddering boy, shaking in every limb, shrank away and merely pointed out the door of the dressing-room.

Miss Tabby had merely time to raise her hands and eyes in mute appeal to heaven, before a shoal of new arrivals—"flower girls," "strawberry girls," "match girls," "morning stars," "evening stars," "springs," "summers," "nuns," "bacchantes," etc., claimed her attention; while a troupe of "brigands," "monks," "troubadours," "clowns," "harlequin," "kings," "crusaders," et cætera, demanded the guidance of Mr. Joy.

And after this thicker and faster they came, crowding one group behind another, until the ushers were nearly demented. When drove after drove had divided and passed to the right or the left, that is, to the ladies' or gentlemen's dressing-rooms, and the stream began to slacken a little, so that they could distinguish individuals, Mr. Joy in turn received and passed a "Puritan preacher," a "cavalier soldier," a "Highlander," a "knight," a "minstrel," the "veiled prophet," a "Switzer," a "Chinese mandarin," a "Russian serf," and black, white, and gray, red, yellow, and blue dominoes, he suddenly exclaimed:

"Good Lord deliver us! What's *that?*"

Miss Tabby, who, to her infinite disgust, had been receiving and passing any number of "fairies," "fisher girls," "soubrettes," "sultanas," et cætera, turned around, and in a quavering voice, inquired:

"What's *what?*"

"Why, *that!*" shuddered Joe, pointing to a ghastly figure that was standing quite still, a few paces from where they stood, trembling.

"It's a skeleton! Oh, my goodness! how did ever IT get here?"

"Yes it *is* a skeleton! Oh, this is too horrible!" gasped Joe, shrinking up against the wall. And his female companion clung close to him.

Meanwhile the "skeleton" stalked towards them.

We, reader, have seen the figure before. But so distinctly was the skeleton of the human body painted in white upon that tight-fitting black suit, that the illusion was perfect; and the wonder was not great that the two poor ignorant servants trembled and gasped, and shrank back.

"Why, if you were not afraid of the Devil, why should you shrink from Death?" demanded the stranger:

"Grinning horribly a ghastly smile."

"I—was not—afraid; only it gives one such a turn!" replied Joe, with chattering teeth.

"Then direct me to a dressing-room," ordered the stranger.

"But—are you—a gentleman's skeleton, or a lady's?" gasped Joe.

"I am neither. I am Death," curtly replied the stranger.

"Lord save us!" ejaculated Miss Tabby.

"Are you going to direct me to a dressing-room?"

"Yes, sure, as soon as I know what sort of a one you want. Are you a gentleman's death, or a lady's?" faltered Joe, who could by no means command his nerves.

"I am a lady's death!" replied the stranger, in a tone so grim that Miss Tabby ejaculated:

"Heaven have mercy on us!"

Joe was about to direct the stranger to the ladies'

dressing-rooms, when his attention was suddenly diverted by the arrival of a crowd of "knights," "Indians," "Welsh bards," "grisettes," "Greek slaves," et cætera, who demanded immediate service. The usher divided them according to their sexes, and then noticed that the ghastly figure of "Death" joined the gentlemen's party and accompanied them to their dressing-room.

CHAPTER XVI.

ON THE WATCH.

False—from head's crown to the foot's sole—false!
To think I never knew it until now,
Nor saw thro' him e'en when I saw him smile;
Saw that he meant this when he wed me,
When he caressed me! Yes, when he kissed my lips!
—BROWNING.

WHILE this busy scene was being enacted below stairs, equally important, if quieter dramas were being performed in the dressing-rooms up-stairs, where the maskers were putting the last finishing touches to their toilets.

In Mrs. Berners' dressing-room, Sybil, the queen of the festival, was alone. Mr. Berners, who had assumed the character of "Harold, the last of the Saxon Kings," had already completed his toilet and gone below stairs, as he said, to take his place near the door to welcome his guests as they should enter the drawing-room.

So Sybil was alone in her apartment. She also had just completed her toilet, and now she stood before the large cheval mirror, surveying the reflection of her figure from its clear surface, where it looked like a framed picture.

Ah! far the most beautiful, far the most terrible figure in the pageantry of the evening would be that of Sybil Berners! She had chosen for her character the unprecedented part of the impersonation of the Spirit of Fire. It suited well with her whole nature. She was a true child of the sun—a fervent Fire Worshipper, if ever there lived one in a Christian community. And now her costume was but the outward sign of the inward fervor. Let me try to describe it.

She wore a robe of chameleon-hued satin, so artfully woven, with a warp of golden thread and woof of crimson silk, that, as with every change of light and shade, it glowed in ruby coals or blazed in amber flames; and as with every motion of her graceful form it flashed around her, she seemed to be clothed in living fire.

She wore a burning garnet, like a live coal on her bosom; and on her brow a golden circle set with garnets, and having golden points set with amber and topaz, and tipped with diamonds, and flashing like little tongues of flame from a circle of fire.

Her mask was of golden gauze, perfectly moulded to her beautiful features.

Never had Sybil Berners worn a dress so perfectly expressive of herself as this, for she herself was Fire!

She had confided the secret of her costume to no one but to her husband, not even to her guest—courtesy did not oblige her to do that; and in order to preserve the secret inviolate, she had on this occasion dressed herself without the assistance of her maid.

Being now ready to join the maskers, she slipped a large dark cloak over her dress, opened the chamber door cautiously to see that the hall was clear, found it to be so at that moment, and slipped out, glided down the front stairs, elbowing crowds that were pushing up, and so passed down to the lower hall, and stole through the multitude that filled it up, back to the rear door. She passed around the outside of the house to the front door, and entered with the swarm of new arrivals. Would the ushers, Joe Joy and Miss Tabby, recognize their lady? That was the question, and that was the test. She passed up with the rest, letting her black cloak slip down to reveal her robe and crown of fire.

"Heaven save us! who comes here? It must be a mermaid from the 'lake that burneth with fire and brimstone for ever and ever.' It's a she, anyhow, and belongs to your department, thanks be to goodness!" whispered Joseph Joy, to his companion in duty.

"This way, ma'am, if you please. Delia, pass this lady on to the ladies' dressing-room," said unconscious Miss Tabby, courtesying and pointing.

And Sybil passed on, smiling to herself to perceive

that not even her old family domestics had recognized her face or form. So, keeping up her stratagem of being one of the masked guests of the ball, she entered the large chamber that had been chosen for the ladies' dressing-room and fitted up with a dozen small dressing-tables and mirrors. Her entrance created a sensation even among that fantastic crowd, each individual of which was a wonder in him or herself.

"Oh! look there!" simultaneously whispered twenty masks to forty others, as they caught sight of her.

"What a marvelous dress! What a splendid creature!"

"What a dazzling costume!"

"She throws us all in the shade."

These were a few of the impulsive ejaculations of admiration that were passed from one to another, as Sybil flashed through the throng and stopped before a dressing-table, where she made a pretence of putting a few finishing touches to her dress.

Then, certain of not having been recognized, and wishing to escape such close scrutiny in such confined quarters, she joined a group of ladies who, having completed their own toilets, were just then passing out of the chamber door into the upper hall, where they were met by their gentleman escorts.

There was no one to meet Sybil; a circumstance that was not of much importance, since there were one or two other ladies of the same party, who, having no escort of their own, had to follow in the wake of others. Nor would Sybil have minded this at all, had she not looked over the balustrades and seen issuing from the little passage leading from Mrs. Blondelle's room, two figures—a gentleman and a lady. The gentleman she instantly recognized as her husband, by his dress as "Harold, the last of the Saxon Kings." The lady she felt certain must be Rosa Blondelle, as she wore the dress of "Edith the Fair," the favorite of the King.

For an instant Sybil reeled under this shock; and then she recovered herself, re-gathered all her strength, and sternly crushing down all this weakness, passed on as a guest among her guests to the door of the drawing-room.

There they were received by a very venerable mask

with a long and flowing white beard, and dressed in a gold 'broidered black velvet tunic, white hose, white gauntlets, and red buskins, and holding a long brazen wand. This was no other than " Father Abe," the oldest man on the manor, personating my " Lord Polonius," that prince of gentlemen ushers and gold sticks in waiting.

While Sybil stood behind the group, she saw her husband and her rival precede every one to the door.

" Names, if you please, sir?" inquired the usher with a bow.

" Harold the Saxon and Edith the Fair," answered Mr Berners in a low voice.

" Mr. Harry Claxton and Miss Esther Clair!" shouted poor old Abe at the top of his voice as he opened wider the door to admit his unknown master and the lady.

" Name, sir, please?" he continued, addressing the next party.

" Rob Roy Macgregor."

" Mr Robert McCracker!" shouted the usher, passing in this mask, and passing immediately to the next with, " Name, missus, please?"

" Fenella the dumb girl," murmured a very shy little maiden, whom the usher immediately announced as " An Ell of a dumb girl!" And so on, he went, making the most absurd as well as the most awful blunders with ladies' and gentlemen's names, as announcing the " Grand Turk" as Miss Ann Burke; for which last mistake the poor old man was not much to blame, as the subject was but a little fellow in a turban and long gown, whom Polonius naturally took to be a woman in a rather fantastic female dress. But when he thundered forth a " Musketeer" as a " mosquito," and a " Crusader" as a " curiosity," and " Joan of Arc" as " Master Johnny Dark," he was quite unpardonable.

Meanwhile Sybil had entered the room, which was blazing with light and resounding with music. As the guests were now nearly all assembled, the gentlemen selected partners and opened the ball with a grand promenade to the music of the grand march in " Faust."

Introductions are of course unnecessary at private masquerades, as well as impracticable at all such festivals; so when the ghastly mask " Death" came up and offered his skeleton arm to Sybil for the promenade, she unhesitatingly accepted it, supposing him all the while to be one of her invited guests.

But in joining the promenaders, he entered the circle at a point immediately in the rear of Harold the Saxon, and Edith the Fair. Death kept his eye on the two, and speaking in a low voice, inquired of his companion ;

" Beautiful mask ! though we may not yet discover ourselves to each other, yet we are at liberty to form a guess of the identity of our friends here ? "

" Yes," answered Sybil, in a low voice. She scarcely understood what she had been asked, or what she had answered ; for her whole attention was absorbed in watching her husband and her rival, who were walking immediately before her—so close, yet so unconscious of her presence ; so near in person, yet so far in spirit !

"—As, for instance, lovely mask," continued Death, "I think I know this 'Fair Edith' as the beautiful blonde who is staying here with our hostess. Am I not right ? "

" Yes," answered Sybil, in the same absent and unconscious manner; for she really had not the slightest idea of what he had been talking about, but only a half-conscious instinct that the best and shortest, as well as the most courteous, way, in which to be rid of him was to agree with all he said. Her whole attention was still painfully absorbed by the pair before her.

" But as for the gentleman, Saxon Harold, I do not recognize him at all ! However, he seems to be quite devoted to his fair Edith, as is most natural ! Fair Edith was his best beloved ! best beloved ? Yes, beloved far beyond his queen ! "

Sybil knew what he was saying now ! She was listening to him with her ears, while she was watching the pair before her with her eyes.

" When Harold's dead body was found on the battle-field, it was not the queen, but Fair Edith, who was sent for to identify it, and to her it was given," continued the stranger.

A half-suppressed cry broke from Sybil's lips.

" What is the matter ? Are they treading on your feet ? " inquired the mask.

"*Some* one is treading on me," murmured Sybil, with a sad double meaning.

"Do not press on us so, if you please, sir!" said Death, turning and staring angrily at the unoffending little Grand Turk, and Fenella the dumb girl, who happened to be immediately in the rear. Having thus brow-beaten the imaginary enemy, Death turned to his companion and said:

"King Harold and Fair Edith were lovers, and these who assume their parts are also lovers, and they take their related parts from a sentimental motive! You are tired! let me lead you to a seat," suddenly exclaimed the stranger, feeling his partner's form drooping heavily from his side.

She was almost fainting, she was almost sinking into a swoon. She permitted her escort to take her to a chair, and to fetch her a glass of water. And then she thanked him, and requested him to select another partner, as she was too much fatigued to go upon the floor again for an hour, and that she preferred to sit where she was, and to watch the masquerade march on before her.

But Death politely declared that he preferred to stand there by her and share her pastime, if she would permit him to do so.

She bowed assent, and Death took up his position at her side.

CHAPTER XVII.

DRIVEN TO DESPERATION.

For only this night, as they whispered, I brought
My own eyes to bear on her so, that I thought,
Could I keep them one half-minute fixed—she would fall
Shriveled!—She fell not; yes, this does it all.—BROWNING.

As the circle revolved before them, Sybil saw no one but Lyon Berners and Rosa Blondelle, and these she saw always—with her eyes, when they were before them; with her spirit, when they had revolved away from them.

She saw him hold close to his heart the arm that leaned on his arm; she saw him press her hand, and play with her fingers, and look love in the glances of his eyes, and speak love in the tones of his voice, although no *word* of love had been uttered as yet.

At last—oh! deliverance from torture!—the music ceased, the promenaders dispersed to their seats.

The relief was but short! The band soon struck up a popular quadrille, and the gentlemen again selected their partners and formed sets. Lyon Berners, who had conducted his fair companion to a distant seat, now led her forth again, and stood with her at the head of one of the sets.

"There! you see! they *are* lovers! I wonder who *he* is?" whispered Death, leaning to Sybil's ear.

Sybil bit her lip and answered nothing.

"Ah! you do not know, or will not tell! Well, will you honor me with your hand in this quadrille?" requested the stranger, with a bow.

Scarcely knowing what she did, for her eyes and thoughts were still following her husband and her rival, Sybil bowed assent, and arose from her seat.

Death took her hand and led her up to the same quadrille, at the head of which Harold the Saxon and Edith the Fair stood, and he placed himself and his partner exactly opposite to, and facing them.

Thus Lyon Berners for the first time in the evening was obliged to see his wife, for of course he knew her by her dress, as she knew him by his dress. She saw him stoop and whisper to his partner, and she surmised that he gave her a hint as to who was their *vis-a-vis*, and gave it as a warning. She fancied here that her confidence had been betrayed in small matters as well as in great, and even in this very small item of divulging the secret of her costume to her rival. And at that moment she took a resolution, which later in the evening she carried out. Now, however, from behind her golden mask she continued to watch her husband and her rival. She noticed, that from the instant her husband had observed his wife's presence, he modified his manner towards his partner, until there seemed nothing but indifference in it.

But this change, instead of being satisfactory to Sybil, was simply disgusting to her, who saw in it only the effect of her own presence, inducing hypocrisy and deception in

DRIVEN TO DESPERATION.

them. And the resolution that she had formed was strengthened.

Meanwhile the only couple that was wanted to complete the quadrille now came up, and the dance began.

Sybil noticed, in an absent-minded sort of a way, how very gracefully her grim partner danced. And the thought passed carelessly through her mind, that if in that most ghastly disguise his manner and address were so elegant and polished, how very refined, how perfect they must be in his plain dress. And she wondered and conjectured who, among her numerous friends and acquaintances, this gentleman could be; and she admired and marveled at the tact and skill with which he so completely and successfully concealed his identity.

She noticed too, in the superficial sort of manner in which she noticed everything except the objects of her agonizing jealousy, that her strange partner watched Rosa as closely as she herself watched Lyon—and she even asked herself:

"Does he know Rosa, and is he jealous?"

Meanwhile the mazy dance went merrily on, heying and setting, whirling and twisting to the inspiring sound of music. And Sybil acted her part, scarcely conscious that she did it, until the set was ended, and she was led back to her seat by her partner, who, as he placed her in it, bowed gracefully, thanked her for the honor she had done him, and inquired if he could have the pleasure of bringing her a glass of water, lemonade, or anything else.

But she politely declined all refreshment.

He then expressed a hope of having the honor of dancing with her again during the evening, and with a final bow he withdrew.

But he did but make way for a succession of suitors, who, in low and pleading tones, besought the honor of her hand in the waltz that was about to begin. But to each of these in turn she excused herself, upon the plea that she never waltzed.

Next she was besieged by candidates for the delight of dancing with her in the quadrille that was immediately to follow the waltz. And she mechanically bowed assent to the first applicant, and excused herself to all others, upon the plea of her previous engagement.

That Sybil consented to dance at all, under the painful circumstances of her position, was due to the instinctive courtesy of her nature, which taught her, that on such an occasion as this, the hostess must not indulge her private feelings, however importunate they might be, but that she must mingle in the amusements of her guests; for she forgot that a masquerade ball was different from all other entertainments in this, that ner masquerade dress put her on an equality with all her guests, and emancipated her from all the duties of a hostess as long as she should wear her mask.

Meanwhile she was looking for her husband and her rival, who had both disappeared. And presently her vigilance was rewarded. They reappeared, locked in each other's arms, and whirling around in the bewildering waltz. And she watched them, all unconscious that she herself was the " observed of all observers," the " cynosure of eyes," the star of that "goodlie company." All who were not waltzing, and many who were waltzing, were talking of Sybil.

" Who is she? What is she? Where did she come from? Does any one know her?" were some of the questions that were asked on all sides.

" She outshines every one in the room," whispered a " Crusader " to a " Quaker."

" I have heard of ' making sunshine in a shady place,' but *she* ' makes sunshine ' even in a lighted place!" observed Tecumseh.

" Who, then, is she?" inquired William Penn.

" No one knows," answered Richard Cœur de Lion.

" But what character does she take?" asked Lucretia Borgia.

" I should think it was a ' Priestess of the sun," surmised Rebecca the Jewess.

" No! I should think she has taken the character of the ' Princess Creusa,' the daughter of Creon, King ot Corinth, and the victim of Medea the Sorceress. Creusa perished, you know, in the robe of magic presented to her as a wedding gift from Medea, and designed to burn the wearer to ashes! Yes, decidedly it is Creusa, in her death robe of fire!" persisted the " gentle Desdemona," who had just joined the motley group.

"You are every one of you mistaken. I heard her announced when she entered—the 'Spirit of Fire,'" said Pocahontas, with an air of authority.

"That is her assumed character! Now to find out her real one."

"Shall I whisper my opinion? Mind, it is *only* an opinion, with no data for a foundation," put in Charlemagne.

"Yes; do tell us who you take her to be," was the unanimous request of the circle.

"Then I think she is our fair hostess."

"Oh-h-h!" exclaimed all the ladies.

"Why do you think so?" inquired several of the gentlemen.

"Because the *correspondence* is so perfect that it strikes me at once, as it ought to strike everybody."

"How? how?"

"The correspondence between her nature and her costume, I mean! The outward glow expresses the inward heat. Believe me, Sybil Berners has been masquerading all her life, and now for the first time appears in her true character—a 'Fire Queen!'"

Such gossip as this was going on all over the room, but only in this circle was the secret of Sybil's character discovered. But soon this discovery found its way through the crowd, and in half an hour after the secret was first revealed, every one in the room knew of it, except the person most concerned. Sybil was surrounded by a circle of admirers, each one of whom, even by the slightest change of tone or manner, revealed their knowledge, for it would have been as much against the laws of etiquette and courtesy to recognize her before she was willing to be recognized, as it would have been to have unmasked her before she was ready to unmask. So they were very guarded in their manners—even more guarded than they needed to be, for Sybil was not critical, she was indeed scarcely observant of them. She was too deeply absorbed in watching her adored husband and her abhorred rival, as twined in each other's embrace, they swam around and around in the dizzy waltz, appearing, disappearing, and reappearing as they made the grand circle of the saloon.

At first they did not see Sybil, entrenched as she was behind her group of admirers; but the moment that they did see her—and Sybil knew that very moment—they modified their manners towards each other. And again Sybil was more disgusted than pleased at what she thought confirmed her worst suspicions of them.

At length the waltz was over. Lyon Berners led his fair partner to a seat, left her there and came to speak to his wife. But it was not until her group of admirers had separated to go in search of partners for the ensuing quadrille, that he had an opportunity of speaking to her privately.

"How are you enjoying yourself?" he inquired, on general principles.

"I am looking on. I am really interested in all these fooleries," answered Sybil evasively, but truly.

"Why were you not waltzing?"

"Why? Because I did not choose and could not have borne to have had my waist encircled by any other man's arm than yours, Lyon," answered his wife, very gravely.

"My darling Sybil, that comes of your old-fashioned notions and country training; and it deprives you of giving and receiving much pleasure," answered Mr. Berners.

And before Sybil could reply to that, the Black Prince came up to claim her promised hand in the quadrilles that were then forming.

Again, as she flashed like fire through and through the mazes of the dance, her elegant figure, her graceful motions, and her dazzling, flame-like dress was the general subject of enthusiastic admiration.

It was impossible but that some of this praise should reach the ears of its object. And equally impossible that her own name should not be coupled with it. So Sybil at length discovered that her identity was known, to some persons certainly—to how many she could not even conjecture.

Suddenly she resolved to try an experiment. She turned to her partner and inquired:

"Do you know me?"

"Not until you permit me to do so, Madam," answered the Black Prince, very courteously.

"Your reply was worthy of a knight and prince! So I permit you to recognize me," said Sybil.

"Then you are our beautiful hostess; and I am happy

to greet you by your real name, Mrs. Berners," said the Black Prince.

"Thanks," answered Sybil. "I saw that many persons knew me, and I wished to ascertain whether you were among their number, and how you and others found me out."

"Some diviner of spirits," laughed the Black Prince, "divined you, not only *through* but *by* your costume, in its correspondence with your character. And as soon as he made this discovery he hastened to promulgate it. Then I, for one, perceived at once that the splendid 'Fire Queen' could be no other than a daughter of 'Berners of the Burning Heart.' And now, Madam! am I permitted to introduce myself by the name I bear in this humdrum world of reality, or has your penetration already rendered such an introduction unnecessary?"

"It is unnecessary. I have just recognized—Captain Pendleton," replied Sybil.

The captain bowed low. And then, to the "forward two" of the leader of the band, he led his partner up to meet their *vis-a-vis*, to "balance," "pass," "change," and go through all the figures of the dance.

And so the dances succeeded each other to the end of the set. And then Captain Pendleton led his beautiful partner back to her seat, and stood talking with her until the music for the waltz commenced.

Then, having solicited her hand for that dance, and having ascertained that she never waltzed, he bowed and withdrew to find a partner elsewhere.

Very soon Sybil saw him whirling around the room with some one of the many unknown flower girls that constituted so large a portion of the company.

Soon after this she saw both her husband and her rival, among the waltzers; but they were not waltzing together. Edith the Fair was whirling around and around the room in the arms of a hermit, while Harold the Saxon was engaged with a pretty nun.

"They know me! they are cautious!" muttered Sybil, biting her lips with suppressed fury; for their forbearance, which she called duplicity, enraged her more than all their flirting had done.

And now she immediately put in execution the resolution that she had formed in the earlier part of the evening. Seeing her new acquaintance Death standing unemployed, she beckoned him to approach.

He came promptly.

"King of Terrors!" she said with assumed levity, "I do not waltz, but I am tired of sitting here. Give me your arm to the other end of the room, and even all around the room, perhaps."

"Spirit of Fire! it will not be the first time I have had the honor of waiting on you or following in your track," said Death, gallantly.

"True; Fire has often preceded Death as his agent," assented Sybil.

"Say rather, that Death has often followed Fire as her servant."

"Enough of this. We seem to be well paired, at least. Let us get up and walk."

Death bowed and offered his arm, and Fire arose and took it. And they walked around the room, keeping outside the circle of the waltzers and near the seats by the walls. But as they walked, many exclamations of admiration, wonder, and awe struck their ears.

"Splendid creature! She moves like a spirit or a flame," exclaimed one.

"What a contrast to her companion! She all life and light, he all darkness and death."

"It looks, as they walk side by side, as if she had burned him up and consumed him to a skeleton of charred bones," said another.

"Horrible! Hush!" imperatively commanded a young lady, whose will, if it did not enforce silence, modified expression.

Meanwhile Fire and Death went three times around the room. Then Fire paused near a little corner *tête-à-tête* sofa, on which a young girl, dressed as Janet Foster the little Puritan, was seated quite alone; and turning to her escort, she said:

"I am tired and thirsty. I will take this vacant seat for a while and trouble you to go and fetch me a glass of lemonade."

"With pleasure!" gallantly assented Death, starting off promptly and zealously to execute her commands.

Sybil seated herself beside the young girl on the sofa and laying her hand upon her shoulder, whispered:

"Trix."

"There!" exclaimed the girl, starting. "Every one knows me, even you."

"Well, everybody knows me also, even you," said Sybil.

"It is very provoking."

"Very."

"When I had taken so much pains to disguise myself too."

"Yes, and I also."

"*You?* Why you took the very means to reveal yourself, wearing a dress so perfectly adapted to your nature Anybod; might have known you," pouted Trix.

"Yes, anybody *might* have known me; but I do not think that anybody *would* have done so, if it had not been for a certain 'expert' who, detecting the 'correspondences,' as he calls them, divulged the secret to the whole room," explained Sybil.

"Well, somebody found you out, and did it by the fitness of your costume too. But as for me, nothing could be more opposite in character than Janet Foster the Puritan maiden, and Beatrix Pendleton the wild huntress. We are about as much alike as sage tea and sparkling hock Why, see here, Sybil; in order to throw every one off the track of me, I took a character as unlike mine as it was possible to find, and yet I have not succeeded in concealing my identity. And this has provoked me to such an extent that I have left the dance."

"And so I find you sulking here? Well, Trix, I will tell you how they found you out. You and I are known to be the two smallest women in the whole neighborhood. After having found me out, through the divination of a magician, it was easy to see that the other small woman must be you."

"Oh, I see; but it is perfectly exasperating!"

"So it is; but you may get some fun out of it yet, Trix, by turning the tables upon them all."

"How? Tell me! I'll do anything to get the better of them."

"I cannot tell you now, for here comes my escort with

my lemonade, and this matter must remain a secret between you and me. But listen: in fifteen minutes from this time slip away and go to my bedroom. You know the way, and you will find it empty. I will join you there, and tell you my plan," said Sybil, in a very low tone.

At that moment her escort arrived with the glass of lemonade.

Sybil received it from him with many thanks, and having offered it first to her companion, who politely declined it, she drank it, sat the empty glass upon the corner of the mantel-piece and then said:

"I will trouble you now, if you please, to take me back to my former seat."

Death bowed and offered his arm. Fire arose, nodded to the little Puritan on the sofa, took the arm of her escort, and walked away.

When she reached her old seat she dismissed her escort and in a few minutes, finding herself for the instant unobserved, she quietly slipped away to her bed-chamber, where she found Beatrix Pendleton already awaiting her.

First of all Sybil locked the door, to insure herself and her companion from interruption. Then she went to the glass and took off her crown of flames and her mask of gold gauze, and drew a long breath of relief as she turned towards her companion, who startled violently, exclaiming:

"Good Heaven, Sybil! how ghastly pale you look! You are ill!"

"Oh, no; only very weary," sighed Sybil, adding then, in explanation, "You know these affairs are very fatiguing."

"Yes, I know, but not to that extent, when you have a house full of trained servants to do everything. Why Sybil, you look as if your fiery dress had burned you to a form of ashes, leaving only a shape that might be blown away with a breath."

"Like another Creusa," answered Sybil, coldly. Then changing her tone, she said, with assumed lightness, "Come, Trix, you want to see some fun, and you shall see it. You and I are of about one size. We will therefore exchange dresses. You shall be the Fire Queen and I will be the Puritan maid. You can sustain the part you will take admirably, and upon occasion can disguise your own voice or imitate mine. I shall do my best to enact the little Puritan. But with all we can do to support the characters, we shall puzzle people to the end of their wits. They will not feel quite sure now as they were an hour ago that I am the Fire Queen, or you the Puritan maid. But they will not know who we are. Come, what have you to say to this?"

"Why, that it is enchanting. I agree to your plan at once."

"All right, then. We have no time to lose. It is half-past ten o'clock now. At twelve supper will be served, when all the guests will lay aside their masks. So you see that we have but an hour and a half to effect our change of dress and hoax our wise companions. Just before supper we must slip up here again and change back, so that we may unmask at supper in our proper disguises."

"All right!" exclaimed Trix, delighted with the plan.

"And there is one more caution I must give you. Keep out of the way of my husband. He knows my character of Fire Queen, and if he should see you near him in that dress, he would be sure to speak to you for me; and if you should attempt to reply, no matter how well you might imitate my voice, your speech would certainly betray you."

"All right! I will keep away from your husband, if I can; but how shall I know him?"

"He is dressed as Harold the last of the Saxon Kings!"

"Oh! is *that* Mr. Berners? And I never suspected it! I thought *that* it was some single man, desperately smitten with the charms of Edith the Fair," continued Beatrix.

"Oh, yes, I dare say you thought, but you were mistaken. Edith the Fair is our guest, Mrs. Blondelle. And she took the character of Edith to support Mr. Berners in Harold, and to be true to these characters they must act as they do; for Harold and Edith were lovers in history," explained Sybil, speaking calmly, though every word uttered by her companion had seemed like a separate stab to her already deeply wounded bosom.

"'Lovers in history' were they? I should take them

to be lovers in mystery now, if I did not know them to be Mr. Berners and Mrs. Blondelle," persisted Beatrix, all unconscious of the blows she was raining upon Sybil's overburdened heart. "However," she added, "I shall keep out of the way of both, for if *he* knew your disguise, be sure that *she* knew it also; and of course both, in daily intercourse with you, know your voice equally well. And if either of them should take me for you and speak to me for you, and I should attempt to reply, I should be sure to betray myself. So I will keep away from both, if I can. If not, if they should come suddenly upon me and speak to me, I shall not answer, but shall turn around and walk silently away as if I were offended with them."

"Yes, do that; that will be excellent," assented Sybil.

"And now, how are you going to support my character, or rather my disguise?" inquired Beatrix.

"By being very silent and demure as Janet Foster; or, if need should be, by carrying on your mood of sullenness as Beatrix Pendleton, masked."

"That will do," agreed Beatrix, with a smile.

All the while they had been speaking, they had also been taking off their fancy dresses. No time was lost, and the exchange of costume was quickly effected.

"Now," said Sybil, "another favor."

"Name it."

"Let me go down first. Then do you wait ten minutes here before you follow me. And when you enter the room keep away from me, as well as from my husband and my guest."

"Very well I will do so. Anything else?"

"Nothing now, thank you," said Sybil, kissing her hand as she left the room.

And Sybil, dressed now in the plain, close-fitting camlet gown and prim white linen cap, cuffs, and collar of the Puritan maid, and with a pale, young looking mask on her face, reëntered the saloon to try her experiment.

She looked around, and soon saw her husband and her rival sitting side-by-side, on the little retired sofa in the corner. They were absorbed in each other's attractions, and did not see her. She glided cautiously into a seat near them.

They were sitting very close together, talking in a very

low tone. Her hand rested in his. At length, Sybil heard her inquire:

"Where is your wife? I have not seen her for some time."

"She has left the room, I believe," answered Mr. Berners.

"Oh, that is such a relief! Do you know that I am really afraid of her?"

"Afraid of her! why? With me you are always perfectly safe. Safe!" he repeated, with a light laugh— "why, of course you are! Besides, what could harm you? Of whom are you afraid? Your friend, my wife, Sybil? She is your friend and would do you only good."

Rosa Blondelle slowly shook her head, murmuring:

"No, Lyon, your wife is not my friend—she is my deadly enemy. She is fiercely jealous of your affection for me, though it is the only happiness of my unhappy life. And she will make you throw me off yet."

"Never! no one, not even my wife, shall ever do that! I swear it by all my hopes of——"

"Hush! do not swear, for she will make you break your oath. She is your wife. She will make you forsake me, or—she will do me a fatal mischief. Oh, I shiver whenever she comes near me. Ah, if you had seen her eyes as I saw them through her mask to-night. They were lambent flames! How they glared on me, those terrible eyes!"

"It was your fancy, dear Rosa; no more than that. Come, shake off all this gloom and terror from your spirit, and be your lovely and sprightly self!"

"But I cannot! oh, I cannot! I feel the burning of her terrible eyes upon me now."

"But she is not even in the room."

(Here Sybil slipped away to a short distance, and joined a group of masks as if she belonged to them.)

"But I shiver as if she were near me now."

Lyon Berners suddenly looked around and then laughed, saying:

"But there is no one near you, dear Rosa, except Death."

"Death!" she echoed with a start and a shudder.

"Why, how excessively nervous you are, dear Rosa,"

said Lyon Berners laying his hand soothingly upon her shoulder.

"Oh, but just reflect what you have just said to me. 'No one near me but Death!' Death near me!" she repeated, trembling.

"Poor child, are you superstitious as well as nervous? It was the mask I meant. The mask that was Sybil's partner in the quadrille which we danced with them," laughed Lyon Berners.

"Oh, yes, I know. And they stood opposite to us. So that we danced with them more than with any one else! And my own hand turned cold every time it had to touch his. What a ghastly mask!"

"Yes, indeed. I wonder any man should choose such a one," added Lyon.

"Who is he? Who is that mask?"

"Indeed I do not know. Some one among our invited guests, of course. But he maintains his incognito so successfully, that even I, who have discovered most people in the room, have not been able to detect his identity. However, at supper all will unmask, and we shall see who he is."

"Look, is he still near me?" inquired Rosa, shaking as if with an ague.

Mr. Berners turned his head, and then answered:

"Yes, just to your left."

"Oh! please ask him to go away! I freeze and burn all in one minute, while he is near!"

That was enough for Lyon Berners. He arose and went to Death, and said:

"Excuse me, friend. No offence is meant; but your rather ghastly costume is too much for the nerves of the lady who is with me. I do not ask you to withdraw to some other part of the room; but I ask you whether you will do so, or whether I shall take the lady away from her resting-place?"

"Oh! I will withdraw! I know that my presence is not ever welcome, though I am not always so easily got rid of!" answered Death as, with a low inclination of his head, he went away.

"Oh! I breathe again! I live again!" murmured Rosa, with a sigh of relief.

DRIVEN TO DESPERATION. 133

"And now you are sufficiently rested, the music is striking up for a lively quadrille, and so, if you please, we will join the dancers and dance away dull care!" said Lyon Berners, rising and offering his arm to Rosa Blondella.

She arose and took his arm.

(Sybil, in her little Puritan's dress moved after them.)

He led her to the head of a set that was about to be formed.

"Oh! there she is!" suddenly exclaimed Rosa.

"Who?"

"Sybil."

"Where?"

"There!"

And Rosa pointed to one of the doors, at which Beatrix Pendleton, in Sybil's disguise, was just entering the room.

"No matter! She! she has taken another direction from this, and will not be near you, dear child; so be at rest," said Lyon Berners soothingly.

"Oh! I am so glad! You don't know how I fear that woman," replied Rosa.

"But you did not use to do so!"

"No! not until to-night! To-night when I met her terrible eyes," said Rosa.

"Come, come, dear! Cheer up," smiled Mr. Berners, encouragingly, as he took her hand and led her to the order—"Forward four!"

The dance began, and Sybil heard no more; but she had heard enough to convince her, if she had not been convinced before, of her guest's treachery and her husband's enthrallment.

She went and sat down quietly in a remote corner, and "bided her time." And waltz succeeded quadrille, and quadrille waltz. At the beginning of every new dance, some one would come up and ask for the honor of her hand, which she always politely refused—taking good care to speak in a low tone, and disguised voice. At length Captain Pendleton came up, and mistaking her for his sister, said:

"Sulking still, Trix?"

Not venturing to speak to him, lest he should discover

his mistake, she shrugged her shoulders and turned away.

"All right! sulk as long as you please. It hurts no one but yourself, my dear," exclaimed the Captain, sauntering off.

She saw Beatrix Pendleton, in her dress, moving merrily through the quadrille, or floating around in the waltz. She heard a gentleman near her say:

"I thought that lady never waltzed. I know she refused me and several others upon the plea that she never did."

And she heard the other lightly answer:

"Oh, well, ladies are privileged to change their minds."

The waltz of which they were speaking came now to an end. Sybil saw Beatrix led to a seat near her own. She also saw her partner bow and leave her. She seized the opportunity and glided up to Beatrix, and whispered:

"There will be but one more quadrille, and then supper will be served. I am going to my room. Do not dance in the next quadrille, but follow me, that we may change our dresses again. We have to be ready to unmask at supper, you know."

"Very well! I will be punctual. I really have enjoyed myself in your dress. And you?"

"As much as I expected to. I am satisfied."

At this moment the music for the quadrille struck up, and gentlemen began to select their partners. Two or three were coming towards Sybil and Beatrix. So with a parting caution to Beatrix to be careful, Sybil left the saloon.

She glided up to her chamber, where she was soon joined by Beatrix.

They began rapidly to take off their dresses, to exchange them.

"Oh, I have had so much amusement!" exclaimed Beatrix, laughing. "Everybody took me for you. And oh, I have received so many flattering compliments intended for you! and I have heard so much wholesome abuse of myself! That I was fast; that I was eccentric; that I was more than half-crazy; that I had a dreadful temper. And you?"

"I also received some sweet flattery intended for the

DRIVEN TO DESPERATION. 135

pretty little Puritan maiden, and learned some bitter truths about myself," answered Sybil.

"How hollow your voice is, Sybil! Bosh! who cares for such double-dealing wretches, who flatter us before our faces and abuse us behind our backs?" exclaimed Beatrix, as she quickly finished her Puritan toilet, and announced herself ready.

Sybil was also dressed, and they went down-stairs and entered the drawing-room together.

The last quadrille before supper was over, the supper-rooms were thrown open, and the company were marching in.

Captain Pendleton hastened to meet Sybil, and another gentleman offered his arm to Beatrix, and thus escorted they fell in the line of march with others.

As each couple passed into the supper-room, they took off their masks, and handed them to attendants, placed for that purpose, to the right and left of the door. Thus, when the company filled the rooms, every face was shown.

There were the usual surprises, the usual gay recognitions.

Among the rest, "Harold the Saxon," and "Edith the Fair" stood confessed as Mr. Berners and Mrs. Blondelle, and much silent surprise as well as much whispered suspicion was the result.

"Is it possible?" muttered one. "I took them for a pair of lovers, they were so much together."

"I thought they were a newly married pair, who took advantage of their masks to be more together than etiquette allows," murmured a second.

"I think it was very improper; don't you?" inquired a third.

"Improper! It was disgraceful," indignantly answered a fourth, who was no other than Beatrix Pendleton, who now completely understood why it was that Sybil Berners wished to change dresses with her, and also how it was that Sybil's voice was so hollow, as she spoke in the bed-chamber. "She wished to put on my dress that she might watch them unsuspected, and she was right. She detected them in their sinful trifling, and she was wretched," said Beatrix to herself. And she looked around to catch a glimpse of Sybil's face. Sybil was sitting too near to be seen. Sybil was on the same side with herself, and only two or three seats off. But Beatrix saw Mr. Berners and Mrs. Blondelle sitting immediately opposite to herself, and with a recklessness that savored of fatuity, still carrying on their sentimental flirtation.

Yes! Rosa was still throwing up her eyes to his eyes, and cooing "soft nonsense" in his ears; and Lyon was still dwelling on her glances and her tones with loverlike devotion. Suddenly assuming a gay tone, she asked him:

"Where is our ghastly friend, Death! I do not see him anywhere in the room, and I was *so* anxious to see him unmasked, that I might find out who he is. Where is he? Do you see him anywhere?"

"No; he is not here yet; but doubtless he will make his appearance presently," answered Mr. Berners.

"Do you really not know who he is?"

"Not in the least; nor does any one else here know," replied Mr. Berners.

Suddenly Rosa looked up, started, and with a suppressed cry, muttered:

"Good heavens! Look at Sybil!"

Mr. Berners followed the direction of her gaze across the table, and even he started at the sight of Sybil's face.

That face wore a look of anguish, despair, and desperation that seemed fixed there forever; for in all its agony of passion that tortured and writhen face was as still, cold, hard, and lifeless as marble, except that from its eyes streamed glances as from orbs of fire.

Mr. Berners suddenly turned his eyes from her, and looked up and down the table. Fortunately now every one was too busily engaged in eating, drinking, laughing, talking, flirting, and gossiping to attend to the looks of their hostess.

"I must go and speak to her," said Lyon Berners in extreme anxiety and displeasure, as he left Rosa's side, and made his way around the table, until he stood immediately behind his wife. He touched her on her shoulder to attract her attention. She started as if **an adder had** stung her, but she never looked around.

"Sybil, my dearest, you are ill. What is the matter?" he whispered, trying to avoid being overheard by others.

"Do NOT touch me! Do *not* speak to me, unless you wish to see me drop dead or go mad before you!" she answered in tones so full of suppressed energy, that he impulsively drew back.

He waited for a moment in dire dread lest the assembled company should see the state of his wife, and then he ventured to renew his efforts.

"Sybil, my darling, you are really not well. Let me lead you out of this crowded room," he whispered, very gently, laying his hand upon her shoulder.

She dashed it off as if it had been some venomous reptile, and turned upon him a look flaming with fiery wrath.

"Sybil, you will certainly draw the attention of our guests," he persisted, with much less gentleness than he had before spoken.

"If you touch me, or speak to me but once more—if you do not leave me on the instant, I *will* draw the attention of our guests, and draw it with a vengeance too!" she fiercely retorted, never once removing from him her flaming eyes.

CHAPTER XVIII.

LYING IN WAIT.

"He is with her; and they know that I know
 Where they are, and what they do; they believe my tears flow
 While they laugh, laugh at me, at me left in the drear
 Empty hall to lament in, for them!—I am here."—BROWNING.

"You are a lunatic, and fit only for a lunatic asylum!" was the angry comment of Lyon Berners, as he turned upon his heel and left his wife.

It was the first time in his life that he had ever spoken angrily to Sybil, or even felt angry with her.

Hitherto he had borne her fierce outbursts of jealousy with "a great patience," feeling, perhaps, that they flamed up from the depths of her burning love for him; feeling, also, that his own thoughtless conduct had caused them.

Now, however, he was thoroughly incensed by the deportment of his wife, and deeply mortified at the effect it might have upon their company.

He went around to the opposite side of the table. He did not again join Rosa, for he dreaded a scene, and even a catastrophe; but he mingled with the crowd, and stood where he could see Sybil, without being seen by her.

Her face remained the same—awful in the marble-like stillness of her agonized features; terrible in the fierceness of her flaming eyes.

This was at length observed by some of the guests, who whispered their comments or inquiries to others. And the hum of voices and the burden of their low-toned talk at length reached the ears or excited the suspicions of Lyon Berners. The ordeal of the supper-table was a frightful trial to him. He longed for it to be over.

At length the longing was gratified—the torture was over. The guests, by twos and by fours, by small groups and large parties, left the supper-room for the saloon, where the musicians struck up a grand march, and the greater portion of the company formed into a leisurely promenade as a gentle exercise after eating, and a prudent prelude to more dancing.

Some among the guests, however, preferred to seat themselves on the sofas that lined the walls, and to rest.

Among these last was Rosa Blondelle, who sat on a corner sofa, and sulked and looked sad and sentimental because Lyon Berners had not spoken to her, or even approached her since he had seen that look on Sybil's face. To the vain and shallow coquette, it was gall and bitterness to perceive that Sybil had still the power, of whatever sort, to keep her own husband and *her* admirer from her side. So Rosa sat and sorrowed, or seemed to sorrow on the corner sofa, from which nobody invited her to rise, for there was a very general feeling of disapprobation against the beautiful blonde.

Sybil also sank upon a side seat, where she sat with that same look of agony turned to marble, on her face. Some one came up and invited her to join in the promenade. Scarcely recognizing the speaker, or comprehending what he said, she arose, more like an automaton than a living woman, and let herself be led away to join the march.

But her looks had now attracted very general attention and occasioned much comment. More than one indiscreet friend or acquaintance had remarked to Mr. Berners:

"Mrs. Berners looks quite ill. I fear the fatigue of this masquerade has been too much for her," or words to that effect.

"Yes," Lyon Berners invariably replied, "she is quite indisposed this evening, suffering indeed; and I have begged her to retire, but I cannot induce her to do so."

"She is too unselfish; she exerts herself too much for the entertainment of her guests," suggested another.

And so the rumor went around the room that Mrs. Berners was suffering from severe illness. And this explanation of her appearance was very generally received; for the outward and silent manifestations of mental anguish are not unlike those of physical agony.

And so, after another quadrille and another waltz, and the final Virginia reel, the company, in consideration of their hostess, began to break up and depart. Some few intimate friends of the family, who had come from a distance to the ball, were to stay all night at Black Hall. These upon their first arrival had been shown to the chambers they were to occupy, and now they knew where to find them. And so, when the last of the departing guests had taken leave of their hostess, and had gone away, these also bade her good-night and retired.

And Sybil remained alone in the deserted drawing-room.

It is sometimes interesting and curious to consider the relative position of the parties concerned, just before the enactment of some terrible tragedy.

The situation at Black Hall was this: The guests were in their chambers, preparing to retire to bed. The servants were engaged in fastening up the house and putting out the lights, only they refrained from interfering with three rooms, where three members of the family still lingered.

In the first of these was the mistress of the house, who, as I said, remained alone in the deserted drawing-room. Sybil stood as if turned to stone, nd fixed to the spot—

motionless in form and face, except that her lips moved and a hollow monotone issued from them, more like the moan of a lost soul, than the voice of a living woman.

"So all is lost, and nothing left but these—REVENGE and DEATH!" she muttered.

The awful spirit of her race overshadowed her and possessed her. She felt that, to destroy the destroyer of her peace, she would be willing to meet and suffer all that man could inflict upon her body, or devil do to her soul! And so she brooded, until suddenly out of this trance-like state she started, as if a serpent had stung her.

"I linger here," she cried, "while they—where are they, the traitor and his temptress? I will seek them through the house; I will tear them asunder, and confront them in their treachery."

Meanwhile where were they, the false friend and the fascinated husband?

Lyon Berners, much relieved from anxiety by the departure of the last guests, but still deeply displeased with his wife, had retired to the little morning parlor to collect himself. He stood now upon the rug, with his back to the smouldering fire, absorbed in somber thought. He loved his wife, bitterly angry as he had been with her this evening, and prone as he was to fall under the spell of the fair siren who was now his temptress. He loved his wife, and he wished to insure her peace. He resolved to break off, at once and forever, the foolish flirtation with a shallow coquette which his deep-hearted Sybil had taken so earnestly. How to do this, occupied his thoughts now. He knew that it would be difficult, or impossible to do it, as long as Rosa Blondelle remained in the same house with himself. He felt that he could not ask her to go and find another home; for to do so would be rude, inhospitable, and even cruel to the homeless and friendless young stranger.

What should he do, then?

It occurred to him that he might make some fair excuse to take Sybil to the city, and spend the ensuing winter there with her, leaving Rosa Blondelle in full possession of Black Hall until she should choose to make arrangements to return to her own country. This or something else must be done, for the flirtation with Rosa

LYING IN WAIT. 141

must never be resumed. In the midst of these good resolutions he was interrupted.

Meanwhile Rosa Blondelle had been as deeply mortified and enraged by the sudden desertion and continued coolness of Lyon Berners, as it was in her shallow nature to be. She went to her own room, but she could not remain there. She came out into the long narrow passage leading to the front hall, and she paced up and down with the angry restlessness of a ruffled cat, muttering to herself:

"She shall not take him from me, even if he is her husband! I *will* not be outrivaled by another woman, even if she is his wife!"

Over and over again she ground these words through her teeth, or other words of the same sort. Suddenly she passed out of the narrow passage into the broad hall, where she noticed that the parlor door was ajar, a light burning within the room, and the shadow of a man thrown across the carpet. She stole to the door, peeped in, and saw Lyon Berners still standing on the rug with his back to the smouldering fire, absorbed in somber thought.

She slipped in, and dropped her head upon his shoulder and sobbed.

Startled and very much annoyed, he gently tried to raise her head and put her away.

But she only clung the closer, and sobbed the more.

"Rosa! don't! don't, child! Let us have no more of this. It is sinful and dangerous! For your own sake, Rosa, retire to your room!" he gently expostulated.

"Oh! you love me no longer! You love me no longer!" vehemently exclaimed the siren. "That cruel woman has compelled you to forsake me! I told you she would do it, and now she has done it."

"'That woman,' Rosa, is my beloved wife, entitled to my whole faith; yet not even for her will I forsake you; but I will continue to care for you, as a brother for a sister. But, Rosa, this must cease," he gravely added.

"Oh, do not say that! do not! do not fling off the poor lonely heart that you have once gathered to your own!" and she clung to him as closely and wept as wildly as if she had been in earnest.

"Rosa! Rosa!" he whispered eagerly, and in great embarrassment, "my child! be reasonable Reflect! you have a husband!"

"Ah! name him not. He robbed and left me, and I hate him," she cried.

"And I have a dear and honored wife whose happiness I must guard. Thus you see we can be nothing to each other but brother and sister. A brother's love and care is all that I can offer you, or that you should be willing to accept from me," he continued, as he gently smoothed her fair hair.

"Then give me a brother's kiss," she sighed. "That is not much to ask, and I have no one to kiss me now! So give me a brother's kiss, and let me go!" she pleaded, plaintively.

He hesitated for a moment, and then bending over her, he said:

"It is the *first*, and for your own sake it must be the *last*, Rosa!" he pressed his lips to hers.

It *was* the last as well as the first; for at the meeting of their lips, they were stricken as under as by the fall of a thunderbolt!

And Sybil, blazing with wrath, like a spirit from the Lake of Fire, stood between them!

Yes! for she looked not human—with her ashen cheeks, and darkened brow, and flaming eyes—with her whole face and form heaving, palpitating, flashing forth the lightnings of anger!

"SYBIL!" exclaimed her husband, thunderstruck, appalled.

She waved her hand towards him, as if to implore or command silence.

"I have nothing to say to you," she muttered, in low and husky tones, as if ashes were in her throat. "But to YOU!" she said, and her voice rose clear and strong as she turned and stretched out her arm towards Rosa, who was leaning in a fainting condition against the wall—"TO YOU, viper, who has stung to death the bosom that warmed you to life—TO YOU, traitress, who has come between the true husband and his wife—TO YOU, thief! who has stolen from your benefactress the sole treasure of her life—TO YOU I have this to say: I will not drive you forth in dishonor from my door this night, nor will I publish your infamy to the world to-morrow, though you have deserved nothing less than these from my hands; but in the morning you must leave the house you have desecrated! for if you do not, or if ever I find your false face here again, I will tread down and crush out your life with less remorse than ever I set heel upon a spider! I will, as I am a Berners! And now, begone, and never let me see your form again!"

Rosa Blondelle, who had stood spell-bound by the terrible gaze and overwhelming words of Sybil, the wronged wife, now suddenly threw up her hands, and with a low cry, fled from the room.

And Sybil dropped her arm and her voice at the same instant, and stood dumb and motionless.

And now, at length, Lyon Berners spoke again.

"Sybil! you have uttered words that nothing on the part of that poor lady should have provoked from you—words that I fear may never be forgotten or forgiven! But—I know that she has a gentle and easy nature. When you are cooler and more rational, I wish you to go to her and be reconciled with her."

"With *her!* I am a Berners!" answered Sybil, haughtily.

"But you bitterly wrong that lady in your thoughts!"

"Bah! I caught her in your arms! on your breast! her lips clinging to yours!"

"The first and last kiss! I swear it by all my hopes of Heaven, Sybil—a brother's kiss!"

Sybil made a gesture of scorn and disgust.

"If I were not past laughing, I should have to laugh now," she said.

"And you will not believe this?"

She shook her head.

"And you will not be reconciled to this injured young stranger?"

"I! I am a lady—'or long have dreamed so'," answered Sybil, haughtily. "At least the daughter of an honest mother And I will not even permit such a woman as that to live under the same roof with me another day. She leaves in the morning."

"The house is yours! You must do as you please!

But this I tell you: that in the same hour which sees that poor and friendless young creature driven from the shelter of this roof, I leave it too, and leave it forever."

If Lyon Berners really meant this, or thought to bring his fiery-hearted wife to terms by the threat, he was mistaken in her character.

"Oh, go!" she answered bitterly—"go! I *will* not harbor *her*. And why should I seek to detain you? Your heart has left me already; why should I wish to retain its empty case? Go as soon as you like, Lyon Berners. Good-night, and—good-bye," she said, and with a wave of her hand she passed from the room.

He was mad to have spoken as he did; madder still to let her leave him so! how mad, he was soon to learn.

CHAPTER XIX.

SWOOPING DOWN.

Twice it called, so loudly called
With horrid strength beyond the pitch of nature;
And murder! murder! was the dreadful cry.
A third time it returned with feeble strength,
But on the sudden ceased; as though the words
Were smothered rudely in the grappled throat,
And all was still again, save the wild blast
Which at a distance growled—
Oh, it will never from the heart depart!
That dreadful cry all in the instant stilled.—BAILLIE.

LYON BERNERS remained walking up and down the room some time longer. The lights were all out, and the servants gone to bed. Yet still he continued to pace up and down the parlor floor, until suddenly piercing shrieks smote his ear.

In great terror he started forward and instinctively rushed towards Rosa's room, when the door was suddenly thrown open by Rosa herself, pale, bleeding from a wound in her breast.

"Great Heaven! What is this?" he cried, as, aghast with amazement and sorrow, he supported the ghastly and dying form, and laid it on the sofa, and then sunk on his knees beside it.

SWOOPING DOWN. 145

"Who, who has done this?" he wildly demanded, as, almost paralyzed with horror, he knelt beside her, and tried to stanch the gushing wound from which her life-blood was fast welling.

"Who, who has done this fiendish deed?" he reiterated in anguish as he gazed upon her.

She raised her beautiful violet eyes, now fading in death; she opened her bloodless lips, now paling in death, and she gasped forth the words:

"She—Sybil—your wife. I told you she would do it, and she has done it. Sybil Berners has murdered me," she whispered. Then raising herself with a last dying effort, she cried aloud, "Hear, all! Sybil Berners has murdered me." And with this charge upon her lips, she fell back DEAD.

Even in that supreme moment Lyon Berners' first thought, almost his only thought, was for his wife. He looked up to see who was there—who had heard this awful, this fatal charge.

All were there! guests and servants, men and women, drawn there by the dreadful shrieks. All had heard the horrible accusation.

And all stood panic-stricken, as they shrank away from one who stood in their midst.

It was she, Sybil, the accused, whose very aspect accused her more loudly than the dying woman had done; for she stood there, still in her fiery masquerade dress, her face pallid, her eyes blazing, her wild black hair loose and streaming, her crimsoned hand raised and grasping a blood-stained dagger.

"Oh, wretched woman! most wretched woman! What is this that you have done?" groaned Lyon Berners, in unutterable agony—agony not for the dead beauty before him, but for the living wife, whom he felt that he had driven to this deed of desperation. "Oh, Sybil! Sybil! what have you done?" he cried, grinding his hands together.

"I? I have done nothing!" faltered his wife, with pale and tremulous lips.

"Oh, Sybil! Sybil! would to Heaven you had died before this night! Or that I could now give my life for this life that you have madly taken!" moaned Lyon.

"I have taken no life! What do you mean? This is horrible!" exclaimed Sybil, dropping the dagger, and looking around upon her husband and friends, who all shrank from her. "I have taken no life! I am no assassin? Who dares to accuse me?" she demanded, standing up pale and haughty among them.

And then she saw that every lowered eye, every compressed lip, every shuddering and shrinking form, silently accused her.

Mr. Berners had turned again to the dead woman. His hand was eagerly searching for some pulsation at the heart. Soon he ceased his efforts, and arose.

"Vain! vain!" he said, "all is still and lifeless, and growing cold and stiff in death. Oh! my wretched wife!"

"The lady may not be dead! This may be a swoon from loss of blood. In such a swoon she would be pulseless and breathless, or seem so! Let me try! I have seen many a swoon from loss of blood, as well as many a death from the came cause, in my military experience," said Captain Pendleton, pushing forward and kneeling by the sofa, and beginning his tests, guided by experience.

His words and actions unbound the spell of horror that had till then held the assembled company still and mute, and now all pressed forward towards the sofa, and bent over the little group there.

"Air! air! friends, if you please! Stand farther off. And some one open a window!" exclaimed Captain Pendleton, peremptorily.

And he was immediately obeyed by the falling off of the crowd, one of whom threw open a window.

"Some one should fetch a physician!" suggested Beatrix Pendleton, whose palsied tongue was now at length unloosed.

And half a dozen gentlemen immediately started for the stables to despatch a messenger for the village doctor from Blackville.

"And while they are fetching the physician, they should summon the coroner also," suggested a voice from the crowd.

"No! no! not until we have ascertained that life is actually extinct," exclaimed Captain Pendleton, hastily; at

SWOOPING DOWN. 147

the same time seeking and meeting the eyes of Mr. Berners with a meaning gaze said :

"If we cannot restore the dead woman to life, we must at least try to save the living woman from unspeakable horrors!"

Mr. Berners turned away his head, with a deep groan.

And Captain Pendleton continued his seeming efforts to restore consciousness to the prostrate form before him, until he heard the galloping of the horse that took the messenger away for the doctor, and felt sure that the man could not now receive orders to fetch the coroner also.

Then Captain Pendleton arose and beckoned Miss Tabby Winterose to come towards him. That lady came forward, whimpering as usual, but with an immeasurably greater cause than she had ever possessed before.

"Close her eyes, straighten her limbs, arrange her dress. She is quite dead," said the Captain.

Miss Tabby's voice was lifted up in weeping.

But wilder yet arose the sound of wailing, as the Scotch girl, with the child in her arms, broke through the crowd and cast herself down beside her dead mistress, crying :

"Oh! and is it gone ye are, my bonny leddy? Dead and gone fra us, a' sae suddenly! Oh, bairnie! look down on your puir mither, wham they have murthered—the born deevils."

The poor child, frightened as much by the wild wailing of the nurse as by the sight of his mother's ghastly form began to scream and to hide his head on Janet's bosom.

"Woman, this is barbarous. Take the boy away from this sight," exclaimed Captain Pendleton, imperatively.

But Janet kept her ground, and continued to weep and wail and apostrophize the dead mother, or appeal to the orphan child. And all the women in the crowd whose tongues had hitherto been paralyzed with horror, now broke forth in tears and sobs, and cries of sympathy and compassion, and—

"Oh, poor murdered young mother! Oh, poor orphaned babe!" or lamentations to the same effect, broke forth on all sides.

"Mr. Berners, you are master of the house. I earnestly exhort you to clear the room of all here, except Miss Winterose and ourselves," said Captain Pendleton in an almost commanding tone.

"Friends and neighbors," cried Lyon Berners, lifting up his voice, so that it could be heard all over the room, "I implore you to withdraw to your own apartments. Your presence here only serves to distress yourselves and embarrass us. And we have a duty to do to the dead."

The crowd began to disperse and move towards the doors when suddenly Sybil Berners lifted her hand on high and called, in a commanding tone:

"STOP!"

And all stopped and turned their eyes on her.

She was still very pale, but now also very calm; the most self-collected one in that room of death.

"I have somewhat to say to you," she continued. "You all heard the dying words of that poor dead woman, in which she accused me of having murdered her; and your own averted eyes accuse me quite as strongly, and my own aspect, perhaps, more strongly than either."

She paused and glanced at her crimsoned hand, and then looked around and saw that her nearest neighbors and oldest friends, who had known her longest and loved her best, now turned away their heads, or dropped their eyes. She resumed:

"The dead woman was mistaken; you are misled; and my very appearance is deceptive. I will not deny that the woman was my enemy. Driven to desperation, and in boiling blood, I might have been capable of doing her a deadly mischief, but bravely and openly, as the sons and daughters of my fiery race have done such things before this. But to go to her chamber in the dead of night, and in darkness and secrecy—! No! I could not have done that, if she had been ten times the enemy she was. Is there one here who believes that the daughter of Bertram Berners could be guilty of that or any other base deed?" she demanded, as her proud glance swept around upon the faces of her assembled friends and neighbors.

But their averted eyes too sorrowfully answered her question.

Then she turned to her husband and lowered her voice to an almost imploring tone as she inquired:

"Lyon Berners, do YOU believe me guilty?"

He looked up, and their eyes met. If he had really believed her guilty he did not now. He answered briefly and firmly :

"No, Sybil! Heaven knows that I do not. But oh! my dear wife! explain, if you can, how that dagger came into your possession, how that blood came upon your hands; and, above all, why this most unhappy lady should have charged you with having murdered her."

"At your desire, and for the satisfaction of the few dear old friends whom I see among this unbelieving crowd, the friends who would deeply grieve if I should either door suffer wrong, I *will* speak. But if it were not for you and for them, I would die before I would deign to defend myself from a charge that is at once so atrocious and so preposterous—so monstrous," said Sybil, turning a gaze full of haughty defiance upon those who stood there before her face, and dared to believe her guilty.

A stern voice spoke up from that crowd.

"Mr. Lyon Berners, attend to this. A lady lies murdered in your house. By whom she has been so murdered we do not know. But I tell you that every moment in which you delay in sending for the officers of justice to investigate this affair, compromises you and me and all who stand by and silently submit to this delay, as accessories, after the fact."

Lyon Berners turned towards the speaker, a grave and stern old man of nearly eighty years, a retired judge, who had come to the mask ball escorting his granddaughters.

"An instant, Judge Basham. Pardon us, if in this dismay some things are forgotten. The coroner shall be summoned immediately. Captain Pendleton, will you oblige me by despatching a messenger to Coroner Taylor at Blackville?" he then inquired, turning to the only friend upon whose discretion he felt he could rely.

Captain Pendleton nodded acquiescence and intelligence, and left the room, as if for the purpose specified.

"Now, dear Sybil, with Judge Basham's permission, give our friends the explanation that you have promised them," said Lyon Berners affectionately, and confidingly taking her hand and placing himself beside her.

For all his anger as well as all her jealousy had been swept away in the terrible tornado of this evening's events.

"The explanation that I promised *you* and those who wish me well," she said emphatically. And then her voice arose clear, firm, and distinct, as she continued.

"I was in my chamber, which is immediately above that occupied by Mrs. Blondelle. My chamber is approached by two ways, first by the front passage and stairs, and secondly by a narrow staircase running up from Mrs. Blondelle's room. And the door leading from her room up this staircase and into mine, she has been in the habit of leaving open. To-night, as I said, I was sitting in my chamber; from causes not necessary to explain now and here, I was too much disturbed in mind to think of retiring to rest, or even of undressing. I do not know how long I had sat there, when I heard a piercing shriek from some one in the room below. Instinctively I rushed down the communicating stairs and into Mrs. Blondelle's room, and up to her bed, where I saw by the light of the taper she was lying. Her eyes were closed, and I thought at first that she had fainted from some fright until, almost at the same instant, I saw this dagger—" here Sybil stooped and picked up the dagger that she had dropped a few minutes before—"driven to its haft in her chest. I drew it out. Instantly the blood from the opened wound spirted up, covering my hand and sleeve with the accusing stains you see! With the flowing of the blood her eyes flew wildly open! She gazed affrightedly at me for an instant, and then with the last effort of her life, for which terror lent her strength, she started up and fled shieking to this room. I, still holding the dagger that I had drawn from her bosom, followed her here. And— you know the rest," said Sybil; and overcome with excitement, she sank upon the nearest chair to rest.

Lyon Berners still held her hand.

Her story had evidently made a very great impression upon the company present. But Lyon Berners suddenly exclaimed:

"Good Heavens! that lady's mistaken charge has put us all off the scent, and allowed the murderer to escape. But it may not yet be too late! Some clue may be left in her room by which we may trace the criminal! Come, neighbors, and let us search the premises."

And Lyon Berners, leaving the shuddering women of the party in the room with Sybil and the dead, and followed by all the men, went to search the house and grounds for traces of the assassin.

CHAPTER XX.

THE SEARCH.

> My friends, I care not, (so much I am happy
> Above a number,) if my actions
> Were tried by every tongue, every eye saw them,
> Envy and base opinion set against them,
> To know my life so even.—SHAKESPEARE.

AND first they went to Mrs. Blondelle's room, and carefully examined every part of it, especially the fastenings of the doors and windows. They all seemed to be right.

"I have a theory of this murder now!" said Mr. Berners, standing in the middle of the room and speaking to the men who were with him.

"Humph! what is it?" coldly inquired old Judge Basham.

"It is this; that as Mrs. Blondelle was known to have possessed jewels of great value, some miscreant came here with the intention to rob her of them."

"Well, and what then?" asked the Judge.

"That this miscreant entered either by the outer door, or by one of these windows, approached the bed of his victim who, being awake and seeing him, shrieked, either before or at the moment of receiving the death wound, and then fainted."

"Humph! what next?" grunted the Judge.

"That first shriek brought my wife running to the rescue. At the sound of her approach, of course the murderer turned and fled, escaping through the outer door or window"

"An ingenious story, and a plausible explanation, Mr. Berners; but one, I fear, that will never convince a jury, or satisfy the public," remarked Judge Basham.

"Nay, and it will na satisfy mysel' neither! It'll na do, gentlemen! The murderer didna come through the outer door, nor the window either! For mysel' fastened them a' before I went to my bed! And yesel's found them fastened when ye cam!" said the Scotch girl Janet, who had now entered the room with the child in her arms.

"But he may have come through the door, my good girl," suggested Mr. Berners, whose very blood seemed to freeze at this testimony of the maid.

"Nay, nay, laird! that will na do either. The murderer could na hae come by the outer door, for mysel' bolted it before I went to bed! And it was still bolted when my puir leddy—Oh, my puir bonny leddy! oh! my puir dear murdered mistress!" broke forth from the girl in sudden and violent lamentations.

"Compose yourself, and tell us all about the bolted door," said Judge Basham.

"Aweel, sir, the door was bolted by mysel', and bolted it stayed until that puir leddy started out of her bed and tore the bolt back, and fled away from before the face of her murderer! too late! oh, too late! for she carried her death wound with her."

"So you see, Mr. Berners, your theory of the murder falls to pieces. This girl's testimony proves that the murderer could not have entered the room, from this floor," said Judge Basham.

"Then he *must* have been concealed in the room," exclaimed Lyon, desperately.

"Nay, nay! that will na do either, laird. Na mon was hid in the room. Mysel' looked into all the closets, and under the bed, and up the chimney, as I always do before I go to sleep. I could na sleep else. Nay, nay, laird! The murderer came in neither by outer door nor window, nor yet lay hidden in the room; for mysel' had fastened the outer door and window, and searched the room before I slept. Nay, nay, laird! The murderer cam by the only way left open—left open because we thought it was safe—the way leading from Mistress Berners' room down to the little stair, and through this door which was not bolted," persisted the Scotch girl.

Lyon Berners' heart seemed turned to ice by these last words. Nevertheless he summoned fortitude to say:

"We must examine and see if there has been a robbery committed. If there *has* been one, then, of course, in the face of all this woman's evidence, it will prove that the robber has done this foul deed."

"I do not see clearly that it will," objected Judge Basham. "However, we will make the examination."

"Your honors need na tak the trouble. Mysel' saw to that too. See, the bureau drawers and wardrobes are all fast locked as me leddy saw me lock them hersel'. And the keys are safe in the pocket of my gown. Nay, nay, lairds, naething is stolen," said Janet.

Nevertheless, Mr. Berners insisted on making the examination. So Janet produced the keys and opened all the bureau drawers, boxes, wardrobes, etc. All things were found in order. In the upper bureau drawer, caskets of jewels, boxes of lace, rolls of bank-notes and other valuables were found untouched. Nothing was missing.

In a word, no clue was found to the supposed murderer and robber; but, on the other hand, every circumstance combined to fix the deed on Sybil.

Lyon Berners felt a faintness like death coming over him, and subduing all his manhood. Unblenchingly, in his own person, he would have braved any fate. But that his wife—his pure, high-toned, magnanimous Sybil, should be caught up and ground to pieces by this horrible machinery of circumstances and destiny! Was this a nightmare? His brain was reeling. He felt that he might go mad. Like the drowning man, he caught at straws. Turning to the Scotch girl, he demanded somewhat sternly:

"And where were you when your mistress was being murdered? where were you, that you did not hasten to her assistance? You could not have been far off—you must in fact have been in that little adjoining nursery."

"And sae I was, laird; and her first screech waked me up and garred me grew sae till I couldna move, and didna move till I heard her screech again and again, and saw her rin across the floor, and tear back the bolt and flecht fra the room, followed close behind by Mistress Berners. And thin mysel' sprang up wi' the bairn in me arms and rin after them, thinking the de'il was behind me. Oh, me puir leddy! oh, me puir, bonny leddy! oh! oh!

oh!" wept and wailed the girl, dropping down on the floor and throwing her apron over her head.

But the cries of the child from the adjoining nursery caused her to start up, and run in there to comfort him.

The searchers left that room, and pursued their investigations elsewhere. They went all through the house without finding any clue to the mystery. They attempted to search the grounds, but the night was pitch-dark, and the rain was falling fast. Finally, they returned to the room of death.

All the ladies and all the servants had gone away. No one remained in it but Sybil and Miss Tabby, watching the dead.

Sybil sat near the head of the body, and Miss Tabby near the feet.

At the sight of his doomed young wife, Lyon Berners senses reeled again.

"She is so inexperienced in all the ways of the world; so ignorant of the ways of the law! Oh, does she know —does she even dream of the awful position, the deadly danger in which she stands? No; she is unconscious of all peril. She evidently believes that the explanation she gave us here, and which satisfies her friends, will convince all others. Oh, Sybil! Sybil! an hour ago so safe in your domestic sanctity, and now—now momentarily exposed to—Heaven! I cannot bear it!" he groaned, as he struggled for self-command and went towards her.

She was sitting with her hands clasped, as in prayer, and her eyes, full of the deepest regret and pity, fixed upon the face of the dead. There was sorrow, sympathy, awe —anything but fear or distrust in her countenance. At the approach of her husband, she turned and whispered gravely:

"She was my rival where I could least bear rivalry; and I thought she had been a successful one. I do not think so now; and now I have no feeling towards her but one of the deepest compassion. Oh, Lyon, we must adopt her poor child, and rear it for our own. Oh! who has done this deed? Some one whose aim was robbery, no doubt. Has any trace been discovered of the murderer?" she inquired.

THE SEARCH. 155

"None, Sybil," he answered, with difficulty.

"Oh, Lyon, such awful thoughts have visited me since I have sat here and forced myself to look upon this sight! For I see in it that which I might have done, had my madness become frenzy ; but even then, not as this was done. Oh, no, no, no! May God forgive me and change my heart, for I have been standing on the edge of an abyss !"

Mr. Berners could not speak. He was suffocating with the feeling that she now stood upon the brink of ruin yawning to receive her.

"Heaven help you, Sybil!" was the silent prayer of his spirit as he gazed on his unconscious wife.

Miss Tabby, who sat whimpering at the feet of the dead, now spoke up :

"I think," she said, wiping the tear-drop from the end of her nose, "I *do* think as we ought not to leave it a-lying here, cramped up onto this sofy, where we can't stretch it straight. We ought to have it taken to her room and laid out on her bed, decent and in order."

"It is true ; but oh, in a shock like this, how much is forgotten!" said Mr. Berners. Then turning to old Judge Basham, who had sank into an easy-chair to rest, but seemed to consider himself still on the bench, since he assumed so much authority, Lyon inquired, "Do you see any objection to the body being removed to a bedroom before the coroner's arrival ?"

"Certainly not. This is not the scene of the murder. You had best take it back to the bed on which she received her death," answered the old Judge.

"Friends," said Mr. Berners, turning to the gentlemen, who had all solemnly and silently seated themselves as at a funeral, "will one of you assist me in this?"

Captain Pendleton, who had just re-entered the room, came promptly up.

"By the way, did you send for the coroner, sir ?" demanded the old Judge, intercepting him.

"Yes, sir, I did," curtly answered the Captain.

"Then I shall sit here until his arrival," observed the Judge settling himself for a nap in his easy-chair.

"That old fellow is in his dotage!" growled Captain Pendleton to himself, as he tenderly lifted the head and shoulders of all that remained of poor Rosa Blondelle. But at the touch of her cold form, the sight of her still face, tears of pity sprang into the young soldier's eyes. Rosa had been a fine woman, and her body was now no light weight. It took the united strength of Captain Pendleton and Mr. Berners to bear it properly from the parlor to the chamber, where they laid it on the bed, and left it to the care of Sybil and Miss Tabby, who had followed them.

Mr. Berners then pulled the Captain into an empty room and whispered hoarsely:

"Did I understand you to tell the Judge that you had sent a messenger for the coroner?"

"Yes; but mind, I sent an old man on an old mule. It will be many hours before he reaches Blackville; many more before the coroner gets here. Good Heavens! Berners, I *had* to do that! Don't you see the awful danger of your innocent wife?" exclaimed Captain Pendleton, in an agitated voice.

"*Don't* I see it? I am not mad, or blind. But you, in the face of this overwhelming evidence—you believe her to be innocent?" demanded Lyon Berners, in a tone of agonized entreaty.

"I *know* her to be innocent! I have known her from her infancy. She might have flown at a rival, and torn her to pieces, in a frenzy of passion; but she could never have struck a secret blow," answered Captain Pendleton, emphatically.

"Thanks! Oh, thanks for your faith in her!" exclaimed Lyon Berners, earnestly.

"But now! *Do* you not see what is to be done? She must be got out of the house before the coroner or any officer of justice arrives," said Captain Pendleton, earnestly

"Oh, this is so sudden and terrible! It is an avalanche —an earthquake! It crushes me. It deprives me of reason!" groaned Lyon Berners, sinking into a chair, and covering his face with his hands.

"Lyon, my friend, arouse yourself! Rise above this agony of despair, if you would save your imperiled wife! She must fly from this house within an hour, and you must accompany her," urged Captain Pendleton.

"I know it! I know it! But oh, Heaven! the an

guish of my heart! the chaos of my thoughts! Pendleton, think for me; act for me; tell me what to do!" cried the strong man, utterly overwhelmed and powerless.

Captain Pendleton hurried into the supper-room, the scene of the late revels, and brought from there a glass of brandy, which he forced his friend to swallow.

"Now listen to me, Berners. Go and call your wife, take her to your mutual room, tell her the necessity of instant flight. She is strong, and will be equal to the occasion. Then, quickly as you can collect all your money and jewels, and conceal them about your person. Dress yourself, and tell her to dress in plain stout weather-proof riding-habits. Do this at once. Meanwhile, I will go myself to the stables, and saddle two of the swiftest horses, and bring them around to the back door, so that no servant need to be taken into our confidence to-night. When I meet you with the horses, I will direct you to a temporary retreat where you will be perfectly safe for the present; afterwards we can think of a permanent place of security. Now, then, courage, and hurry!"

"My friend in need!" fervently exclaimed Lyon Berners, as they parted.

"I have further suggestions to make when we meet again. I have thought of everything," Captain Pendleton called after him.

Lyon Berners went in search of Sybil, to the chamber of death, which was now restored to order, and dimly lighted.

CHAPTER XXI.

SYBIL'S FLIGHT.

'Tis well—my soul shakes off its load of care;
'Tis only the obscure is terrible;
Imagination frames events unknown,
In wild, fantastic shapes of hideous ruin,
And what its fears creates.—HANNAH MORE.

UPON the snow-white bed the form of Rosa Blondelle, wrapped in pure white raiment, was laid out. Very peaceful and beautiful she looked, her fair face, framed in its pale gold hair, wearing no sign of the violent death by which she died.

At her head sat Sybil, looking very pale, and shedding silent tears.

At her feet sat Miss Tabby, whimpering and muttering.

Within the little nursery, beyond the chamber, the Scotch girl sat, crying and sobbing.

Lyon Berners softly approached the bed, and whispered to Sybil.

"Dearest, come out, I wish to speak to you."

She silently arose and followed him. He was silent until they had reached their own room.

"Sit down, Sybil," he then said, as calmly as he could force himself to speak.

She sank into a seat and looked at him inquiringly, but fearlessly.

He stood before her, unable to proceed. It was terrible to him to witness her utter unconsciousness of her own position—more terrible still to be obliged to arouse her from it.

She continued to regard him with curiosity, but without anxiety, waiting silently for what he should say to her.

"Sybil," he said at length, as soon as he was able to speak—"Sybil you are a brave and strong spirit! You can meet a sudden calamity without sinking under it."

"What is it?" inquired his wife, in a low tone.

"Sybil, dearest Sybil! there is no time to break the bad news to you; brace yourself to hear it abruptly."

"Yes! tell me."

"Sybil, listen, and comprehend. The circumstances that surround this mysterious murder are of a character to compromise you so seriously, that you may only find safety in immediate flight."

"Me!—flight!" exclaimed Mrs. Berners, dilating her dark eyes in amazement.

Mr. Berners groaned in the spirit, as he replied:

"Yes, Sybil, yes! Oh! my dearest, attend and understand, and be strong! Sybil, hear. The quarrel you were known to have had with this poor woman; the threats you used on that occasion; the dagger in your hand; the blood on your wrist, and above all the words of the dying woman charging you with her death. All these form a chain of circumstantial and even direct evidence that will drag you down—I cannot say it!" burst forth Lyon in an accession of agony.

Sybil's dark eyes opened wider and wider in amazement, but still without the least alarm.

"It is enough, oh, Sybil, to repeat to you that your only safety is in instant flight," he exclaimed, dropping his face upon his hands.

"Flight!" echoed Sybil, staring at him. "Why should I take refuge in flight? I have done nothing criminal, nor will I do anything so ignominious as to fly from my home, Lyon," she added, proudly.

"But, Sybil—Oh, Sybil! the circumstantial evidence——"

"Why, I explained all that!" replied Mrs. Berners naïvely. "I told you all how it was: that when I heard her scream, I ran to see what was the matter and I drew the dagger from her bosom, and then the blood spirted up and sprinkled me! It was terrible enough to see and bear that without having to hear and endure such a preposterous suspicion! And it is all easy enough for any honest mind to understand my explanation."

"Oh, Sybil! Sybil! that indeed—I mean your presence at her death, with all its concurrent circumstances might be explained away! But the dying woman's last solemn declaration, charging you as her murderess, that was the most direct testimony! Oh, Heaven, Sybil! Sybil! prepare for your flight; for in that is your only hope of safety! Prepare at once, for there is not an instant to be lost!"

"Stop!" said Sybil, suddenly and solemnly—"Lyon Berners, do *you* believe that dying declaration to have been true?"

"No! as the Lord hears me, I do not Sybil! I know you were incapable of doing the deed she charged upon you. No! I am sure she spoke in the delirium of sudden death and terror," said Lyon Berners earnestly.

"Nor will any one else who knows me, believe it! So be tranquil. I am not guilty, nor will I run away like a guilty one. I will stay here and tell the truth," said Sybil composedly.

"But, oh, good Heavens! telling the truth will not help you! The law deals with *facts*, not *truths!* and judges of facts as if they were truths. And oh! my dear Sybil! the lying facts of this case involve you in such a net of circumstantial evidence and direct testimony as renders you liable to arrest—nay, certain to be arrested and imprisoned upon the charge of murder! Oh, my dear, most innocent wife! my free, wild, high-spirited Sybil! even the sense of innocence could not save you from imprisonment, or support you during its degrading tortures! *You* could not bear—*I* could not bear for you, such loss of liberty and honor for one hour—even if nothing worse should follow! But, Sybil, worse may, worse *must* follow! Yes, the *very worst!* Your only safety is in flight! instant flight! And oh! Heaven! how the time is speeding away!" exclaimed the husband, beside himself with distress

During the latter part of his speech the wife had started to her feet, and now she stood staring at him, amazed, incredulous, yet firm and brave.

"Rouse yourself to the occasion, Sybil! Oh! for my sake, for Heaven's sake, collect your faculties and prepare for flight," he passionately urged.

"I am innocent, and yet I must fly like the guilty? Lyon, for your sake, and only for yours, I will do it," she answered gravely, and sadly.

"We must not call assistance, nor stop to compliment each other. Pack quickly up what you will most need for yourself, in a traveling bag, and I will do the same for myself," explained Lyon Berners, suiting the action to the word by shoving into his valise some valuable papers, money, razors, a few articles of clothing, etc.

Sybil showed more promptitude and presence of mind than might have been expected of her. She quickly collected her costly jewels and ready money, and change of under-clothing, combs, and brushes, and packed them in a small traveling bag.

"We go on horseback," quickly explained Lyon Berners, as he locked his valise.

Swiftly and silently Sybil threw off her masquerading dress, that she had unconsciously worn until now, and dropped it on the floor, where it lay glowing like a smouldering bonfire. She then put on a water-proof riding habit, and announced herself ready.

"Come, then," said Lyon Berners, taking up both bags, and beckoning her to follow him silently.

They slipped down the dark stairs and through the deserted halls, and reached the back door, where, under the shelter of a large hemlock-tree, Captain Pendleton held the horses. It was dark as pitch, and drizzling rain. They could see nothing, they could only know the whereabouts of their "friend in need," and their horses, by hearing Captain Pendleton's voice speaking through the mist in cautious tones, and whispering:

"Lock the door after you, Berners, so as to secure us from intrusion from within. And then stop there under the porch until I come and talk to you."

Mr. Berners did as he was requested to do, and then stood waiting for his friend, who soon came up.

"You have got all you will need on your journey, have you not?" inquired the Captain.

Mr. Berners replied by telling his friend exactly what he had brought.

"All that is very well, but people require to eat and drink once in a while. So I have put some sandwiches, and a bottle of wine from the supper-table, into your saddle-bags. And now, in the hurry, have you decided upon your route?"

"Yes; we shall endeavor to reach the nearest seaport, Norfolk probably, and embark for some foreign country, no matter what, for in no place but in a foreign country can my unhappy wife hope for safety," mournfully replied Lyon Berners.

"Endeavor to reach Norfolk! That will never succeed. You will be sure to be overtaken and brought back before you go a score of miles on that road," declared Captain Pendleton, shaking his head.

"Then, in the name of Heaven, what *will* do?" demanded Mr. Berners, in a tone of desperation.

"You must find a place of concealment, and then take time to disguise yourself and your wife, so that neither of you can be recognized, before you venture upon the road to Norfolk. You see, Lyon you are the better lawyer, but I am the better strategist! I graduated among the war-paths and the ambushes of the Redskins on the frontier."

"But where shall I find such a piece of concealment?"

"I have thought of that."

"You think of everything."

"Ah! it is easy to show presence of mind in other people's confusion! Almost as easy as it is to bear other people's troubles!" said the Captain, attempting a jest, only to raise his friend's drooping spirits. "But now to the point, for we must be quick. You know the 'Haunted Chapel?'"

"The old ruined church in the cleft on the other side of the Black Mountain?"

"Yes; that is the place. Its deep solitude and total abandonment, with its ghostly reputation, will be sure to secure your safety. Go there; conceal yourselves and your horses as well as you can. In the course of to-morrow, or to-morrow night, I will come to you with such news and such help as I may be able to bring."

"Thank you. Oh, thank you. But what are words? You are a man of deeds. Your presence of mind has saved us both!" said Lyon Berners earnestly.

"And now to horse," said Captain Pendleton, taking Mrs. Berners under his guidance, while Mr. Berners brought on the valise and traveling bag.

Captain Pendleton placed Sybil in her saddle, whispering, encouragingly,

"Be strong and hopeful. This necessary flight is a temporary evil, intended to save you from a permanent, and even perhaps a fatal wrong. Be patient, and time shall vindicate you and bring you back."

"But oh! to leave my home, and the home of my fathers! to leave it like a criminal, when I am innocent! to leave it in haste, and not to know if I may ever return," cried Sybil, in a voice of anguish.

"It is a fearful trial. I will not mock you by denying that it is. Yes, it is a terrible ordeal! but one, Mrs. Berners, that you have heroism enough to bear," replied Captain Pendleton, as he bowed over her extended hand and gave her the reins.

Lyon Berners was also mounted. They were ready to

start. With a mutual "God bless you," the friends parted.

Lyon and Sybil took the dark road.

Captain Pendleton unlocked the door that had been locked by Mr. Berners, but as he pushed to open it he felt an obstruction, and instantly afterwards heard some one run away.

"A listener," he thought, in dismay as he pursued the fugitive. But he only caught a glimpse of a figure disappearing through the front door and into the darkness without, in which it was lost.

"An eavesdropper!" he exclaimed, in despair. "An eavesdropper! Who now can be assured of her safety? Oh, Sybil! you rejected my hand, and very nearly ruined my life! But this night I would die to save you," he sighed, as he went and joined the gentlemen who were sitting up watching, or rather dozing, in the parlor, while waiting for the physician's or the coroner's arrival.

"Where is Mrs. Berners?" inquired the old Judge, rousing himself up.

"She retired to her chamber about an hour ago," answered Captain Pendleton, telling the truth, but not the whole truth, as you will perceive.

"Hum, ha, yes; well, and where is her husband?

"He followed her there," answered the Captain, shortly.

"Ha, hum, yes, well. The coroner is long in coming," grumbled the Judge.

"It is some distance to Blackville, sir, and the roads are rough and the night is dark," observed the Captain.

"Well, yes, true," agreed the old man, subsiding into his chair and into his doze.

Captain Pendleton threw himself into a seat, but had not sat long before the parlor door opened, and his sister appeared at it and called to him in a low voice.

He arose, and went to her.

"Come out into the hall here; I want to speak to you, Clement," said Miss Pendleton.

He went out.

Then his sister inquired, in a voice full of anxious entreaty:

"Clement, *where* is Sybil?"

"She went to her room a little more than an hour ago,"

answered the brother, giving his sister the same answer that he had given the Judge.

"Clement, I must go to her, and throw my arms around her neck and kiss her. I must not tell her in so many words that I know she is innocent, for to do that would be to affront her almost as much as if I should accuse her of being guilty; for she will rightly enough think that her innocence should not be called into question, but should be taken for granted. So I must not say a word on that subject, but I *must* find her and embrace her, and make her feel that I know she is innocent. Who is with her?"

"Her husband is with her, Beatrix, and so you cannot of course go to her now."

"Oh, but I am so anxious to do so. Look here, Clement. I stood there among the crowd this evening, gazing upon that bleeding and dying woman, until the sight of her ghastly form and face seemed to affect me as the Medusa's head was said to have affected the beholder, and turn me into stone. Clement, I was so petrified that I could not move or speak, even when she appealed to us all to know whether any among us could believe her to be capable of such an act. I could not speak; I could not move. She must have thought that I too condemned her, and I cannot bear to rest under that suspicion of hers. I must go to her now, Clement."

"Indeed you must not, Trix. Wait till she makes her appearance: that will be time enough," answered her brother.

"Oh, this is a horrible night; I wish it were over. I cannot go to bed; nobody can. The ladies are all sitting huddled together in the dressing-room, although the fire has gone out; and the servants are all gathered in the kitchen, too panic-stricken to do anything. Oh, an awful night! I wish it were morning."

"It will soon be daylight now dear Beatrix. You had better go and rejoin your companions."

And so the brother and sister separated for the night; Beatrix going to sit and shudder with the other ladies in the dressing-room, and Clement returning to the parlor to lounge and doze among the gentlemen.

Only his anxiety for Sybil's safety so much disturbed his repose, that if he did but drop into an instant slumber he started from it in a vague fright. So the small hours of the morning wore on and brought the dull, drizzly, wintry daylight.

Meanwhile Lyon and Sybil Berners rode on through mist and rain.

CHAPTER XXII.

THE HAUNTED CHAPEL.

> "The chapel was a ruin old,
> That stood so low, in lonely glen,
> The Gothic windows high and dark
> Were hung with ivy, brier, and yew."

THE Haunted Chapel to which Mr. and Mrs. Berners were going was in a dark and lonely gorge on the other side of the mountain across Black River, but near its rise in the Black Torrent. To reach the chapel, they would have to ride three miles up the shore and ford the river, and then pass over the opposite mountain. The road was as difficult and dangerous as it was lonely and unfrequented.

Lyon and Sybil rode on together in silence, bending their heads before the driving mist, and keeping close to the banks of the river until they should reach the fording place.

At length Sybil's anguish broke forth in words.

"Oh! Lyon, is this nightmare? Or is it true that I am so suddenly cast down from my secure place, as to become in one hour a fugitive from my home, a fugitive from justice! Oh! Lyon, speak to me. Break the spell that binds my senses. Wake me up. Wake me up," she wildly exclaimed.

"Dear Sybil, be patient, calm, and firm. This is a terrible calamity. But to meet calamity bravely, is the test of a true high soul. You are compelled to seek safety in flight, to conceal yourself for the present, to avoid a train of unmerited humiliations that even the consciousness of innocence would not enable you to bear. But you have only to be patient, and a few days or weeks must bring the truth to light, and restore you to your home."

"But flight itself looks like guilt; will be taken as additional evidence of guilt," groaned Sybil.

"Not so. Not when it is understood that the overwhelming weight of deceptive circumstantial evidence and deceptive direct testimony had so compromised you as to render flight your only means of salvation. Be brave, my own Sybil. And now, here we are at the ford. Take care of yourself. Let me lead your horse."

"No, no; that would embarrass you, without helping me. Go on before, and I will follow."

Lyon Berners plunged into the stream. Sybil drew up her long skirts and dashed in after him. And they were both soon splashing through the Black River, blacker now than ever with the double darkness of night and mist. A few minutes of brave effort on the part of horses and riders brought them all in safety to the opposite bank, up which they successfully struggled, and found themselves upon firm ground.

"The worst part of the journey is over, dear Sybil. Now I will ride in advance and find the pass, and do you keep close behind me," said Lyon Berners, riding slowly along the foot of the mountain until he came to a dark opening, which he entered, calling Sybil to follow him."

It was one of those fearful passes so frequently to be found in the Alleghany Mountains, and which I have described so often that I may be excused from describing this. They went in, cautiously picking their way through this deeper darkness, and trusting much to the instinct of their mountain-trained steeds to take them safely through. An hour's slow, careful, breathless riding brought them out upon the other side of the mountain.

As they emerged from the dark labyrinth, Lyon Berners pulled up his horse to breathe, and to look about him. Sybil followed his example.

Day was now dawning over the broken and precipitous country.

"Where is that chapel of which you speak? I have heard of it all my life, but I have never seen it; and beyond the fact that it is on this side of the mountain, and not far from the Black Torrent, I know nothing about it," said Sybil.

"It is near the Black Torrent; almost under the bed of

the cascade, in fact. And we shall have to turn our horses' heads up stream again to reach it," answered Lyon Berners.

"You know exactly where it is; you have been there, perhaps?" inquired Sybil.

"I have seen it but once in my life. But I can easily find it. It is not a frequented place of resort, dear Sybil But that makes it all the safer as a place of concealment for you," said Lyon Berners, as he started his horse and rode on.

Sybil followed him closely.

Day was broadening over the mountains, and bringing out a thousand prismatic colors from the autumn foliage of the trees, gemmed now with the rain drops that had fallen during the night.

"It will be quite clear when the sun rises," said Lyon, encouragingly to Sybil, as they went on.

He was right. Sunrise in the mountains is sometimes almost as sudden in its effects as sunrise at sea. The eastern horizon had been ruddy for some time, but when the sun suddenly came up from behind the mountain, the mist lifted itself, rolled into soft white wreaths and crowned the summits, while all the land below broke out into an effulgence of light, color, and glory.

But people who are flying for life do not pause to enjoy scenery, even of the finest. Lyon and Sybil rode on towards the upper banks of the Black River, hearing at every step the thunder of the Black Torrent, as it leaped from rock to rock in its passionate descent to the valley.

At length they came to a narrow opening in the side of the mountain.

"Here is a path I know," said Mr. Berners, "though its entrance is so concealed by undergrowth as to be almost impossible to discover."

Lyon Berners dismounted, and began to grope for the entrance in the thicket of wild-rose bushes, that were now closely covered with scarlet seed-pods that glowed, and rain-drops that sparkled, in the rays of the morning sun.

At length he found the path, and then he returned to his wife, and said:

"We cannot take our horses through the thicket, dear Sybil. You will have to dismount and remain concealed in here until I lead them back across the river, where I will turn them loose. There will be a great advantage gained by that move. Our horses being found on the other side, will mislead our pursuers on a false scent."

While Lyon Berners spoke, he assisted his wife to alight from her saddle, and guided her to the entrance of the thicket.

"This path has not been trodden for a score of years, I can well believe. Just go far enough to be out of sight of any chance spy, and there remain until I return. I shall not be absent over half an hour," said Mr. Berners, as he took leave of Sybil.

She sank wearily down upon a fragment of a rock, and prepared to await his return.

He mounted his own horse, and led hers, and so went his way down the stream to the fording place.

He successfully accomplished the difficult task of taking both horses over the river to the opposite bank, where he turned them loose.

Next with a strong pocket jack-knife he cut a leaping pole from a sapling near, and went still farther up the stream to the rapids, where, by a skilful use of his pole and dexterous leaping from rock to rock, he was enabled to recross the river almost dry-shod.

He rejoined Sybil, whom he found just where he had left her.

She was sitting on a piece of rock, with her head bowed upon her hands.

"Have I been gone long? Were you anxious or lonely dearest?" he inquired, as he gave her his hand to assist her in rising.

"Oh, no! I take no note of time! But oh! Lyon, *when shall I wake?*" she exclaimed in wild despair.

"What is it you say, dear Sybil?" he gently asked.

"When shall I wake—wake from this ghastly nightmare, in which I seem to myself to be a fugitive from justice! an exile from my home! a houseless, hunted stranger in the land! It *is* a nightmare! It can *not* be real, you know! Oh, that I could wake!

"Dear Sybil, collect your faculties. Do not let despair

drive you to distraction. Be mistress of yourself in this trying situation," said Lyon Berners, gravely.

"But oh, Heaven! the crushing weight and stunning suddenness of this blow! It is like death! like perdition!" exclaimed Sybil, pressing her hands to her head.

Lyon Berners could only gaze on her with infinite compassion, expressed in every lineament of his eloquent countenance.

She observed this, and quickly, with a great effort, from a strong resolution, throwing her hands apart like one who disperses a cloud, and casts off a weight, she said:

"It is over! I will not be nervous or hysterical again. I have brought trouble on you, as well as on myself, dear Lyon; but I will show you that I can bear it. I will look this calamity firmly in the face, and come what may, I will not drag you down by sinking under it."

And so saying, she gave him her hand, and arose and followed him as he pushed on before, breaking down or bearing aside the branches that overhung and obstructed the path.

Half an hour of this difficult and tedious traveling brought them down into a deep dark dell, in the midst of which stood the "Haunted Chapel."

It was an old colonial church, a monument of the earliest settlement in the valley. It was now a wild and beautiful ruin, with its surroundings all glowing with color and sparkling with light. In itself it was a small Gothic edifice, built of the dark iron-gray rock dug from the mountain quarries. Its walls, window-frames, and roof were all still standing, and were almost entirely covered by creepers, among which the wild rose vine, now full of scarlet berries, was conspicuous.

A broken stone wall overgrown with brambles enclosed the old church-yard, where a few fallen and mouldering gravestones, half sunk among the dead leaves, still remained.

All around the church, on the bottom of the dell, and up the sides of the steeps, were thickly clustered foresttrees, now glowing refulgent in their gorgeous autumn livery of crimson and gold, scarlet and purple.

A little rill, an offspring of the Black Torrent, tumbled down the side of the mountain behind the church, and ran frolicking irreverently through the old graveyard. The great cascade was out of sight, though very near, for its thunder filled the air.

"See," said Sybil, pointing to the little singing rill; "Nature is unsympathetic. She can laugh and frolic over the dead, and, besides, the suffering."

"It would seem, then, that Nature is wiser as well as gladder than we are; since she, who is transitory, rejoices while we, who are immortal, pine," answered Lyon Berners pleased that any thought should win her from the contemplation of her misfortune.

He then led the way into the old ruined church through the door frames, from which the doors had long been lost. The stone floor, and the stone altar still remained; all else within the building was gone.

Lyon Berners looked all around, up and down the interior, from the arched ceiling to the side-walls with their window spaces and the flagstone floor with its mouldy seams. The wild creeping vines nearly filled the window spaces, and shaded the interior more beautifully than carved shutters, velvet curtains, or even stained glass could have done. The flagstone floor was strewn with fallen leaves that had drifted in. Up and down, in every nook and corner of the roof and windows, last year's empty bird nests perched. And here and there along the walls, the humble "mason's" little clay house stuck.

But there seemed no resting-place for the weary travelers, until Sybil, with a serious smile, went up to the altar and sank upon the lowest step, and beckoned Lyon to join her saying:

"At the foot of the altar, dear Lyon, there was sanctuary in the olden times. We seem to realize the idea now."

"You are cold. Your clothes are all damp. Stop! I must try to raise a fire. But you, in the meantime, must walk briskly up and down, to keep from being chilled to death," answered Lyon Berners very practically, as he proceeded to gather dry leaves and twigs that had drifted into the interior of the old church.

He piled them up in the center of the floor, just under the break in the roof, and then he went out and gathered sticks and brushwood, and built up a little mound. Lastly he took a box of matches from his pocket and struck a light, and kindled the fire.

The dried leaves and twigs crackled and blazed, and the smoke ascended in a straight column to the hole in the roof through which it escaped.

"Come, dear Sybil, and walk around the fire until your clothes are dry, and then sit down by it. This fire, with its smoke ascending and escaping through that aperture, is just such a fire as our forefathers in the old, old times enjoyed, as the best thing of the kind they knew anything about. Kings had no better," said Lyon Berners, cheerfully.

Sybil approached the fire, but instead of walking around it, she sat down on the flagstones before it. She looked very weary, thoroughly prostrated in body, soul and spirit.

"What are we waiting for, in this horrible pause?" she inquired at length.

"We are waiting for Pendleton. He is to bring us news, as soon as he can slip away and steal to us without fear of detection," answered Lyon Berners.

"Oh, Heaven! what words have crept into our conversation about ourselves and friends too! 'Steal,' 'fear,' detection!' Oh, Lyon!—But there, I will say no more. I will *not* revert to the horror and degradation of this position again, if I can help it," groaned Sybil.

"My wife, you are very faint. Try to take some nourishment," urged Lyon, as he began to open the small parcel of refreshments thoughtfully provided by Captain Pendleton.

"No, no, I cannot swallow a morsel. My throat is parched and constricted," she answered.

"If I only had a little coffee for you," said Lyon.

"If we only had liberty to go home again," sighed Sybil, "then we should have all things. But there: indeed I will not backslide into weak complaints again," she added, compunctuously.

"Modify your grief, dear Sybil, but do not attempt entirely to suppress it. Nature is not to be so restrained," said Lyon Berners, kindly.

There was silence between them for a little while, during which Sybil still sat down upon the flagstones, with her elbows resting on her knees, and her head bowed upon the palms of her hands; and Lyon stood up near her with an attitude and expression of grave and sad reflection and self-control.

At length Sybil spoke:

"Oh, Lyon! who could have murdered that poor woman, and brought us into such a horrible position?"

"My theory of the tragedy is this, dear Sybil: that some robber, during the confusion of the fancy ball, found an opportunity of entering and concealing himself in Mrs. Blondelle's room; that his first purpose might have been simple robbery, but that, being discovered by Mrs. Blondelle, and being alarmed lest her shrieks should bring the house upon him and occasion his capture, he impulsively sought to stop her cries by death; and then that, hearing your swift approach down the stairs leading into her room, he made his escape through the window."

"But then the windows were all found, as they had been left, fastened," objected Sybil.

"But, dearest, you must remember that these windows, having spring bolts, may be fastened by being pushed to from the outside. It is quite possible for a robber, escaping through them to close them in this manner to conceal his flight."

"That must have been the case in this instance. Everybody must see now that that was the manner in which the miscreant escaped. Oh, Lyon! I think we were wrong to have left home."

"No, dear Sybil, we were not. Our only hope is in the discovery of the real murderer, and that may be a work of time; meanwhile we wish to be free, even at the price of being called fugitives from justice."

"Lyon, that poor child! If we ever go home again, we must adopt and educate him."

"We will do so, Sybil."

"For, oh! Lyon, although I am entirely innocent of that most heinous crime, and entirely incapable of it, yet when I remember how my rage burned against that poor woman only an hour before her death, I feel—I feel as if I were half guilty of it! as if—Heaven pardon me!—I might, in some moment of madness, have been wholly guilty of it! Lyon, I shudder at myself!" cried Sybil, growing very pale.

THE HAUNTED CHAPEL. 173

"You should thank Heaven that you have been saved from such mortal sin, dear wife, and also pray Heaven always to save you from your own fierce passions," said Mr. Berners, very gravely.

"I have breathed that thanksgiving and that prayer with every breath I have drawn. And I will continue to do so. But, oh! Lyon, all my passions, all my sufferings grew out of my great love for you."

"I can well believe it, dear wife. And I myself have not been free from blame; though in reality your jealousy was very causeless, Sybil."

"I know that now," said Sybil, sadly.

"And now, dearest, I would like to make 'a clean breast of it,' as the sinners say, and tell you all—the whole head and front of my offending' with that poor dead woman," said Mr. Berners, seating himself on the floor beside his wife.

Sybil did not repel his offered confidence, for though her jealousy had died a violent death, she was still very much interested in hearing his confession.

Then Lyon Berners told her everything, up to the very last moment when she had surprised them in the first and last kiss that had ever passed between them.

"But in all, and through all, my heart, dear wife, was loyal in its love to you," he concluded.

"I know that, dearest Lyon—I know that well," replied Sybil.

And with that tenderness towards the faults of the dead, which all magnanimous natures share, she forbore to say, or even to think, how utterly unprincipled had been the course of Rosa Blondelle from the first to the last of their acquaintance with that vain and frivolous coquette.

Sybil was now almost sinking with weariness. Lyon perceived her condition, and said:

"Remain here, dear Sybil, while I go and try to collect some boughs and leaves to make you a couch. The sun must have dried up the moisture by this time."

And he went out and soon returned with his arms full of boughs, which he spread upon the flagstones. Then he took off his own overcoat and covered them with it.

"Now, dear Sybil," he said, "if you will divest yourself of your long riding skirt, you may turn that into a blanket to cover with, and so sleep quite comfortably."

With a grave smile Sybil followed his advice, and then she laid herself down on the rude couch he had spread for her. No sooner had her head touched it, than she sank into that deep sleep of prostration which is more like a swoon than a slumber.

Lyon Berners covered her carefully with the long riding skirt, and stood watching her for some minutes. But she neither spoke nor stirred; indeed, she scarcely breathed.

Then, after still more carefully tucking the covering around her, he left her, and walked out to explore the surroundings of the chapel.

CHAPTER XXIII.

THE SOLITUDE IS INVADED.

> Oh, might we here
> In solitude live savage, in some glade
> Obscured, where highest woods impenetrable
> To star, or sunlight, spread their umbrage broad
> And brown as evening; cover us, ye pines,
> Ye cedars with innumerable boughs,
> Hide us where we may ne'er be seen again.—BYRON.

NOTHING could be more lonely and desolate than this place. It was abandoned to Nature and Nature's wild children. Of the birds that perched so near his hand; of the squirrels that peeped at him from their holes under the gravestones, he might have said with Alexander Selkirk on Juan Fernandez,

"Their tameness is shocking to me."

There was a great consolation to be derived from these circumstances, however; for they proved how completely deserted by human beings, and how perfectly safe for the refugees, was this old "Haunted Chapel."

Too deeply troubled in mind to take any repose of body, Lyon Berners continued to ramble about among the

THE SOLITUDE IS INVADED.

gravestones, which were now so worn with age that no vestige of their original inscriptions remained to gratify the curiosity of a chance inspector.

Above him was the glorious autumn sky, now hazy with the golden mist of Indian summer. Around him lay a vast wilderness of hill and dell covered with luxuriant forests, now gorgeous with the glowing autumn colors of their foliage.

But his thoughts were not with this magnificent landscape. They wandered to the past days of peace and joy before the coming of the coquette had "made confusion" with the wedded pair. They wandered to the future, trying to penetrate the gloom and horror of its shadows. They flew to Black Hall, picturing the people, prevising the possibilities there.

How he longed for, yet dreaded the arrival of Captain Pendleton! Would there be danger in his coming through the open daylight? What news would he bring?

The verdict of the coroner's jury? Against whom must this verdict be given? Lyon Berners shuddered away from answering this question. But it was also possible that before this the murderer might have been discovered and arrested. Should this surmise prove to be a fact, oh, what relief from anguish, what a happy return home for Sybil! If not—if the verdict should be renered against *her*,—nothing but flight and exile remained to them.

While Lyon Berners wandered up and down like a restless ghost among the gravestones, his attention was suddenly arrested by the sound of a crackling tread breaking through the bushes. He turned quickly, expecting to see Captain Pendleton, but he saw his own servant instead

"Joe!" he exclaimed, in a tone of surprise.

"Marser!" responded the man, in a voice of grief.

"You come from Captain Pendleton? What message does he send? How is it at the house? Has the coroner come? And oh! has any clue been found to the murderer?" anxiously inquired Mr. Berners.

"No, marser, no clue an't been found to no murderer. But the house up there is full of crowners and constables, as if it was the county court-house, and Cappin Pendulum managing everything."

"He sent you to me?"

"No, marser, nor likewise knowed I come."

"Joe! *who* has sent you here?" inquired Mr. Berners.

"No one hasn't, marser," answered Joe, dashing the tears from his eyes, and then proceeding to unstrap a large hamper that he carried upon his shoulders.

"No one! Then how came you here?" demanded Mr. Berners, uneasily.

Now, instead of answering his master's question, Joe sat down upon his hamper, and wept aloud.

"What is the matter with you?" inquired Mr. Berners.

"You axed me how I comed here," sobbed Joe, "just as if I could keep away when she and you was here in trouble, and a-wanting some one to look arter you."

"But how did you know we were here?" anxiously questioned Mr. Berners.

"I wa'n't a listening at key-holes, nor likewise a-eavesdropping, which I consider beneath a gentleman to do; but I was a-looking to the back shutters, to see as they was all safe arter the fright we got, and I hearn somebody a-talkin, which I was sure was more bugglers; so I made free to wait and hear what they said."

"It was Captain Pendleton and myself, I suppose," said Mr. Berners, much annoyed.

"Jes so, sir; it wer Capping Pendulum and yourself, which it hurt me to the heart as you should have trusted into Capping Pendulum and not into me—a old and valleyed servant of the family."

"And so, Joe, you overheard the whole matter?"

"Which I did, sir, and shocked I was to think as any false charges should cause my dear young missus to run away from home in the night-time, like a fusible slave. And hurt I was to think you didn't trust into me instead of into he."

"Well, Joe, it appears to me that you were resolved to take our trust, if we did not give it to you. What brought you here this morning?"

"Coffee, sir," gravely answered Joe, getting up off the hamper and beginning to untie its fastenings.

"*What?*" demanded Mr. Berners, gathering his brows into a frown.

"COFFEE!" reiterated Joe, as he took from the hamper a small silver coffee-pot, a pair of cups and saucers, spoons, plates, and knives and forks, a bottle of cream, and several small packets containing all that was needful for breakfast.

"Joe! this was very kind and thoughtful of you; but was it quite safe for you to come here with a hamper on your back in open day?" inquired Mr. Berners.

"Lord bless you, sir! safe as safe! I took by-paths, and didn't see a creetur, not one! Why, lord, sir, you had better a-trusted into me from the beginning, than into Capping Pendulum. Bress your soul, marser, there an't that white man going, nor yet that red injun, that can aiqual a colored gentleman into hiding and seeking!"

"I can well believe that."

"Why, marser!—but you don't 'member that time I got mad long o' old Marse Bertram Berners, 'bout blaming of me for the sorrell horse falling lame; and I run away?"

"No."

"Well, I was gone three months, and not five miles from home all that time! And all the constables looking arter me for law and order; and all the poor white trash hunting of me for the reward; and not one of 'em all ever struck upon my trail, and me so nigh home all the while!"

"Well, but you were found at last," suggested Mr. Berners.

"Who, *me?* No, *sir!* And I don't think as I should a-been found yet; 'cause it was a funny kind of life, that run-a-way life, a dodging of the man-hunters; but you see, marser, I sort o' pined arter the child—meaning Miss Sybil, who was then about four years old. And, moreover, it was fotch to me by a secret friend o' mine, as the child was likewise a pining arter me. So I up and went straight home, and walked right up before old marse, and took off my hat and told him as how *I* was willin' to forgive and forget, and let by-gones be by-gones like a Christian gentleman, if he would do the same."

"And of course your master at once accepted such magnanimous terms."

"Who, *he?* Why, Marse Lyon! he looked jes as if he'd a-knocked me down! Only, you see, the child—meaning Miss Sybil—was a sitting on his knee, which, soon as ever she saw me, she ran to me, and clasped me round one leg, and tried to climb up in my arms; which I took her up at once; and old marster, he couldn't knock me down then, if it had been to have saved his life."

"So peace was ratified."

"Yes, Marse Lyon; which I telled you all this here nonsense jes to let you know how good I was at hiding and seeking. And, Marse! the horses come home all right."

"They did! I am glad of that."

"This was the way of it being all right, sir! You see I knowed, when I heard you were going to ride to this old church, as you couldn't get the horses through this thicket, but would have to turn them loose, to find their way home. And I knowed how if any other eyes 'cept mine saw them, it would set people to axing questions. So I goes out to the road, and watches till I sees 'em coming; when I takes charge of 'em, and gets 'em into the stables quiet, and no one the wiser."

"Well done, Joe! But tell me, my good man, are we missed yet? Has any one inquired for us?"

"Plenty has axed arter you both, Marse! But as no one but me and Capping Pendulum knowed where you was gone, and as I locked your door, and took the key, most of the folks still think as how Miss Sybil has gone to bed, overcome by the ewents of the night, and as how you is a watching by her, and a taking care of her."

"That also is well."

"But, Marse, how is Miss Sybil, and where is she?" inquired the faithful servant, looking about himself.

"She is very much prostrated by fatigue and excitement, and is now sleeping in the church."

"Thanks be to the Divine Marster as she *can* sleep," said Joe, reverently.

"And now," he continued, as he replaced it on his head, "I will kindle a fire and make the coffee, and may be she may wake up by the time it is ready."

"Kindle a fire out here, Joe! Will not the smoke be seen, and lead to our discovery?" inquired Lyon Berners, glancing at the slender column of smoke from the fire in church, that he himself had kindled, and now for the first time struck with the sense of the danger of discovery to which it might have exposed Sybil.

THE SOLITUDE IS INVADED.

"Lord, Marse!" replied Joe, showing his teeth, "we are too far from any human being for any eye to see our smoke. And even if it wasn't so, bless you, there are so many mists rising from the valley this morning, that one smoke more or less wouldn't be noticed."

"That is true," admitted Mr. Berners.

Meanwhile Joe busied himself with lighting a fire. When it was burning freely, he took the kettle and filled it from the little stream that flowed through the churchyard.

"Now, Marse Lyon, in about ten minutes I will set you down to as good a breakfast, almost, as you could have got at home," said Joe, as he raised three cross-sticks over the fire, and hung the kettle over the blaze, gipsy fashon.

While Joe was at work, Mr. Berners went into the church to look after Sybil.

She was still sleeping the heavy sleep of utter mental and bodily prostration. For a few minutes he stood contemplating her with an expression of countenance full of love and pity, and then after adjusting the covering over her, and collecting together the brands of the expiring fire to light up again, he left the church.

On going outside, he found that Joe had spread a cloth and arranged a rude sort of picnic breakfast upon the ground.

"The coffee is ready, Marse Lyon; but how about the Missus?" inquired the man, as he stirred down the grounds from the top of the pot.

"She is still sleeping, and must not be disturbed," answered Mr. Berners.

"Well, Marse Lyon, I reckon as how you can relish a cup of coffee as well as she; so please to let me wait on you, sir."

Mr. Berners thanked Joe, and threw himself down upon the ground, and made such a breakfast as a hungry man *can* make, even under the most deplorable circumstances."

"Now you know, sir, when the Missus wakes up, be it longer or shorter, I can make fresh coffee for her in ten minutes," said Joe, cheerfully.

"But you cannot stay here very long. You'll be missed from the house," objected Mr. Berners.

"Please, sir, I have so well provided for all that, that I can stay till night. Bless you, sir, I told my fellow-servants as I was going to take some corn to the mill to be ground, and was agoin' to wait all day to fetch it home; and so I really did take the corn, and told the miller I should come arter it this evening, and so I shall, and take it home all right, accordin' to my word."

"That was a very politic proceeding, Joe; but how could you account to them for the hamper you brought away, and which must have excited suspicion, if not inquiry?"

"Bless you, sir, I wasn't fool enough to let them see the hamper. All they saw was the two bags of corn as I rode out of the gate with. I had filled the hamper on the sly, and hid it in the bushes by the road, until I went by and picked it up."

"Still better, Joe! But your horse? what horse did you ride, and what have you done with him?"

"I rode Dick, which I have tied him fast in the deep woods on the other side of the river. I crossed over the rapids with the help of a pole," explained Joe.

While they were speaking, a step was heard crushing through the dried brushwood, and another moment Captain Pendleton, pale, sad, and weary, stood before them.

CHAPTER XXIV.

THE VERDICT AND THE VISITOR.

Can such things be,
And overcome us like a summer cloud
Without our special wonder?—SHAKESPEARE.

"PENDLETON! oh! Heaven, Pendleton! What news?" exclaimed Lyon Berners, starting up to greet him.

"Good Heaven! Berners! How is this? Another—a servant taken into your confidence, and trusted with the secret of your retreat!" cried Captain Pendleton in dismay.

THE VERDICT AND THE VISITOR.

"He is trustworthy! I will vouch for his fidelity! But oh! Pendleton! What news? what news?" exclaimed Lyon Berners in an agony of impatience.

"The worst that you can anticipate!" cried Captain Pendleton in a voice full of sorrow.

"Oh! my unhappy wife! The coroner's jury have found their verdict then?" groaned Lyon.

Captain Pendleton bowed his head. He was unable to reply in words.

"And that verdict is—Oh! speak! let me hear the worst!—that verdict is——"

"Wilful Murder!" muttered Pendleton in a hoarse and choking voice.

"Against—against—whom?" gasped Lyon Berners, white as death.

"Oh, Heaven! *You know!* Do not ask me to sully her name with the words!" cried Captain Pendleton utterly overcome by his emotions.

"Oh, my unhappy wife! Oh, my lost Sybil!" exclaimed Lyon Berners, reeling under the blow, half expected though it might have been.

There was silence for a few minutes. Pendleton was the first to recover himself. He went up to his friend, touched him on the shoulder, and said:

"Berners, rouse yourself; the position requires the exertion of your utmost powers of mind and body. Calm yourself, and collect all your faculties. Come now, let us sit down here and talk over the situation."

Lyon permitted the captain to draw him away to a little distance, where they both sat down side by side, on a fallen tombstone.

"In the first place, how is your wife, and who does she sustain herself under this overwhelming disaster." inquired Captain Pendleton, forcing himself to speak composedly.

"I do not think my dear innocent Sybil was able fully to appreciate the danger of her position, even as she stood before the rendering of that false and fatal verdict, she was so strong in her sense of innocence. She seemed to suffer most from the lesser evils involved in her exile from home,"

"Where is she, then?"

"Sleeping heavily in the church there; sleeping very heavily, from the united effects of mental and bodily fatigue and excitement."

"Heaven grant that she may sleep long and well. And now, Berners, to our plans. You must know that I kept a horse saddled and tied in the woods down by the river, and as soon as that lying verdict was rendered, I hurried off, leaped into my saddle and galloped here. I forded the river, and have left my horse just below here, at the entrance of this thicket. I must soon mount and away again on your service."

"Oh, my dear Pendleton, how shall I ever repay you?"

"By keeping up a stout heart until this storm-cloud blows over, as it must, in a few days or weeks. But now to business. How came this man Joe here?"

Mr. Berners explained how Joe had overheard all their conversation while they were making their arrangements, and taken pains to co-operate with them, and had followed them here with some necessary provisions. And he, Mr. Berners, closed with a eulogy on Joe's fidelity and discretion.

"I am very glad to hear what you tell me, for it relieves my mind of a very great weight. I knew that there had been a listener to our conversation, for I almost ran against him as I went into the house; but as he made his escape before I could identify him, I was very anxious on the subject. So you may judge what a burden is lifted from my mind by the discovery that he was no other than honest Joe, whom Providence sent in the way. But why he ran from me, I cannot imagine.

"He was a little jealous, a little sulky, and somewhat fearful of being blamed, I suppose. But tell me, Pendleton, has our flight been discovered yet?" inquired Mr Berners, anxiously.

"No, nor even suspected; at least, not up to the time that I left Black Hall. Mrs. Berners was supposed to be in her chamber. I warned all the men, and requested my sister to caution all the women, against knocking at her door."

"And I, who must have been expected to be on the spot?" asked Lyon.

"You were often asked for. Fortunately for you,

THE VERDICT AND THE VISITOR. 183

there is a well-known weakness in human nature to pretend to know all about everything that may be inquired into. And so, every time you chanced to be inquired for by one party, you were accounted for by another. Some said you were with Mrs. Berners; others that you had gone to Blackville on pressing business connected with the tragedy. And these last authorities came to be believed; so that when I slipped away I left the people momentarily expecting your return."

" Whom did you leave there?"

"Everybody—the coroner's jury and all the guests of the house, who had been detained as witnesses."

" Then all our friends heard the fatal verdict?"

" All."

" Was there—a warrant issued?" gasped Lyon Berners, scarcely able to utter the words.

" Ah, yes; the issue of the warrant was the first intimation I had of the fatal nature of the verdict. It was put in the hands of an officer, with orders to be on the watch and serve it as soon as Mrs. Berners should come out of her chamber, but not to knock at the door, or molest her while she remained in it."

Lyon Berners groaned deeply, and buried his face in his hands.

" Come, come! bear up, that you may sustain *her!*" said Captain Pendleton. "And now listen: Your flight, as I told you, was not suspected up to the time I left Black Hall. It will not be discovered probably until late this evening, when it will be too late for the authorities to take any immediate measures of pursuit. We have, therefore, this afternoon and to-night to perfect our plans. Only you need to bring steady nerves and a clear head to the task."

" What do you suggest, Pendleton?"

" First of all, that during this night, which is ours, all necessary conveniences be brought here to support your life for a few days, for you must not leave this safe refuge immediately—to do so would be to fall into the hands of the law."

" I see that," sighed Mr. Berners.

" I, then, with the help of this faithful Joe, will bring to you here to-night such things as you and Mrs. Berners will actually need, for the few days that you must remain. As to all your affairs at the Hall, I counsel you to give me a written authority to act for you in your absence. I have brought writing materials for the purpose; and when you have written it, I will myself take it and drop it secretly into the post-office at Blackville, so that it may reach me regularly through the mail, and help to mislead everybody to whom I shall show it, into the idea that you have gone away through Blackville. Will you write it now?" inquired Captain Pendleton, drawing from his pocket a rolled writing-case, containing all that was requisite for the work.

"A thousand thanks, Pendleton. I do not see how in the name of Heaven we could have managed without you," replied Berners, as he took the case, unrolled it on his knee, and proceeded to write the required "power of attorney."

"And now," said the Captain, when he received the document, "now we must be getting back. The sun is quite low, and we have much to do. Come, Joe, are you ready?"

"Yes, Massa Capping; ready and waitin' on you too. I ought to be at the mill now, 'fore the miller shuts it up."

Captain Pendleton then shook hands with Mr. Berners, and Joe pulled his front lock of wool by way of a deferential adieu, and both left the spot and disappeared in the thicket.

But it was not until the last sound of their retreating steps, crashing through the dried bushes, had died away, that Lyon Berners turned and went into the church.

As he entered, a singular phenomenon, almost enough to confirm the reputation of the place as "haunted ground," met his view.

All in one instant his eyes took in these things: First, Sybil covered over with the dark riding skirt, and still sleeping by the smouldering fire; but sleeping uneasily, and muttering in her sleep. Secondly, the four prints of the western windows laid in sunshine on the floor. Thirdly, a *shadow* that slipped swiftly athwart this sunshine, and disappeared as if it had sunk into the floor on the right of the altar. And in the same moment Sybil,

THE VERDICT AND THE VISITOR. 185

with a half-suppressed shriek, started up, and stared wildly around, exclaiming:

"Oh! what is this? Where am I? Who was she?"

Lyon Berners hastened to his wife, saying soothingly:

"Sybil, wake up, darling; you have been dreaming."

"But what does all this mean? Where are we? What strange place is this?" she cried, throwing back her long dark hair, and shading her eyes with her hands, as she gazed around.

"Dearest wife, take time to compose yourself, and you will remember all. A sudden and terrible catastrophe has driven us from our home. You have had a heavy sleep since that, and you find it difficult to awake to the truth," said Lyon Berners tenderly, as he sat down by her side, and sought to soothe her.

"Oh! I know now! I remember all now! my fatal fancy ball! Rosa Blondelle's mysterious murder! Our sudden flight! All! O! Heavens, all!" cried Sybil, dropping her face upon her hands.

Lyon Berners put his arm around her, and drew her to his bosom. But he did not speak; he thought it better to leave her to collect herself in silence.

After a few moments, she looked up again, and looked all around the church, and then gazed into her husband's eyes, and inquired:

"But Lyon, who was *she?* and where has she gone?"

"Who was who, dear Sybil? I don't understand," answered Mr. Berners, in surprise.

"That gipsy-like girl in the red cloak, who was bending over me, and staring into my face, just as you came in?"

"There was no such girl near you, or even in the church, my dear," said Mr. Berners.

"But indeed there was; she started away just as I woke up."

"My dearest Sybil, you have been dreaming."

"Indeed no; I saw her as plainly as I see you now; a girl in a red cloak, with such an elfin face I shall never forget it; such small piercing black eyes; such black eyebrows, depressed towards the nose, and raised high towards the temples, giving such an eldritch, mischievous, even dangerous expression to the whole dark countenance; and such wild black hair streaming around her shoulders."

"A very vivid dream you have had, dear wife, and that is all."

"I tell you no! she was bending over me; looking at me; and she fled away just as I woke up."

"My darling, I will convince you out of your own mouth. She ran away, you say, just as you woke up; therefore you did not see her after you were awake, but only while you slept, in your dreams. Besides, dear, I was here when you woke up, and I saw no one near you, or even in the building," persisted Lyon Berners—though at that moment he did recall to mind *the shadow* that he had seen slip past all the sunshine on the floor, and disappear as if it had sunk under the slabs on the right side of the altar.

"Lyon," said Sybil, solemnly, "I do not like to contradict you, but as I hope to be saved, I saw that girl, not in a dream, but in reality; and since you do not know anything about her, I begin to think the apparition mysterious and alarming. Let me tell you all about it."

"Well, tell me, dear, if to do so will do you any good," said Mr. Berners indulgently, but incredulously.

"Listen, then. I was in a *dead sleep*, oh, such a deep dead sleep, that I seemed to be away down in the bottom of some deep cave, when I felt a heavy breathing or panting over my face, and was conscious of somebody leaning over me, and looking at me. I tried to wake, but could not. I could not lift myself up out of that deep dark cave of sleep. But at last I felt a hand near my throat, trying to unfasten this golden locket that contains your miniature. Then I struggled, and succeeded in throwing off the spell and waking up As soon as I opened my eyes I saw the wild eldritch face, with its keen bright black eyes and queer eyebrows, and snake-like black locks, running down over the red cloak. The instant I saw this, I cried out, and the girl fled, and you hurried up. Now call that a dream if you can, for I tell you I saw that figure start up and run away from me as plainly as I saw you come up. One event was as real as the other," concluded Sybil.

Lyon Berners did not at once reply, for he thought

THE VERDICT AND THE VISITOR.

again of the flitting *shadow* he had seen cross the sunshine, and disappear as if it had sunk into the flagstones on the right side of the altar. And he mentally admitted the bare possibility that some intruder had entered the church and looked upon Sybil in her sleep, and fled at her awakening. But fled whither? The windows were very high, the wall was smooth beneath them; no one could have climbed to them, for there was no foothold or handhold to assist one in the ascent, and there was but the one door by which he himself had entered, at the same moment the strange visitor was said to have fled, and he was quite sure that no one had passed him. Besides, the shadow that he had seen vanished beside the altar, at the upper end of the church. Lyon Berners knew not what to think of all that he had seen and heard within the last quarter of an hour. But one thing was quite certain, that it was absolutely necessary to Sybil's safety to ascertain whether any stranger had really entered the church, or even come upon the premises.

"Well," inquired Sybil, seeing that he still remained silent, "what do you think now, Lyon?"

"I think," he answered promptly, "that I will search the church."

"There is not a hiding-place for anything bigger than a rat or a bird," said his wife, glancing around upon the bare walls, floor, and ceiling.

Nevertheless Lyon Berners walked up to the side of the altar where he had seen the shadow disappear. Sybil followed close behind him. He examined the altar all around. It was built of stonework like the church; that was the reason it had stood so long. But he experienced a great surprise when he looked at the side where shadow had vanished; for there he found a small iron-grated door, through which he dimly discerned the head of a flight of stone steps, the continuation of which was lost in the darkness below. Glancing over the top of the door, he read, in iron letters, the inscription:

"DUBARRY. 1650."

"What is it, dear Lyon?" inquired Sybil, anxiously looking over his shoulder.

"Good Heaven! It is the family vault of the wicked old Dubarrys, who once owned all the land hereabouts, except the Black Valley Manor, and who built this chapel for their sins; for of them it might not be said with truth, that 'all their sons were true, and all their daughters pure,' but just exactly the reverse. However, they are well forgotten now!"

"And this is their family vault?"

"Yes; but I had almost forgotten its existence here."

"Lyon, can my mysterious visitor have hidden herself in that vault?"

"I can search it, at any rate," answered Mr. Berners, wrenching away at the grated door.

But it resisted all his efforts, as if its iron bars had been bedded in the solid masonry.

"No," he answered; "your visitor, if you had one, could not possibly have entered here. See how fast the door is."

"Lyon," whispered Sybil, in a deep and solemn voice, "Lyon, could she possibly have come out from there?"

"Nonsense, dear! Are you thinking of ghosts?"

"This is the 'Haunted Chapel,' you know," whispered Sybil.

"Bosh, my dear; you are not silly enough to believe that?"

"But my strange visitor?"

"You had no visitor, dear Sybil; you had a dream, and your dream had every feature of nightmare in it—the deep, death-like, yet half-conscious and much disturbed sleep; the sense of heavy oppression; the apparition hanging over you; the inability to awake; even the grappling at your throat, and the swift disappearance of the vision immediately upon your full awakening—all well-known features of incubus," replied Mr. Berners But again he thought of the shadow he had seen; now, however, only to dismiss the subject as an optical illusion.

Sybil sighed deeply.

"It is hard," she said, "that you won't trust to my senses in this affair."

"Sweet wife, I would rather convince you how completely your senses have deceived you. Your imagination has been excited while your nerves were depressed. You have heard the legend of the Haunted Chapel, and while sleeping within it you conjured up the heroine of the

THE VERDICT AND THE VISITOR. 189

story in your dream where she immediately took the form of incubus."

"I!—the legend! What are you talking of, Lyon? I have heard the church called the Haunted Chapel indeed, but I never even knew that there was any story connected with it," exclaimed Sybil, in surprise.

"Really? Never heard the legend of 'Dubarry's Fall'?" inquired Mr. Berners, with equal surprise.

"Never, upon my word."

"Well, it is an old tradition; forgotten like the family with whom it was connected. I heard it in my childhood; but it had slipped my memory until your graphic description of the gipsy girl in the red cloak recalled it to my mind, and led me to believe that your knowledge of the legend had so impressed your imagination as to make it conjure up the heroine of the legend."

"What is the legend? Do tell me, Lyon."

"Not now, dearest. You must first have some coffee, which a faithful friend has provided for us.

"Captain Pendleton?" eagerly inquired Sybil.

"No, dear, our servant Joe. I do not expect to see Captain Pendleton until nightfall," added Lyon Berners, for he tried to anticipate and prevent any troublesome questions that Sybil might ask, as he wished to save her from needless additional pain as long as he possibly could.

"And Joe is here with us?" inquired Sybil, cheerfully.

"No, dear; he has returned home; but will come again to-night."

"But what news did he bring?"

"None. We will hear from Captain Pendleton to-night. Now you must have some coffee; and then I will tell you the 'Legend of the Haunted Chapel;' for that legend, Sybil, may well account for your vision, whether we look on it from my point of view or from yours—as illusion or reality," said Lyon Berners.

"Or, stay," he added, reflectively; "it is too cold for you to sup in the open air. I will bring the things in here."

"Well, let me go with you, to help to bring them in, at least," pleaded Sybil.

"What! are you really afraid to stay here alone?" inquired Lyon, smiling, with an attempt at pleasantry.

"No, indeed; but all smells mouldy inside this old church. At least it does since the sun set, and I would like to go out and get a breath of fresh air," replied Sybil quite seriously.

"Come, then," said Lyon.

They went out together.

The fire that had been built by Joe was now burnt down to embers; but the coffee-pot sat upon these embers, and the coffee was hot.

Lyon Berners took it up, while Sybil loaded herself with crockery ware and cutlery.

They had turned to go back to the church, when Sybil uttered a half-suppressed cry, and nearly dropped her burden.

"What's the matter?" cried Mr. Berners.

"Look!" exclaimed Sybil.

"Where?"

"At the east window."

Mr. Berners raised his eyes just in time to see a weird young face, with wild black hair, and a bright red mantle flash downward from the window, as if it had dropped to the floor.

There was no dream now; not even an optical illusion. The reality of the vision was unquestionable.

"This is most strange," exclaimed Mr. Berners.

"It is the same face that bent over me, and woke me up," answered Sybil, with a shudder.

"It is some one who is concealed in the church, and whom we shall be sure to discover, for there is but one exit by the front door; and if she comes out of that, we shall see her; or if she remains in the building, we shall be sure to find her there. Since I saw the face drop from the window, I have carefully watched the door. Do you also watch it, my dear Sybil; so that the creature, whatever it is, may not pass us," said Mr. Berners, as he strode on rapidly towards the church, followed by his wife.

They entered together, and looked eagerly around.

Though the sun had set some ten minutes before, yet the "after glow" shone in through the six tall Gothic window spaces, and revealed clearly every nook and corner of the interior. Their strange inmate or visitor, whichever she might be, was nowhere to be seen.

THE VERDICT AND THE VISITOR.

With an impatient gesture, Mr. Berners set down the coffee-pot, and hurried towards the door of the vault, and looked through the iron grating. But he could see nothing but the top of those stairs, the bottom of which disappeared in the darkness.

He then shook the door; but it firmly resisted all his strength. The bars appeared to be built into the solid masonry.

"This is really confounding to all one's intelligence," exclaimed Lyon Berners, gazing around in perplexity.

"It is indeed. But it is well that you have seen this mystery with your own eyes, for if you had not done so, you never would have believed in it," said Sybil, gravely shaking her head.

"Nor do I believe in it, now that I have seen it."

"Then you will not trust the united evidence of your own eyes and mine."

"No, Sybil; not for a prodigy so out of nature as that would be," replied Lyon Berners, firmly.

"Well, then, tell me the legend of the Haunted Chapel, for you hinted that that legend must have some connection with this apparition."

"A seeming connection, at the very least; but I cannot tell it to you now—not until you take something to eat and drink, for you have not broken your fast since morning."

"Nor have I hungered since morning," replied Sybil, with a sigh.

Mr. Berners went up to the smouldering embers of the fire that he had lighted in the morning on the stone floor of the church; and he drew together the dying brands, put fresh fuel on them, and soon rekindled the flame.

And the husband and wife sat down beside it; and while Sybil ate and drank with what appetite she could bring to the repast, Lyon Berners, to pass off the heavy time, related to her the legend of the Haunted Chapel.

CHAPTER XXV.

THE FALL OF THE DUBARRYS.

>But, soft! behold, lo, where it comes again!
>I'll cross it, though it blast me.—Stay, illusion!
>If thou hast, any sound, or use of voice,
>Speak to me!—SHAKESPEARE.

"THE Dubarrys," he began, "were a French Roman Catholic family of distinction. A cadet of that family came over to Virginia among the earliest English settlers of the colony.

"As is the case of the more important among his Anglican comrades, he obtained a very large tract of land by Royal patent. He built his hut and fixed his abode here, not a hundred yards from the spot where this church now stands.

"He took an Indian girl for a wife, and continued to live a wild huntsman sort of life in the wilderness; only breaking it sometimes by going down to Jamestown, twice a year, to buy such necessaries of civilized life as the wilderness could not furnish, and to hear news from any ship that might have come in from the old country; and above all, to take a holiday among civilized pleasure-seekers—for such existed even in the primitive settlement of Jamestown.

"In due course of time, a family of half-breed sons and daughters grew up around him, and the little primitive hut gave place to a substantial stone lodge.

"And the country around was becoming settled. The Berners had got a grant of the Black Valley, and had built the first part of Black Hall, which has since been added to in every generation, until it has grown to its present dimensions.

"About this time also, Charles Dubarry was inspired with a certain ambition for his eldest son, a densely ignorant, half-Indian youth of nineteen; and hearing that the two young sons of Richard Berners of Black Hall were to be sent to England to be educated, he proposed that his own 'black boy,' as he called his handsome dark-eyed heir, should go with them. And as the three lads had been forest companions for some years, the proposal of old Dubarry was gladly accepted, and the three young men sailed in company for England.

"They spent ten years in the old world, and returned, as they had set out, together. It was after their return that the close friendship of a young lifetime was turned to the deadliest enmity. It happened in this manner:

"The country, during their absence, had grown a great deal in population. Every rich valley among these mountains had its white proprietor. In the Valley of the Roses—so named, because at the time it was taken possession of by its first proprietor it was fairly carpeted and festooned all around and about with the wild-rose vine—dwelt one Gabriel Mayo, a gentleman of fortune, taste, and culture. He had a family of fair daughters, of whom old Charles Dubarry, with his national gallantry and proneness to exaggeration, had said, that 'they were all the most beautiful girls in the world, and each one more beautiful than all the others.'

"Be that as it may, it is certain that there were five lovely maidens, ranging from fifteen years to twenty-one to choose from. Yet who can account for human caprice, especially in such matters? The three young men—Louis Dubarry, and John and William Berners—all fixed their affections upon Florette Mayo, the youngest beauty.

"Fierce and bitter was the rivalry between the lovers. But the young girl returned the love of John Berners, and married him, and became your ancestress, as you know, Sybil.

"And from that time to the time of the extinction of the American branch of the Dubarry family, a feud, as fierce and bitter, if not as warlike, as any that ever raged between rival barons of the middle ages, prevailed between the Berners and the Dubarrys.

"I come now to the period just before the breaking out of the Old French War, when the first rude stone lodges in these valleys had given place to handsome and spacious manor houses, and when the then proprietor of the Dubarry estate had erected a magnificent dwelling on the site of his first rough cottage. He called the mansion the

Château Dubarry, a name which the country people quickly changed into Shut-up Dubarry.

"The last name was not inappropriate, for a more morose, solitary, and misanthropical man never lived than Henry Dubarry, the builder of that house. He neither visited nor received visits, but remained selfishly 'shut-up' in the paradise of art and letters that he had created within his dwelling.

"He had a wife, a son, and two daughters, all of whom suffered more or less from this isolation from their fellow-beings. So it was a great relief to the son when he was sent, first to the William and Mary College of Williamsburg for five years, and afterwards to Oxford for five more.

"After the departure of the son and brother, the mother and sisters suffered more and more seriously from the gloom and horror of their isolation, and in the course of years utterly succumbed to it. First the mother died, then the elder sister; and then the younger sister, left alone with her recluse father in that awful house, became a maniac.

"Under these circumstances, the father wrote to his son to come home. But selfishness, not love, ruled that young man, as it had ruled his fathers. He had graduated with honors, and won a 'fellowship' at the University, and he was about to start for the fashionable European tour. He wrote home to this effect, and went on his farther way.

"He remained abroad until summoned home by two events—the deaths of his father and sister, and the necessity of raising money for himself.

"He came home, but not alone. He brought with him a gipsy girl of singular beauty, who seemed to be passionately attached to him, and whom he loved as much as it was in his selfish nature to love anything.

"He placed her at the head of his household, and his simple servants obeyed her as their mistress; and his sociable neighbors, willing to forgive old rebuffs, called upon the young pair.

"But their visits were not kindly received, and not in any case returned. And the report went around the neighborhood, that Philip Dubarry was as morose and selfish as his father had been before him. And so the house was abandoned, as it had been in the days of the old man and the idiot girl.

"But by and by other rumors, darker and more dishonorable to the master and mistress of Shut-up Dubarry, crept out among the people. These rumors were started by the Dubarry servants, in their gossiping with other family servants in the chance meeting in church or village. They were to the effect that Philip Dubarry often quarreled fiercely with his gipsy wife, and even threatened to send her back to her native country, and that Gentiliska, or Iska, as she was more commonly called, wept and raved and tore her black hair by turns.

"It is the old sad tale, dear Sybil. At length the cultivated scholar and unprincipled villain grew tired of his beautiful but ignorant gipsy wife, who was a wife only in justice and not in law. He frequently left home for long absences. He spent his winters in the cities, and his summers in a round of visits to hospitable country houses, leaving her at all seasons to pine and weep, or rage and tear her hair in the gloomy solitude of Shut-up Dubarry. But for all this, whenever he did condescend to visit his home, she received him with an eagerness of welcome—a perfect self-abandonment to joy, that knew no bounds. And when he left her again, her despair was but the deeper, her anguish the fiercer. And all this was duly reported by that indefatigable corps of reporters, the domestics of the house.

"At last came the crisis. Philip Dubarry sent down an agent who opened the doors of Shut-up Dubarry, and brought into it an army of workmen, to repair, refurnish and decorate the mansion-house. In vain Gentiliska asked questions; the workmen either could not or would not give her any satisfaction. "It was the master's orders," they said, and nothing more. To no one in the world were "the master's" orders more sacred than to his loyal gipsy wife. She bowed in submission, and let the workmen do their will. All the summer season was occupied with the work. But by the first of October the house was thoroughly renewed, within and without, so that it seemed like a palace in the midst of Paradise; and the gipsy wife wandered through the house and grounds in a delight that was only damped by the long-continued absence of her husband.

"At length, near the middle of the month, at the height of the hunting season, Philip Dubarry arrived. But the eager welcome of his wife was met with coldness and petulance, that wounded and enraged her. She gave way to a storm of grief and fury. She wept and raved and tore her hair, as was her way when fiercely excited. But now he had not the least patience with her, or the least mercy on her. He had ceased to love her and to want her, and so, in acting out his selfish and demoniac nature, he did not hesitate to treat her with cruel scorn and ignominy. He told her that she was not his wife, and never had been so. He called her ill names, and bade her pack up and go, he cared not where, so it was out of his sight, for he hated her; and out of his house also, for she dishonored it; and that, after being repaired and refurnished, it must also be purified of *her* presence, before he could bring into it the fair maiden whom he was about to make his wife.

"Then all her fury suddenly subsided, and she became calm and resolute unto death. She assured him that she never would leave the house; that she was his wife, and the house's mistress; and she had the right to remain, and would remain. Whereupon he broke out into furious oaths, swearing that if she did not go, he would put her out by force. Then she answered, in these memorable words, that have come down to us in tradition:

"'My body you may thrust forth from my home, but my spirit never! Living or dead, in the flesh or the spirit, I will stay in this house as long as its walls shall stand! Nay, though you were to pull this house down to eject me, in the flesh or the spirit, I would enter in and possess the next house you should build! And should you venture to bring here, or there, a bride to supplant me, in the flesh or the spirit I will blast and destroy her. So help me the gods of my people.'

"For a moment the ruthless and dauntless man stood appalled by the awful spirit he had raised in that slight form. But when he did recover himself it was to fall into a transport of fury, in which he seized the girl and hurled her violently through the open window. Fortunately

THE FALL OF THE DUBARRYS.

they were on the ground floor, so the fall was not great, and she was, besides, light in form and agile as a cat. She fell on her hands and feet upon a thick carpet of the dead leaves that strewed the lawn.

"For a moment she lay where she had fallen, breathless from the shock; then she lifted herself slowly up. One arm hung useless by her side; it was dislocated at the shoulder joint; but the other was raised to heaven, and she muttered some words in her native tongue, and then turned and walked away until she disappeared in the woods.

"'I hope she'll drown herself according to rule, and there will be an end,' the fiendish wretch was heard to mutter. No one was allowed to follow her. She probably *did* drown herself, but that was by no means the end. Well, the gipsy girl is said to have kept her word.

"The third day thereafter, as a boy in search of eagle's eggs was climbing the highest fastnesses of the Black Mountain, his eyes were attracted by the glow of something scarlet lying on a ledge of rocks about half-way down the course of the Black Torrent. Agile as any chamois hunter of the Alps, the boy let himself down, from point to point, until he reached the ledge, upon which the dead body of the gipsy girl was found. It was crushed by the fall, and sodden by the white foam of the cascade that continually rolled over it.

"The boy hastened away to spread the news. With the greatest difficulty the body was recovered, and conveyed to Shut-up Dubarry. The inquest that sat upon it rendered the simple verdict, 'Found Dead;' for whether the death were accidental or suicidal, or whether it resulted from the fall upon the rocks, or from the waters of the cascade, the Dogberries of that jury could not decide.

"The gipsy girl was buried; and her brutal protector coarsely professed himself to be greatly relieved by her death. And he assembled all his servants before him, and forbade them, under the penalty of his heaviest displeasure, ever to mention the name of Gentiliska to the lady he was about to bring home as his wife. These slaves knew their master, and in great fear and trembling they each and all solemnly promised to obey him. Then he left home for the eastern part of the State from which he was to bring his bride. On this occasion he was gone a month.

"It was in the middle of the month of November that he returned to Shut-up Dubarry, bringing with him his fair young bride. She was a Fairfax, from the county that was named after her family. She was unquestionably a lady of the highest and purest order, and the neighboring gentry, ever pleased to welcome such an one among them, called on her, invited her to their houses, and gave dinner or supper parties in her honor.

"Philip Dubarry, who had recently fretted at the galling 'ban' under which, for the transient love of the gipsy girl, he had voluntarily placed himself, now rejoiced at being delivered from it, and entered with all the zest of novelty into the social pleasures of the place. He loved his beautiful and high-born wife with both passion and pride, and she loved some imaginary hero in his form, and was happy in the illusion. Thus all went merry as a marriage bell until one dark and dismal day in December, when the rain fell in floods and the wind raved around the house, and the state of the weather kept the newly married couple closely confined within doors, his bride turned to him, and inquired quietly:

"'Who is that little dark-haired girl with the piercing black eyes, and in the short red cloak, that I see so often around the house?'

"'What did you say?' inquired Philip Dubarry, in a quavering voice.

"Who is that little girl in the red cloak, who seems so much at home in the house? Is she deaf and dumb? I speak to her, but she never answers me; generally indeed, she goes away as soon as she perceives that I notice her. Who is she, Phil?' and the young wife looked at her husband for an answer. But his face was that of a corpse, and his form was shaking with an ague fit, for the guilty are ever cowardly.

"But his wife mistook the cause of his agitation. Forgotten in an instant was the question she had asked, and upon which she had placed no sort of importance; and she went to her husband and took his hand, and gazed into his face, and asked him, for Heaven's sake, to tell her what was the matter.

"He told her a lie. He faltered out between his chattering teeth, that he feared he was struck with a congestive chill; that the sudden and severe change in the weather had affected him;—and more to the same effect.

"She hurried out and prepared a hot drink of brandy, boiling water, and spices, and she brought it to him and made him drink it.

"Under this powerful stimulant he revived. But she had, in the fear and excitement of the hour, utterly forgotten the inquiry she had put to him, and no more would have been said of it, had not he, in fearful interest, resumed the subject.

"'You were asking me about—one of the servants, were you not? he inquired.

"'Oh, yes. But never mind! sit still, and keep your feet to the fire until you get warm. Never mind about gratifying my foolish curiosity now,' she answered, thoughtfully.

"'My chill is already gone, thanks to your skilful nursing! What chill could resist your warm draughts? But now about your question. What was it?'

"'Oh, nothing much! I only asked you who was the little girl with the red cloak, who is so silent and shy that she never answers me when I speak to her, and always shrinks away whenever she finds herself observed.'

"The trembling wretch was ready with his falsehood. He answered:

"'Oh! she is the child of a poor couple on the mountain, and comes to the house for cold victuals; but she is, as you have observed, very shy; so I think you had better leave her to herself.'

"'Yes: but are you sure she is to be trusted? For, shy as she is in other matters, she is bold enough to intrude into the most private parts of the house, and at the most untimely hours of the night,' remarked the lady.

"'Indeed!' muttered the guilty man, in a sepulchral tone.

"'Indeed and indeed! Why, only last night, when we came home at midnight, from Mrs. Judge Mayo's ball, when you lingered below stairs to speak to the butler, and I ran up into my own room alone, I saw this strange looking little creature, with the streaming black hair and the red cloak, standing before my dressing-glass! Now what do you think of that?'

"'She—she—she has been a sort of a pet of the family, and has had the run of the house, coming in and out of all the rooms at all hours, like any little dog,' answered the conscious criminal, in a quivering voice.

"'*That* must be reformed at once!' said the Fairfax bride, drawing herself up with much dignity, and also perhaps with some jealous suspicion.

"'It shall, by my soul! I will give orders to that effect,' quivered Philip Dubarry.

"'Nay, do not take that trouble. It is *my* prerogative to order my household, and I shall do it,' proudly answered the lady.

"And here the matter might have ended, but for that interest Philip Dubarry felt in the subject. He remembered the most awful threat of his betrayed gipsy wife: 'In the flesh or in the spirit, to dwell in the house as long as its walls should stand! In the flesh or in the spirit, to blast and destroy the bride he should bring there to take her place.' Up to this time he had never had any reason to suppose that the gipsy girl had kept her word. He had never seen nor heard of anything unusual about the house. But now when his wife spoke of this silent inmate in the red cloak, he recognized the portrait all but too well, and his guilty soul quaked with fear. And yet he was not superstitious. He was a son of the eighteenth century, which was much more incredulous of the supernatural than the nineteenth, with all its mysterious spiritual manifestations, can be. He was a scientific and practical man. Yet he shuddered with awe as he listened to the description given by his unconscious wife of this strange visitant. And he could not forbear to question her.

"'Did you speak to the girl when you found her in your room at midnight?' he inquired.

"'Yes, certainly; I asked her how she came to be there so late. But instead of answering my question, she glided silently away.'

"'Have you spoken to any of the servants of this girl's intrusion into parts of the house where she had no business to come?'

THE FALL OF THE DUBARRYS. 201

"'No, not until this morning; for I never really felt interest enough in the little creature that I only casually met in the passage of the house, until I found her in my bedroom at midnight. So this morning I described her to the housekeeper, and asked who she was, and who gave her liberty to intrude into my bedroom so late. And what do you think old Monica answered?'

"'I'm sure I don't know.'

"'She crossed herself, and cried out, 'Lord have mercy on all our souls! You have seen her!' I inquired, 'Seen who?' But she answered, 'Nothing. Nobody. I don't know what I'm talking about. My head's wool-gathering, I believe.' Nor could any further questioning of mine draw from her any more satisfactory answer. And so I came to you for an explanation. And you tell me that she is Milly Jones, the child of poor parents, living on the mountain, and that she comes here for broken victuals and old clothes. Very well. In future I shall pension the poor family on the mountain, for I would not have any fellow-creature in my reach to suffer want; but I shall do it on condition that Miss Milly Jones stays home, and helps her mother with the family cooking and washing, instead of losing her time by day and her sleep by night in wandering through all the rooms of a gentleman's house, and taking possession of a lady's bed-chamber.'

"You see this bride never imagined a ghost, but strongly suspected a sweetheart, and so she was a little surprised when her husband answered:

"'Do so, my dear; and may Heaven grant that you may get rid of this unpleasant visitor at once and forever.'

"And as he said this, Philip Dubarry arose and went into his library and rung the bell, and to the servant who answered it, he said:

"'Send Monica the housekeeper here.'

"In a few minutes Monica entered the room.

"'Did I not order you, on pain of my heaviest displeasure, never to annoy Mrs. Dubarry by so much as the mention of the gipsy girl's name to her?' sternly demanded Philip Dubarry.

"The old woman fell down upon her knees, and lifted up both her hands, and exclaimed:

"And no more I haven't, master, not once! But that don't do no good, for *she walks!*

"'Who walks, you old fool?'"

"'*She*, the gipsy girl, master. *She walks*, and the missis sees her as well as we do!"

"'We? Whom do you call "we," you insupportable idiot?'

"'Me and Ben the man-servant, and Betty the chambermaid, and Peggy the parlor maid. All see her, master. We never, none of us, see her before the missis was brought home; but ever since that, we see her every day; we see just as much of her as we used to see when she was alive!' answered the woman, groveling and weeping.

"'*Where* do you see her, or fancy you see her, lunatic?' fiercely demanded Philip Dubarry.

"'Everywhere, master! We meets her on the stairs; we sees her sitting at the head of the table, as soon as the meal is ready, and before the mistress comes to take the place; and we sees her lying in the unmade beds of a morning; but always, as soon as we screams, as scream we must, at such an object, master, she vanishes away!" answered the housekeeper.

"Philip Dubarry was awed and almost silenced—*almost*, but not quite, for he was the very sort of hero to browbeat others the most fiercely when he was himself the most frightened. He rallied himself.

"'Look you here!' he furiously exclaimed; 'all this that you have just told me is the most wicked and abominable falsehood and absurdity! And now take notice! IF EVER I hear of one more word being uttered on this subject in this house, or out of it, by any one of you, under any circumstances whatever, by my blood, I will make you all wish that you had never been born! Repeat this to your fellow-servants, and order them from me to govern their tongues accordingly. Now go!' he thundered at the poor old woman, who hastily picked herself up, and hurried out of the room

CHAPTER XXVI.

THE SPECTER.

It was about to speak
And then it started like a guilty thing,
Upon a fearful summons.—SHAKESPEARE.

"PHILIP DUBARRY remained walking up and down the floor, foaming with impotent rage, as well as trembling with a vague and awful terror. He had a practical and scientific mind, and could understand everything that might be governed by known laws. But he could not understand this unwelcome visitant, that had appeared to every one else in the house but himself. He was an arbitrary and despotic man who enforced his will upon all connected with him, and ruled all flesh with a rod of iron. But he could not rule the spirit, and he knew it. He could not lay this ghost of his guilt.

"There was one grain of truth in the ton of falsehood that he had told to his unconscious wife, to account for the apparition seen by her. There really was a Milly Jones, the daughter of a poor family on the mountains, and she really did come occasionally to the house to ask for broken victuals and old clothes; but instead of being a beautiful black-eyed and black-haired little gipsy, in the picturesque red cloak, she was a pale-faced, light-haired, poor-spirited looking creature, in a faded calico frock, and an old plaid shawl; and instead of being the family pet, with the run of the house, she was the family nuisance, strictly prohibited from passing the bounds of the servants' hall.

"So when that day, being a rainy day, and therefore highly favorable for attention to domestic matters, Mistress Alicia Dubarry called the house-steward to her presence, and ordered him to send a small pension of two dollars a week to the Jones family, with an intimation that Miss Milly need not come to collect it, the order was promptly executed, to the satisfaction of all the domestics; and poor Milly, glad to be relieved from her fatiguing journey and degrading mendicity, was seen no more at Shut-up Dubarry.

"But Mrs. Dubarry did not therefore get rid of her visitor. Not more than three days had elapsed since the issuing of her order, when, one evening between the lights, she entered her own bedroom, and saw the girl in the red cloak sitting quietly in the easy-chair beside the fire.

"'How dare you come here, after the message I sent you? Get up and begone, and let me never catch you here again,' angrily demanded the lady.

"The apparition melted into air; but as it disappeared, the words came, like a sigh borne upon the breeze:

"'*I wait.*'

"The lady was about to dress for an evening party, and so she paid no attention to any chance sound.

"But the next morning she met the girl in the hall, and the next evening in the parlor; again she passed the figure on the stairs, or encountered it in the drawing-room. The lady lost patience, and sent for the house-steward to her presence.

"'Did I not command that that girl should not come here again?' she sternly demanded.

"'Yes, my lady,' respectfully answered the man.

"'Then how is it that she comes here as much as ever?'

"'My dear lady, she have never entered the house since your ladyship gave the order that she was not so to do.'

"'But she has. I have seen her here at least a half a dozen times.'

"'Dear lady, I dare not contradict you; but poor Milly Jones has been down with the pleurisy for these two weeks past, and could not have got out of her bed, even if your ladyship had ordered her to come.'

"'Isaac, is this true?'

"'True as truth, your ladyship, which you can find it out for yourself by riding up to the hut and seeing the poor girl, which it would be a charity so to do.'

"'And you say she has not been here for a fortnight?'

"'No, madam.'

"'Then, in the name of Heaven, WHO is it that I meet so often?' slowly and sternly demanded Mrs. Dubarry.

"Old Isaac solemnly shook his gray head, and answered never a word.

"'What do you mean by that? Speak! I will have an answer. Who is this silent girl in the red cloak, I ask?' repeated the lady.

"'Madam, I don't know. And that is what I meant when I shook my head,' replied the old man, trembling.

"'You don't know! do you dare to mock me?'

"'Far from it, my lady; but goodness knows I don't know.'

"'But you have seen her?'

"'Dear, my lady, I don't know who she is, nor dare I speak of her; the master has forbidden us so to do. Dear madam, ask the master; but oh, for pity sake, do not ask me further,' pleaded the old man, very humbly.

The lady turned white with jealousy. There was but one interpretation she could put upon this mystery.

"'Go and say to your master that I would feel much obliged if he would come to me here,' she said, grimly seating herself.

"The trembling old man went to the kennels, where Mr. Dubarry was busy doctoring a favorite setter, and delivered his message. Dubarry was still enough in love with his three months wife to come quickly at her call.

"'Philip!' exclaimed the lady, as soon as she saw him enter the room, 'once for all, I wish to know who is this girl in the red cloak; and why I am daily insulted with her presence in this house?'

"Dubarry went pale, as usual, at the mention of the apparition; but he faltered out with what composure he could command:

"'I—I told you who she is—Milly Jones."

"'No; begging your pardon, she is *not* Milly Jones. Milly Jones has been ill with pleurisy, at home on the mountain, for the last two weeks; and I have sent her a pension of two dollars a week, No; this is no Milly Jones, and I insist on knowing who she is!'

"'Then, if she is not Milly Jones, she is a creature of your own imagination, for no other living girl comes to the house,' answered Dubarry doggedly.

"'You will not tell me who she is? Very well. When next I see her, *she* shall tell me, silent as she is,' said the lady grimly setting her teeth.

"Dubarry arose with a sigh, and went back to his ailing setter; but his thoughts brooded over the subject of the apparition.

"The lady kept her word at a fearful cost. For the remainder of the day, her conduct towards her husband was so cold and repelling as to wound and offend him. So it happened that when the hour for retiring came that night, she went up to her chamber alone. She had but time to reach the room, when all the household was startled by a piercing shriek and a heavy fall.

"Mr. Dubarry, soon followed by all the servants, rushed up-stairs to Mrs. Dubarry's bedroom. They found the lady extended on the floor in a deep swoon. She was raised and laid upon the bed, and proper means taken to revive her. When at length she opened her eyes, and recognized her husband, she signed for every one else to leave the room; and when they had done so, she turned and took his hand and kissed it, and fixed her wild and frightened eyes upon him and whispered in an awe-struck tone:

"'Phil, dear, I wronged you. I took that creature in the red cloak to be a sweetheart of yours, Phil, but it was not; it was—*a specter!*'

There was silence between them for a minute, during which she never took her scared eyes from his pale face. He was the first to speak. Summoning up as much resolution as he could muster, he affected a light laugh, and answered:

"'Specter! My sweet wife, there is no such thing.'

"'Ah, but—but—if you could have seen what I saw, *felt what I felt!*'

"'Nonsense, dear one. You were the subject of an optical illusion.'

"'No, I was not. Hush! let me tell you what happened. I came up into this room. It was warm and ruddy with the fire-light and the lamp-light; and in the glow I saw the girl standing between the hearth and the bed. I spoke to her, asking her how she dared intrude into my most sacred privacy; and then she silently glided from the spot. But I told her she should not leave the room until she had given some account of herself. And I put forth my hand to stop her, but the moment I did so I received a shock as from some powerful galvanic battery! a tremendous shock that threw me down upon my face. I knew no more until I came to my senses and found myself here, with you watching over me. Now, Philip, tell me that was an optical illusion, if you dare," said the lady, solemnly.

"'Yes, love, I dare. I tell you that what you saw *was* an optical illusion.'

"'—But what I felt?'

"'—Was a slight—a very slight attack of catalepsy. Both the vision and the fit, dear, took their rise in some abnormal state of the nervous system,' said Philip Dubarry; and feeling almost pleased with his own explanation of the mystery, he tried to persuade himself that it was the true one.

"But his wife turned her face to the wall, saying, however:

"'Well, at any rate, I am glad that the girl in the red cloak is not flesh and blood, Phil. I would rather she should be an "optical illusion" or a fit of "catalepsy," or even a "specter," than a sweetheart of yours, as I first took her to be.'

"'Be not afraid. You have no living rival, Alicia,' answered her husband.

"And the reconciliation between the husband and the wife was complete from that time forth.

"But somehow the condition of the lady was worse than before.

"*She was haunted.*

"She knew herself to be haunted; but whether by a spectral illusion or a real specter, she could not know. In the glow of the fire-light, in the shadow of the bed-curtains, in the illuminated drawing-room, on the dark staircase, wherever and whenever she found herself alone, the vision of the girl in the red cloak crossed her path. She did not speak to it or try to stop it again. She did not wish to risk another such an electric shock as should 'cast her shuddering on her face.' But her health wasted under the trial. Her nerves failed. She grew fearful of being left alone for an instant; nothing would induce ner to go into any room in the house without an attendant. She contracted a habit of looking fearfully over her shoulder, and sometimes suddenly screaming.

"Nor was the mistress of the house the only sufferer from this 'abnormal state of the nervous system,' as the master of the house preferred to call the mystery. The servants grew so much afraid to move about the building alone, that their usefulness was much impaired. And at length one after another ran away, and took to the woods and mountain caves, preferring to starve or beg rather than live in luxury in the haunted house. New servants were procured to supply the places of the old ones, until the latter could be brought back; but none of them stayed long; nothing could induce them to remain in the 'haunted house.' The story of the gipsy girl's ghost got around in the neighborhood. Not all the despotic power of Mr. Dubarry could prevent this. The house came to be pointed out and avoided by the ignorant and superstitious, as a haunted and accursed spot. Even the more intelligent and enlightened portion of the community gradually forsook it; for it was not very agreeable to visit a family where the mistress was so full of 'flaws and starts' that, even at the head of her own table, she would often startle the whole company by suddenly looking over her right shoulder and uttering a piercing scream.

"And so the house was abandoned by high and low, rich and poor alike. And the worthy gossips of the neighborhood wisely nodded over their tea-cups, and declared that the deserted condition of the house was but a just retribution for the sins of its master.

"And in the meantime the health of the mistress grew worse and worse. The most serious fears were entertained for her life and reason, death or insanity seeming to be the most probable issue of her malady. Medical advice was called in. The doctor, either in complaisance or sincerity, agreed with Mr. Dubarry's theory of the patient's condition, ascribing her illness to an 'abnormal state of the nervous system,' and he advised change of air and scene, and he held forth good hopes that within a very few months, when the young wife should become a mother, her health might be perfectly reëstablished.

"Under these circumstances, early in the new year, Mr. Dubarry took his wife to Williamsburg, to spend the winter among the gaieties of the colonial Governor's court.

"The haunted house was shut up, and left to itself. Not a man or woman could be found to live in it, for love or money.

"In the glories of the colonial capital, Mrs. Dubarry completely recovered from her nervous malady. She was visited by no more 'optical illusions' or 'cataleptic' fits. She even grew to regard her former visitations in the same way in which her husband pretended to view them— as mere nervous phenomena. And as the fashionable season at Williamsburg closed, and as the spring opened, Mrs. Dubarry expressed an ardent desire to return to 'Shut up Dubarry' for her confinement. 'The heir of the manor should be born on the manor,' she said.

"Mr. Dubarry had great doubts about the safety of this measure, and attempted to dissuade his wife from it; but she was firm in her purpose, and so she carried it.

"It was early in the royal month of June that the young wife was taken back to her country home. Shut-up Dubarry looked as little like a 'haunted house' as any house could look: waving woods, sparkling waters, blossoming trees, blooming flowers, singing birds—all the richness, beauty and splendor of summer turned it into a paradise. Besides, Mrs. Dubarry brought down half a dozen young cousins of both sexes with her, and they filled the house with youthful life. Under these circumstances, the old servants were tempted back. And all went on very well until one day one of the young girls suddenly spoke out at the full breakfast-table, and asked:

"'Alicia, who is that strange, silent girl, in the red cloak, that is always following you about?'

"Mrs. Dubarry grew deadly pale, set down the cup that she had held in her hand, but she did not attempt to speak.

"'Have I said anything wrong? I did not mean to do so. I am sure I beg pardon, if I have,' faltered the young cousin, looking from the pale face of Mrs. Dubarry to the troubled countenance of Mr. Dubarry.

"'I am very sorry if I have said anything wrong,' repeated the little cousin, in dismay.

"'No, no, you have said nothing amiss; but it is a very painful subject; let us drop it,' replied Mr. Dubarry rather inconsistently. And every one around the table silently wondered what the matter could be.

"When breakfast was over, and the husband and wife found themselves alone together, Mrs. Dubarry seized his arm, and whispered:

"'Oh, Philip! the specter has not gone!'

"'My dearest Alicia! you have not fancied that you have seen it lately?'

"'No, no; but *she* has seen it! Kitty has seen it *always following me!* She took it for a real girl, as I did at first!'

"What could Philip Dubarry say to all this? Only one thing:

"'My darling, I cannot have your nerves shaken in this manner. You had no such visitations as these while we stayed at Williamsburg. And so to Williamsburg we will return immediately. Tell your maid to pack up this afternoon, and we will set out to-morrow. No objections, Alicia! for I tell you we must go.'

"She saw that his resolution was fixed, and she made no opposition to it. She rang for her maid, and gave the necessary directions. And then, feeling very unwell, she sent down an excuse to her company, and retired to bed.

"At twelve o'clock that night, while the young people were enjoying themselves in some round game in the drawing-room, and Mr. Dubarry was doing all that he could to promote their entertainment, the whole party was startled by a terrific cry coming from Mrs. Dubarry's chamber. All paused for a breathless instant, and then rushed tumultuously up the stairs. At the door of the bed-chamber, Mr. Dubarry turned around and waved them all back. Then he entered the chamber alone. All seemed quiet there then. The moonlight came flickering through the vine leaves on the outside of the open window, and fell fitfully upon the face and form of Alicia Dubarry, who was sitting up in bed, staring straight before her.

"Mr. Dubarry locked the door before he approached the bed.

THE SPECTER.

"'Alicia,' he said, 'my dear Alicia, what is the matter?'

"'It is doom! It is doom!' she answered in an awful voice, without removing her eyes from some object between the foot of the bed and the moonlit window.

"'Compose yourself, dear wife, and tell me what has happened.'

"'Look! Look! for yourself!' she cried, her finger extended, and following the direction of her eyes.

"'My sweet Alicia, there is nothing there but the tremulous shadow of the vine leaves cast by the moonlight,' said Mr. Dubarry, persuasively, as he went and drew the curtain before the window, and then struck a match and lighted a lamp.

"But her eyes were never removed from the spot where she had gazed.

"'It is there yet!' she cried.

"'What is there, good Alicia? there is nothing there, indeed!'

"'Yes, the dead woman and dead child! Do you not see them?'

"'See! no! you are in one of your nervous attacks; but to-morrow we will leave this place, and you will have no more of them.'

"'Hush! No! I shall never leave this place again.'

"'You shall start by sunrise to-morrow.'

"'Hush! listen! I will tell you what happened. I was sleeping well, very well, when suddenly I was awakened with a tremendous shock. I started up in bed and saw *her*—the terrible girl! She was standing at the foot of the bed looking at me, and pointing to something that lay upon the floor. I looked and saw—there it is yet!—the dead woman, with the dead babe on her bosom! I shrieked aloud, for I knew the woman was myself, and the babe was my own! And as I shrieked, she vanished, as she always does; but the dead woman and child remained! And there they are yet! Oh! cover them over, Philip! cover them over! Cover them from my sight, for I have no power to withdraw my eyes from them, she exclaimed in wild excitement.

"Almost beside himself with distress, Philip Dubarry

seized a large table cover and threw it down over the spot upon which her eyes were fixed.

"'Ah! it is of no use! it is of no use! I see them still! they rise above the covering! they lie upon it!' she cried, in terrific emotion, shaking as if with an ague fit.

"'Lie down,' said Philip Dubarry, compelling himself to be calm, for the sake of trying to calm her. And he took her and laid her back upon the pillow. But still she raved, like one in high fever and delirium.

"I have received my sentence! I am doomed! I am doomed! I have seen my own corpse, and the corpse of my child!" she cried. And then a violent convulsion seized her.

"Nearly maddened by terror and despair, Philip Dubarry rushed from the room and loudly called for assistance. The chamber was soon filled with the members of the household, not one of whom knew what to do, until the entrance of the old housekeeper, who sent everybody out, and requested Mr. Dubarry to dispatch a carriage for the family physician.

"Before morning the doctor arrived. But the convulsions and the delirium of the lady increased in violence until just at the dawn of day, when she gave birth to an infant boy, who breathed and died.

"Then just before her own death, she recovered her senses and grew very calm. She asked to see her child. When the nurse brought it, she kissed its cold face, and bade her lay it by her side. Then the lady called her husband, and whispered so faintly that he had to lean his ear to her lips to hear her words. She said:

"'The vision is realized in the dead mother and the dead babe! But, Philip! *for whose sin do we die?*'

"Before he could make a reply, if any reply had been possible, she was gone.

"The mother and babe were buried together. The company at Shut-up Dubarry broke up in the greatest consternation. The story of the vision, real or imaginary, that had caused the lady's death, got out. All the neighborhood talked of it, and connected it with the fate of the hardly-used gipsy girl, whose spirit was said to haunt the house.

"Mr. Dubarry became a prey to the most poignant grief

and remorse. He shut himself up in his desolate house, where he was abandoned by all his neighbors, and by all his servants, with the exception of the old housekeeper and house-steward, whose devotion to the family they had served so long, retained them still in the service of its last and most unhappy representative.

"But awful stories crept out from that house of gloom. 'Twas said that the master was always followed by the specter of the gipsy girl—that he could be heard in the dead of night walking up and down the hall outside of his chamber door, raving in frenzy, or expostulating with some unknown and unseen being, who was said to be the specter that haunted the house.

"At length, unable to endure the misery of solitude and superstitious terrors, Mr. Dubarry took an aged Catholic priest to share his home. Under the influence of Father Ingleman, Philip Dubarry became a penitent and a devotee. At that time this church was but a rude chapel, erected over the old family vault. But now, by the advice of the old priest, Mr. Dubarry rebuilt and enlarged the chapel, for the accommodation of all the Catholics in the neighborhood. He also added a priest's house. And Father Ingleman said mass every Sunday, while waiting for another priest to be appointed to the charge.

"This rebuilding and remodeling amused the miserable master of the manor, during the latter part of the summer and the autumn following his wife's death. But with the coming of the winter, returned all his gloom and horror. And the good old priest, so far from being able to help his patron, was himself so much affected in health and spirits by this condition of the house, that he begged and obtained leave to retire to the little dwelling beside the church.

"The awful winter passed away.

"But on one stormy night in March, the mansion house took fire. It was said that the haunted master of the house, in a fit of desperation, actually set it on fire, with the purpose of burning out the ghost. At all events, it seems certain that he would permit nothing to be done to stop the flames.

The house was burned to the ground. The houseless master took refuge with Father Ingleman, in the priest's dwelling by the church. But there also the specter followed him, nor could all the exorcisms of Father Ingleman with 'candle, bell, and book,' avail to lay the disturbed spirit.

"Philip Dubarry, half a maniac by this time, sent away the priest, pulled down the priest's house, and took up his abode in the body of the church itself, which was thenceforward deserted by all others. But here also the specter was supposed to have followed him. At length he disappeared. No one knew whither he went. Some said that he had gathered together his money and departed for a foreign country; others, that he had drowned himself in the Black River, though his body never was found. Some said that he had cast himself down headlong from some mountain crest, and his bones were bleaching in some inaccessible ravine; while others, again, did not hesitate to say that the devil had flown away with him bodily.

"The fate of the last of the Dubarrys is unknown. The estate, unclaimed, is held in abeyance. The house, burned to the ground, has never been restored. The church, thereafter known as the Haunted Chapel, has crumbled into the ruin that you see. And such, dear Sybil, is the story of the 'Fall of the Dubarrys.'"

CHAPTER XXVII.

FEARFUL WAITING.

> Still the wood is dim and lonely,
>   Still the plashing fountains play,
> But the past with all its beauty,
>   Whither has it fled away?
> Hark! the mournful echoes say,
>   Fled away!   —A. A PROCTOR.

"AND the apparition that we both saw was like that of the gipsy girl in the ghostly legend," said Sybil, musingly.

"Yes; in the matter of the red cloak—a very common garment, dear Sybil. Such a resemblance reminds us of Paganini's portrait which the child said was like him, 'about the fiddle,'" replied Lyon Berners, with an effort towards pleasantry, which was very far indeed from his heart; for he was oppressed with grief and dread. He was anxiously looking forward to the arrival of Captain Pendleton; and fearing for the effect his disclosures must have upon his beloved Sybil, who seemed still so utterly unable to realize her position. She seemed almost satisfied now, so that Lyon was near her, and she was the only object of his care. So disengaged was her mind, at this hour, from all real appreciation of her situation, that she had leisure to feel interested in the tale that Lyon had told her. She again reverted to it.

"But the likeness was not only in the red cloak, it was in the whole gipsy style. I spoke of that, even before you had told me anything about the gipsy girl," persisted Sybil

Before Lyon could answer her, steps were heard approaching.

"There is Pendleton," exclaimed Mr. Berners, and he arose and hurried forward to meet the visitor.

"Hush! come out here a moment," he whispered, drawing Captain Pendleton outside the chapel. "Sybil knows nothing of that verdict as yet. I wish to keep it from her knowledge as long as possible—forever, if possible. So, if you have more bad news to tell, tell it now and here to me," he added.

"Berners," began the Captain—but then he paused in pity.

"Go on," said Lyon.

"My friend, the flight of your wife and yourself, if not absolutely ascertained, is strongly suspected. An officer watches your closed chamber door. Two others have been dispatched to Blackville, to watch the ferry. By tomorrow merning the flight, so strongly suspected now, will be fully discovered. This is all I have to say in private. And now, perhaps we had better not linger any longer here, lest Mrs. Berners may suspect something, if possible, even more alarming than the truth," said Captain Pendleton.

"You are quite right," admitted Lyon Berners, and they entered the chapel together.

Sybil sprang up to meet them.

"What news, Captain? Is the murderer discovered? May we return home?" she eagerly inquired.

"No. madam; the murderer has not yet been discovered, nor do I think it would be prudent in you yet to return home," replied the Captain, feeling relieved that her questions had taken forms that enabled him to reply truly to them without divulging the alarming intelligence of the verdict of the coroner's jury.

He unstrapped a portmanteau from his shoulders and threw it down near the fire, and seated himself upon it. Then turning to Mr. Berners, he said:

"I have made arrangements with your faithful Joe to bring certain necessaries to this place to-night. They cannot, you know, be brought to this spot by the same direct route that we took in coming here. But as soon as the moon goes down, which will be about one o'clock, Joe will launch a boat just below Black Hall and come across the river with all that is most needed. There he will find a cart and horse waiting for him. He will load the cart and drive it up here to the entrance of the thicket."

"But that cart, Pendleton?"

"Yes! you will wonder how I got it there without exciting suspicion. It was done in this way. I ordered Joe to bring it boldly up in front of the house, and to put in it the boxes containing my own and my sister's masquerade dresses, and to take them over to our place. Joe understood and obeyed me, and drove the cart to Blackville, and crossed the river at the ferry, under the very eyes of the constable stationed there to watch. He brought the cart down this bank, and left it concealed in a clearing of the wood. He will watch his opportunity, as soon as it is dark enough to swim across the river, and launch the boat and fill it with the necessaries that he will secretly obtain from Black Hall. It is a business that will require considerable tact and discretion; or at least, great secretiveness and cautiousness," added Captain Pendleton.

"And these Joe, like all his race, possesses in excess," observed Lyon Berners.

"Are the guests all gone away from the house?" inquired Sybil.

"Nearly all. My sister remains there for the present to watch your interests, Mrs. Berners. The old Judge also, to superintend legal processes; but even he will go away in the morning, I think."

While they spoke, a loud sneeze and then a cough was

heard outside, and then Joe walked in, with a doubled up mattress on his head.

"This here is moving under difficulties, Master," he panted, as he laid the mattress down on the stone floor.

"How ever did you get that along the narrow path through the thicket, Joe?" inquired Sybil.

"You may well ax that, Missis. I had to lay it down endways, and drag it. Howsever, I has got all the things through the worst part of the way now, and they's all out in the churchyard," answered Joe, recovering his breath, and starting for the remaining goods.

He soon returned, bringing in a small assortment of bedding, clothing, and so forth. And in another trip he brought in a small supply of food and a few cooking utensils.

"That's all. And now, Miss Sybil, if you would only let me live here along o' you and Marse Lyon, and wait on to you bofe, I could make myself very much satisfied into my own mind," he said, as he laid down the last articles, and stood to rest himseif.

"But you know, Joe, that you can serve us better by remaining at Black Hall," said Sybil, kindly.

"Now, Marser Capping Pendelum, I hope them there fineries in the boxes, as you told me to bring away, for a blind from our place, won't take no harm along of being left out in the woods all night, for it was there underneaf of a pile of leaves and bushes as I was obligated for to leave them."

"They'll not take cold, at all events, Joe," said Captain Pendleton, good-naturedly.

By this time, the fire on the stone floor had become so low that it was quite dark in the chapel. But among the little necessities of life brought by Joe, was a small silver candlestick and a few slim wax candles. One of these was lighted, and gleamed faintly around, striking strangely upon the faces of the group gathered near the smouldering fire.

The friends sat and talked together, and arranged as far as they could their plans for future movements. It was not until near day that Captain Pendleton arose to depart, saying:

"Well, Berners, I do dislike to leave you and Mrs. Berners here alone again, especially as I fear that you will not go to sleep, as you ought to do. I see that Mrs. Berners' eyes are still wide open—"

"I slept so long in the afternoon," put in Sybil.

"But at all events, I am forced to leave you before light. It is not quite safe now to be seen in open daylight, traveling this road so often. To-night I will come again, and bring you further news, and perhaps more comfort Come, Joe."

Joe, who had fallen asleep over the fire, now slowly woke up and lifted himself from the floor.

The Captain shook hands with his friends, and followed by Joe, left the chapel.

Sybil then went and spread out the mattress, and put the pillows and covering upon it, and persuaded Lyon to lie down and try to sleep, as he had not slept for two nights past. She said that she herself could not sleep, but that she would sit close by him, so as to be ready to arouse him, on the slightest indication of danger.

Very reluctantly he yielded to her pleadings, and stretched himself upon the mattress. She went and gathered the smouldering coals and brands together, so that the fire might not go entirely out, and then she returned and sat down beside her husband.

He took her hand in his, and clasping it protectingly, he closed his eyes and fell asleep.

She sat watching the little fire, and brooding almost to insanity over the strange revolution that a few hours had made in her life, driving her so suddenly from her own hereditary manor-house, her home of wealth and honor and safety, out into the perilous wilderness, a fugitive from the law.

Yet not once did Sybil's imagination take in the extreme horror of her position. She thought that she had been brought away by her husband to be saved from the affront of an arrest, and the humiliation of a few days' imprisonment. That anything worse than this could happen to her, she never even dreamed. But even this to the pure, proud Sybil would have been almost insupportable mortification and misery. To escape all this she was almost willing to incur the charge of having fled from justice, and to endure the hardships of a fugitive's life.

FEARFUL WAITING. 219

"And oh! through all there was one consolation so great, that it was enough to compensate for all the wretchedness of her position. She was assured of her husband's love, beyond all possibility of future doubt. He was by her side, never to leave her more!

This was enough! She closed her hand around the beloved hand that held hers, and felt a strange peace and joy, even in the midst of her exile and danger.

Perhaps in this stillness she slumbered a while, for when she lifted her head, the chapel, that had been dark before, but for the gleaming of the little fire, was now dimly filled with the gray light of dawn.

She saw the shapes of the pointed windows against the background of heavy shadows and pale lights, and she knew that day was coming. She did not stir from the spot lest she should wake her husband, whose hand held hers. All was still in the chapel, so still that even the faint sweet sounds of wakening nature could be heard—the stirring of the partridge in her cover, the creeping of the squirrel from her hole, the murmur of the little brook, the rustle of the leaves, and, farther off, the deep thunder of the cascade, and the detonating echoes of the mountains.

Sybil sat motionless, and almost breathless, lest she should disturb her beloved sleeper. But the next moment she could scarcely forbear screaming aloud; for there passed along the wall before her a figure that, even in the dim light, she recognized as the strange visitant of the preceding day. It came from the direction of the altar, and glided past each of the four windows and vanished through the door. When Sybil had repressed her first impulse to scream, self-control was easy, so she sat quietly holding her husband's hand, though much amazed by what she had again seen.

Day broadened, and soon the rays of the rising sun, striking through the east windows, and lighting on the face of the sleeper, awoke him.

He looked into the face of his wife, and then along the walls of the chapel, with a bewildered expression of countenance. This had been his first sleep for two nights, and it had been so deep that he had utterly forgotten the terrible drama of the two last preceding days, and could not at once remember what had happened, or where he was.

But as he again turned and looked into Sybil's face, full memory of all flashed back upon him. But he did not allude to the past; he merely said to Sybil:

"You have not slept, love."

"I have not wished to do so," she answered.

"This is a very primitive sort of life we are living, love," he said, with a smile, as he arose from the mattress.

"But it is not at all an unhappy one," answered Sybil; "for, oh, since you are with me, I do not care much about anything else. Destiny may do what she pleases, so that she does not part us. I can bear exile, hunger, cold, fatigue, pain—anything but parting, Lyon!"

"Do not fear that, love; we will never part for a single day, if I can help it."

"Then let anything else come. I can bear it cheerfully," smiled Sybil. While they talked they were working also. Sybil was folding up the bedclothes, and Lyon was looking about for a bucket, to fetch water from the fountain. He soon found one, and want upon his errand.

Sybil followed him with two towels. They washed their hands and faces in the stream, and dried them on the towels. And then they went higher up the glen, and caught a bucketful of delightful water from the crystal spring that issued from the rocks.

They returned to the chapel, and together they made the fire and prepared the breakfast.

It was not until they were seated at their primitively arranged breakfast, which was laid upon the flagstones of the chapel floor—it was not, in fact, until they had nearly finished their simple meal, that Sybil told Lyon of the apparition she had seen in the early dawn, to come up as if from the floor to the right of the altar, and glide along the east wall of the chapel, past the four gothic windows, and disappear through the door.

"It was a morning dream, dear Sybil; nothing more," said Lyon, sententiously; for in the broad daylight he believed in nothing supernatural, even upon the evidence of his own senses.

"If that were a morning dream, then the sight that we saw together yesterday was but a dream, and you are but a dream, and life itself is but a dream," replied Sybil, earnestly.

"Well, at all events, what we have both, either separately or together, seen and experienced, must be something perfectly natural and commonplace, although we may not either of us be able to understand or explain it. My private opinion and worse misgiving is, that there is some woman concealed about the place. If ever I find myself in arm's length of that little gipsy, I shall intercept her, even at the risk of receiving such a spiritual-shock as that which struck Mrs. Alicia Dubarry to the ground," said Lyon facetiously, for he might well make a jest of this lighter affair of the chapel mystery to veil the deep anxiety he felt in the heavy matter of their affliction.

The husband and wife passed this second day of hiding tediously enough. She made the little housekeeping corner of the chapel tidy, by folding up and putting aside all their bedclothes and garments, and by washing and arranging their few cooking utensils. He brought in wood and brush, which he broke up and piled in another corner, to have it near at hand to replenish the fire. Also, he brought water from the spring; and then with no other instrument than his pocket-knife, he made a trap and set it to catch rabbits.

Then they rambled together through the wilderness around the chapel, and the better they grew acquainted with the wild neighborhood, the surer they felt of their safety in its profound solitude.

Their only anxiety connected with their security in this place, was upon the subject of the mysterious visitant. It was incomprehensible by any known law of nature.

They talked of this mystery. They reverted to all the so-called "authenticated ghost stories" that they had ever read or heard, and that they had hitherto set down to be either impostures or delusions.

But now here was a fact in their own experience that utterly confounded their judgment, and the end of their discussion on the subject left them just where they had been at its commencement. They resolved, however, to divulge the whole matter to Captain Pendleton, to whom they had not yet even hinted it, and to ask his counsel; and they looked forward with impatience to the evening visit of this devoted friend.

As it was growing cold towards the setting of the sun

they turned their steps again towards the chapel. It was quite dark when they reached it. Their fire had nearly gone out, but he replenished it, and she began to prepare the evening meal.

While she was still engaged in this work, the sound of approaching footsteps warned them that Captain Pendleton was near. Lyon Berners went out to meet him.

CHAPTER XXVIII.

A GHASTLY PROCESSION.

> If charnel-houses and our graves must send
> Those that we bury back, our monuments
> Shall be the maws of kites.—SHAKESPEARE.

"WELL?" exclaimed Mr. Berners, eagerly.

"Well, the flight is now discovered beyond all doubt. Search-warrants have been issued. *My* house is to be searched among the rest," replied Captain Pendleton.

"What else?"

"Arrangements are being made for the funeral of the dead woman. They will bury her the day after to-morrow in the churchyard at Blackville."

"And what else?"

"Nothing, but that I would not permit Joe to accompany me to-night. More precaution is now necessary to insure your safety."

"And that is all?"

"Yes."

"Then come in and see Sybil."

They went in together, where Mrs. Berners greeted Captain Pendleton with her usual courtesy, and then immediately repeated her anxious questions.

"Has the murderer been discovered? May we go home?"

"Not yet, dear Madam!" answered Pendleton to both questions, as he sat down by the fire.

"I have something to tell you, Pendleton, and to ask your advice about," began Lyon Berners. And he related the mysterious vision that had thrice crossed their path.

"Oh! it is a form of flesh and blood! We don't be-

A GHASTLY PROCESSION.

lieve in apparitions at this age of the world! But this indeed must be looked to! If you have seen her three times, of course she has seen you," said Captain Pendleton in much anxiety.

"Most certainly she knows of our presence here, if she knows nothing else about us," replied Mr. Berners.

"Then it is useless to attempt to conceal yourselves from her. She must be laid hold of, talked with, and won or bribed to keep our secret—to help us if possible. We must find out whether she will serve our purpose. If she will, it will all be quite right, and you may remain here until it is safe to depart; but if she will not, it will be all entirely wrong, and you must leave this place at all hazards," concluded Captain Pendleton.

"Yes, it is very well for you to talk of intercepting her, but you had just as well try to intercept a shadow as it glides past you," put in Sybil, with a wise nod.

"The attempt shall be made, at all events," determined Mr Berners.

Sybil was in the act of putting the supper—not on the table, for table there was none in the chapel—but on the cloth spread upon the flag-stones, when Captain Pendleton to give a lighter turn to their talk, said:

"You may put a plate for me also, Mrs. Berners! I have not yet supped, and I'm glad I have got here in time to join you."

"I am glad too! We are getting quite comfortably to housekeeping here, Captain. And Lyon has set his traps, and we shall soon have game to offer you when you come to visit us," replied Sybil quickly, responding to his gayety.

"If I had only a gun, and could venture to use it, it would be a great relief, and we should be very well supplied," smiled Lyon.

"Yes! if you had a gun, and should venture to use it, you would soon bring a *posse comitatus* down upon you; We will have no reverberations of that sort, if you please, Lyon," recommended the Captain.

And then they all sat down around the table-cloth, and Sybil poured out and served the coffee.

Now, whether they were very thirsty, or whether the coffee was unusually good, or whether both these causes combined to tempt them to excess, is not known; but it is certain that the two gentlemen were intemperate in their abuse of this fragrant beverage; which proves that people can be intemperate in other drinks, as well as in alcoholic liquors. This coffee also got into their heads. Their spirits rose; they grew gay, talkative, inspired, brilliant. Even Sybil, who took but one cup of coffee, caught the infection, and laughed and talked and enjoyed herself as if she were at a picnic, instead of being in hiding for her life or liberty.

In a word, some strange exhilaration, some wonderful intoxication pervaded the little party; but the most marvelous symptom of their case was, that they talked no nonsense—that while, under their adverse and perilous circumstances, such gayety was unnatural and irrational, yet their minds were clear and their utterances brilliant. And this abnormal exaltation of intellect and elevation of spirit continued for several hours, long into the night.

Then the great reaction came. First Sybil grew very quiet, though not in the least degree sad; Lyon Berners evinced a disposition rather to listen than to talk; and finally Captain Pendleton arose, and saying that this had been one of the strangest and pleasantest evenings he had ever passed in his life, took leave of his friends and departed.

Sybil was very sleepy, and as soon as their guest was gone she asked Lyon to help her with the mattress: that she was so drowsy she could scarcely move. He begged her to sit still, for that he himself would do all that was necessary. And with much good-will, but also much awkwardness, he spread the couch, and then went to tell Sybil it was ready. But he found her with her head upon her knees, apparently fast asleep. He lifted her gently in his arms, and carried her and laid her on the mattress. And then, feeling overcome with drowsiness, he threw himself down beside her, and fell into a profound sleep.

But Sybil, as she afterwards told, did not sleep so deeply. It seemed, indeed, less sleep than stupor that overcame her. She was conscious when her husband raised her up in his arms and laid her on the bed; but she was too utterly oppressed with stupor and weariness to lift her eyes to look, or open her lips to speak, or, even after he had laid her down, to move a limb from the position into which it fell.

So she lay like one dead, except in being clearly conscious of all that was going on around her. She knew when Lyon laid down, and when he went to sleep. And still she lay in that heavy state, which was at once a profound repose and a clear consciousness, for perhaps an hour longer, when suddenly the stillness of the scene was stirred by a sound so slight that it could only have been heard by one whose senses were, like hers at that time, preternaturally acute. The sound was of the slow, cautious turning of a door upon its hinges!

Without moving hand or foot, she just languidly lifted her eyelids, and looked around upon the dim darkness.

There was a faint glow from the smouldering fire on the flagstone floor, and there was a faint light from the starlit night coming through the windows. By the aid of these she saw, as in a dream, the door of the vault wide open!

In her profound state of conscious repose there was no fear of danger, and no wish to move. So, still as in a dream, she witnessed what followed.

First a dark, shrouded figure issued from the vault, and turned around and bent down towards it, as if speaking to some one within. But no word was heard. Then the figure backed a pace, drawing up from the steps of the vault what seemed to be a long narrow box. As this box came up, it was followed by another dark, shrouded figure, who supported its other end. And as the two mysterious apparitions now stood beside the altar, Sybil saw that the box that they held between them was a coffin!

" Nor was that all. While they moved a little down the side wall, they were follow by two other strange figures, issuing from the vault in the same order, and bearing between them, in the same manner, a second coffin; and as they, in their turn, filed down the side wall, they also were followed by still two others coming up out of the vault, and bringing with them a third coffin!

And then a ghastly procession formed against the side wall. Three long shadowy coffins borne by six dark shrouded figures, filed past the gothic windows, and disappeared through the open chapel door.

Sybil clearly saw all this, as in a nightmare from which she could not escape; she still lay motionless, speechless, and helpless, until she quite lost consciousness in a profound and dreamless sleep. So deep and heavy was this sleep, that she had no sense of existence for many hours. When at length she did awake, it seemed almost to a new life, so utterly, for a time, was all that had recently past forgotten. But as she arose and looked around, and collected her faculties, and remembered her position, she was astonished to see by the shining of the sun into the western windows, that it was late in the afternoon, and that they had slept nearly all day, for her husband was still sleeping heavily.

Then she remembered the horrible vision of the night, and she looked anxiously towards the door of the vault. It seemed fast as ever. She got up and went to look at it. It *was* fast, the bars firmly bedded in the solid masonry, as they had been before.

What then had been the vision? She shuddered to think of it. Her first impulse was now to arouse her husband and tell him what had happened. But her tenderness for him pleaded with her to forbear.

"He sleeps well, poor Lyon! let him sleep," she said, and she threw a shawl around her shoulders, and went out of the chapel to get a breath of the fresh morning air.

She had to pass among the gray old gravestones lying deep in the bright-colored dew-spangled brushwood. As she picked her way past them, she suddenly stopped and screamed.

Captain Pendleton was lying prostrate, like a dead man at the foot of an old tree!

With a strong effort of the will, she controlled herself sufficiently to enable her to approach and examine him. He was not dead, as she had at first supposed; but he was in a very death-like sleep.

She arose to her feet, and clasped her forehead with both hands while she tried to think. What could these things mean? The unnatural exhilaration of their little party on the previous evening; the powerful reaction that prostrated them all in heavy stupor or dreamless sleep, that had lasted some fifteen hours; the ghastly procession she had seen issue from the open door of the old vault, and march slowly down the east wall of the church, past all the gothic windows, and disappear through the front door; the spell that had so deeply bound her own faculties, that she had neither the power nor the will to call out; their visitor overtaken by sleep while on his way to mount his horse, and now lying prostrate among the gravestones? What could all these things mean?

She could not imagine.

However much she might have wished to spare her husband's rest up to this moment, she felt that she must arouse him now. She hurried back into the church, and went up to the little couch and looked at Lyon.

He was moving restlessly, and mutterly sadly in his sleep. And now she felt less reluctance to wake him from his troubled dream. She shook him gently, and called him.

He opened his eyes, gazed at her, arose up in a sitting posture, and stared around for a moment, and then seeing his wife, exclaimed:

'Oh! is it you, Sybil? What is this? the chapel seems to be turned around." And he gazed again at the western windows, where the sun was shining, and which he mistook for the eastern, supposing the time to be morning.

"The chapel has not turned around, Lyon; but the sun has. It is late in the afternoon, and that is the declining and not the rising sun that you see."

"Good gracious, Sybil! Have I slept so late as this? Why did you let me?"

"Because I slept myself; we all slept; even to Captain Pendleton, who must have been overpowered by sleep on his way to his horse; for I have just found him lying among the gravestones."

"What? Who? Pendleton asleep among the gravestones? Say that again. I don't understand."

Sybil briefly repeated her statement.

Lyon started up, shook himself as if to arouse all his faculties, and then went and douched his head and face with cold water, and finally, as he dried them, he turned to Sybil and said:

"What is all this that you tell me? Where is Pendleton? Come and show me."

Sybil led the way to the spot where their friend lay in his heavy sleep.

"Good Heaven! He must have fallen down, or sunk down here, within three minutes of leaving the church!" exclaimed Lyon Berners, gazing on the sleeper.

"Something must have happened to us all, dear Lyon. Do you remember how unreasonably gay we all were at supper last evening? We, too, who had every reason to be very grave and even sad? And do you remember the reaction? When we all grew so drowsy that we could hardly keep our eyes open? And then there was something else, which I will tell you of by and by. And now we have all slept fifteen or sixteen hours. Something strange has happened to us," said Sybil, slowly.

"Something has, indeed. But now we must arouse Pendleton. Good Heaven! he may have caught his death by sleeping out all night," exclaimed Mr. Berners, as he stooped down and shook the sleeper.

But it was not without difficulty that Lyon succeeded in arousing Captain Pendleton, who, when he was fairly upon his feet, reeled like a drunken man.

"Pendleton, Pendleton, wake up! What, man! what has happened to you?" exclaimed Lyon, trying to steady the other upon his feet.

"Too late for roll-call. Bad example to the rank and file," murmured the Captain, with some remnant of a camp-dream lingering in his mind.

Mr. Berners shook him roughly, while Sybil dipped up a double handful of water from a little spring at their feet, and threw it up into his face.

This fairly aroused him.

"Whew-ew! Phiz! What's that for? What the demon's all this? What's the matter?" he exclaimed, sneezing, coughing, and sputtering through the water that Sybil had flung into his face.

"What's all this?" exclaimed Lyon Berners, echoing his question. "It is that we are all robbed and murdered, and carried into captivity, for all I know," he added, smiling, as he could not fail to do, at the droll figure cut by his friend.

"How the deuce came I here?" demanded Pendleton, glaring around with his mouth and eyes wide open. "Is this enchantment?"

"Something very like it, Pendleton. But come, man,

A GHASTLY PROCESSION. 229

this is no laughing matter. It is very serious. Therefore rouse yourself and collect your faculties. You will need them all, I assure you," gravely replied Lyon Berners.

" But—how in thunder came I here? " again demanded the Captain, shivering and staring around him.

" We cannot tell. My wife found you here about half an hour ago. You are supposed to have been overcome by drowsiness, while on your way to your horse, and to have sunk down here and slept from that time to this—some sixteen hours."

" Good—! I remember taking leave of you both, after our lively supper of last evening, and starting for the thicket, and giving way just here to an irresistible feeling of drowsiness, and sinking down with the dreamy idea that I would not go to sleep, but would soon arise and pursue my journey. And I have lain here all night!" he exclaimed in astonishment.

" Yes, and all day !" added Lyon, solemnly.

" How is it that I was not awakened before?" demanded the Captain, with an injured look.

" Because we ourselves were in the same condition. It is not more than fifteen minutes since my wife awakened me."

" In the name of heaven, then, what has befallen us all?" demanded the Captain in amazement.

" That is what we must try to find out. You must help us. I have been thinking rapidly while standing here, and the result is, that I judge we have all been drugged with opium ; but whether by accident or with design, or if with design, by whom, or with what purpose, I cannot even imagine; though I do vaguely connect the fact with the mysterious visitant of the chapel," replied Mr. Berners.

While he spoke they all turned their steps towards the chapel. And with his concluding words, they entered it in company.

The " housekeeping corner " of the chapel was in a state of confusion very much at variance with the young housekeeper's fastidiously tidy habits.

The supper dishes lay upon the table-cloth on the floor, where they had been uncared for by the drugged and drowsy pair. And the little bed remained unmade, as it had been left by them when they ran out to look after Captain Pendleton.

Sybil saw all this at a glance, and with a flush; and forgetting for a moment everything else, she bade her husband and his guest stop where they were until she had put her " house " in order.

In this limited manner of domestic economy, it took Sybil but ten minutes to make the bed and wash the dishes. And, meanwhile, Lyon Berners made up the fire, and Clement Pendleton brought a pail of fresh water from the fountain.

Sybil began to prepare the breakfast, but none of the party felt like eating it.

" And that is another sign of opium! We have no appetite," observed Lyon Berners, as they sat down around the table-cloth; and instead of discussing the viands before them, they discussed the events of the preceding day and night.

Lyon Berners remembered that Sybil and himself had spent nearly the whole of the preceding afternoon in rambling through the woods; and he suggested as the only solution of the mystery that, during their absence some one had entered the chapel, and put opium in their food and drink.

" ' Some one ;' but whom ? " inquired Captain Pendleton, incredulously.

" Most probably the girl whom we have seen here," answered Mr. Berners.

" But for what purpose do you think she drugged your drink ? "

" To throw us into a deep sleep for many hours, which would enable her to come and go, to and from the chapel, undiscovered and unmolested."

" But why should she wish to come back and forth to such a dreary, empty old place as this ? "

" Ah! that I cannot tell; at that point conjecture is utterly baffled," answered Lyon.

" Yes; because conjecture has been pursuing a phantom —a phantome that vanishes upon being nearly approached. I cannot accept your theory of the mystery, Berners; and what is worse, I cannot substitute one of my own," said Captain Pendleton, shaking his head.

A GHASTLY PROCESSION. 231

"And now *I* have something to reveal," said Sybil, solemnly.

"Another morning dream?" inquired Lyon, while Pendleton looked up with interest.

"No; a reality—a ghastly, horrible reality," she answered.

And while both looked at her with strange, deep interest and curiosity, she related her sepulchral experiences of the night. When with pale cheeks and shuddering frame she described the six dark, shrouded forms that had come up out of the vault, bearing long shadowy coffins, which they carried in a slow procession down along the east wall, past the Gothic windows and out at the front door, her two listeners looked at her and then at each other, in amazement and incredulity.

"It was an opium dream," said Mr. Berners, in a positive manner.

"It would be useless, dear Lyon, for me to tell you that I was rather wider awake then than I am now, yet I really was," said Sybil, with equal assurance.

"And yet you did not lift hand or voice to call my attention to what was going on."

"I did not wish to do it; my will seemed palsied. I could only gaze at the awful procession and think how ghastly it was, and thinking so, I sank into a dreamless sleep, and knew no more until I woke up this afternoon."

"Meanwhile let us go and look at the door of the vault. You say the door was wide open?" inquired Captain Pendleton.

"Of course it was wide open: that is, wide open last night when those horrible forms came up out of the vault; but this morning it was fast enough," answered Sybil.

"Oh!" exclaimed Mr. Berners.

"I know what that 'oh!' means, Lyon. But I hope before we leave this chapel that you will find out that I can distinguish a dream from a dreadful reality," observed his wife.

Meanwhile they had reached the iron door of the vault. It was fast. Pendleton took hold of the iron bars and tried to shake it; but the bars were bedded in solid stone, and the door was immovable. Then he looked through the grating down into the depths below, but he only saw the top of the staircase, the bottom of which disappeared in the darkness.

"My dear Mrs. Berners," he then said, turning to Sybil, "I do not like to differ with a lady in a matter of her 'own experience,' but as we are in search of the truth, and the truth happens to be of the most vital importance to our safety, I feel constrained to assure you that this door, from its very appearance, assures us that it cannot have been opened within half a century, and that consequently your 'own experience' of the last night cannot have been a reality, but must have been a dream."

"I wish you could dream such a one, and then you would know something about it," answered Sybil.

"I think you will have to come to my theory about the opium," put in Mr. Berners, "especially as I have pursued my 'phantom' one stage farther in her flight, and am able to assign a possible motive for her secret visits to the chapel."

"Ah! do that, and we will think about agreeing with your views. Now then the motive," exclaimed Pendleton.

"A lover."

"Oh!"

"Yes, a lover. She comes here to meet him; and not liking eye-witnesses to the courtship, she drugged us," said Mr. Berners, triumphantly.

"That is the most violent and far-fetched theory of the mystery. Nothing but our desperate need of an elucidation could excuse its being put forward," said Captain Pendleton, drily. Then he spoke more earnestly: "Berners, whatever may be the true explanation of all that we have experienced here, one thing seems certain: that your retreat here is known to at least one person, who may or may not be inimical to your interests. Now my advice to you is still the same. Stop this girl the first time you see her again, and compel her to give an account of herself. Conceal your names and stations from her, if possible, and in any case bribe her to silence upon the subject of your abode here. If it were prudent, I should counsel you to leave this chapel for some other place of concealment; but really there seems now more danger of moving than in keeping still. So I reiterate my

A GHASTLY PROCESSION. 233

advice, that you shall enlist this strange girl in your interests."

"But before cooking your hare, you must catch it," said Sybil. "We may see this visitant a dozen times more, but we will never be able to stop her. She appears and vanishes! Is seen and gone in an instant! But, Captain Pendleton, I will tell you what I wish you to do for me."

"I will do anything in the world that you wish, except believe in ghosts."

"Then you will bring me a crowbar, or whatever the tool or tools may be with which strong doors may be forced. I want that grated iron door forced open, that we may go down into that vault and see what it holds."

"Good Heavens Mrs. Berners!" he exclaimed, striking a theatrical attitude.

> "'Would'st bid me burst
> The loathsome charnel-house, and
> Spread a pestilence?'"

"I want to see what is in it; and I *will*," persisted Sybil.

"Bring the tools when you come again, Pendleton, and we will open the door, and examine the vault," added Mr. Berners.

"Ugh! you will find it full of coffins and skeletons—

> "'And mair o' horrible and awfu'
> Whilk e'en to name wad be unlawfu'.'"

"You are in a poetical mood, Pendleton."

"And you are in a sepulchral one. Both effects of the opium, I suppose."

While they talked the sun went down.

Captain Pendleton remained with his friends until the twilight deepened into darkness; and then, promising to return the next night, and wondering where he should find his horse, or how he should get home, he took leave and departed.

The strange life of the refugees in the Haunted Chapel seriously interfered with their hitherto regular and healthful habits. They had slept nearly all day, when they should have been awake. And now they intended to watch all night, partly because it was impossible for them to sleep any more then, and partly because they wished to stop their mysterious visitant, in the event of her reappearance.

But the girl in the red cloak came not that night, no, nor even the next day; nor did any other mysterious visitor or unusual event disturb their repose, or excite their curiosity.

Late that night their faithful friend returned, according to his promise. He told them that he had found his poor horse still in the thicket where he had left him, with water and grass in his reach. That he had got home in safety, where his absence had not excited any anxiety, because his sister had supposed him to be at Black Hall.

He then described the funeral of Rosa Blondelle, which had taken place that day, and which had been attended not only by all the county gentry, who had gathered to show their respect and sympathy for the dead, but also by crowds of all sorts of people, who came in curiosity to the scene.

And then, taking advantage of a few minutes during which Sybil was engaged in her housekeeping corner of the chapel, he told Mr. Berners that the search-warrants having failed to find the fugitives, a rumor had been spread that they had certainly left the neighborhood on the morning of the murder, and that they had been seen at Alexandria, by a gentleman who had just come from that city.

"This story," added Captain Pendleton, "is so confidently reported and believed, that an officer with a warrant has been this day dispatched to Annapolis."

"Oh! good Heaven! How zealously her old neighbors do hunt my poor guiltless Sybil," groaned Mr Berners.

"Take courage! This rumor, together with the journey of the officer to Annapolis, opens a way for your immediate escape. So I propose that you prepare to leave this place to-morrow night, and take a bee line to Norfolk. There you must take the first outward bound ship for Europe, and remain abroad until you can with safety return home."

At this moment Sybil came up.

Without mentioning to her the existence of the warrants which were out against her, and which was the only part of Captain Pendleton's communication that it was expedient to conceal from her, Lyon Berners, with a smile of encouragement, told her that they were to leave the Haunted Chapel the next night, to go to Norfolk.

"And we cannot even yet go home?" sighed Sybil.

"No, dear wife; it would scarcely yet be prudent to do so. But we can go to Europe, and travel over the Continent, and see the wonders of the Old World, leaving our friend here with a power of attorney to manage our estate and collect our revenues, and remit us money as we require it. We can stay abroad and enjoy ourselves until such time as justice shall be done, and we can return to our home, not only with safety, but in triumph," replied Lyon Berners, cheerfully.

Sybil too caught the infection of his cheerful manner, whether that were real or assumed, and she too brightened up.

The friends then discussed the details of the projected flight.

"In the first place," began Captain Pendleton, "you must both be so well disguised as to seem the opposite of yourself in rank, age, and personal appearance. You, Lyon must shave off your auburn beard, and cut close your auburn hair, and you must put on a gray wig and a gray beard—those worn by your old Peter, in his character of Polonius at your mask ball, will, with a little trimming, serve your purpose. Then you must wear a pair of spectacles and a broad-brimmed hat and an old man's loose fitting, shabby traveling suit. I can procure both the spectacles and the clothes from the wardrobe of my deceased father. Mrs. Berners, too, should cut her hair short, and wear a red wig and a plain dress. The wig you wore as Harold the Saxon will suit very well, with a little arrangement. Then I can procure the dress from my sister. You must travel as a poor old farmer, and your wife must go as your red-headed illiterate daughter. You are both excellent actors, and can sustain your parts very well."

"Dear me!" said Sybil, half crying, half smiling; "I have been warned that it is never well to begin any enterprise of which one does not know the end. And I'm sure when I undertook to give a mask ball and take a character in it, I had not the slightest idea that the masquerade would last longer than a night, or that I should have to continue to act a character."

"Never mind, darling; it is but for a season. Go on, Pendleton. You seem to have settled everything in your own mind for us. Let us hear the rest of your plan," said Mr. Berners.

"It is this," continued the Captain. "I will bring these disguises to you to-morrow night. I will also have a covered cart, loaded with turnips, potatoes, apples, and so forth; I will have this cart driven by your faithful Joe down to the Blackville ferry-boat, in which of course he can cross the river, with his load of produce unsuspected and unquestioned."

"Or even if some inquisitive gossip should ask him where he might be going, Joe would be ready with his safe answer. He can beat us in baffling inquiry," put in Sybil.

"Like all his race," laughed Lyon.

"The chance you have mentioned is provided for. Joe is instructed to answer any haphazard questioner, that he is bringing the load to me, which will be the truth."

"But proceed, dear Pendleton. Develop your whole plan," urged Mr. Berners.

"Well, then, once safe on this side of the river, Joe will drive the cart to some convenient spot, to which I myself will guide you."

"Ah, how much trouble you take for us, Pendleton sighed Lyon.

"Not at all. As far as I am concerned, it is a piquant adventure. Try to look at it in that light. Well, to our subject. When you reach the cart you can put your wife inside, and then mount the driver's seat, and start upon your journey like a plain old farmer going to market to sell his produce. As you will have but the one pair of horses for the whole journey, you will see the necessity of making very short stages, in order to enable them to complete it."

"Certainly."

"And now listen! Because you must make these

A GHASTLY PROCESSION.

short stages and frequent stoppages, and because you must avoid the most traveled roads, it will be necessary for you to take a map of the State, and follow the most direct route to Norfolk."

"Which is not the turnpike road used by the mail stage-coaches, for that diverges frequently five or ten miles to the right or left of the line, to take in the populous villages," put in Lyon Berners.

"Yes; I see you comprehend me! Well, I should farther advise you, when you reach Norfolk, to put up at some obscure inn near the wharves, and to embark in the very first ship that sails for Europe, even if it should set sail within an hour after your arrival."

"You may rest assured that we shall not loiter in Norfolk," said Mr. Berners.

"As for the draught horses and cart, if you have time, you can sell them. If not, you can leave them at the livery stable, and on the day of sailing post me a letter containing an order to receive them."

"You can think of everything, dear Pendleton."

"I can't think of anything else just now," replied Captain Pendleton.

"Well, then, we will have some supper," said Sybil rising to prepare it.

"I declare, I never in all my life supped out so frequently as I have done since you two have been housekeeping in this old Haunted Chapel! And by the way, talking of that, have you seen any more apparitions? any more spectral gipsy girls? or shrouded forms? or shadowy coffins? or open vaults? eh, Mrs. Berners?" laughingly inquired Captain Pendleton.

"No, nothing unusual has disturbed us, either last night or to-day. But now, talking of open vaults, have you brought the crowbar to force the door, sir?" said Sybil, turning sharply to the Captain.

"Yes, dear, Mrs. Berners; since I promised to bring it, I felt bound to do so; though I hope you will not really have it put to use."

"Just as soon as supper is over, I will have that door forced open. I will see what that mysterious vault holds," said Sybil, firmly.

And she almost kept her word.

As soon as they had finished the evening meal, she arose and called upon the gentlemen to go with her and force the door of the vault.

And they went and inserted the crowbar between the grating and the stone work, and wrenched with all their united strength; but their efforts availed nothing, even to move the door.

They gave over their exertions to recover their breath, and when they had got it they began again with renewed vigor; but with no better success. Again they stopped to breathe, and again they re-commenced the task with all their might; but after working as hard as they could for fifteen minutes longer, they again ceased from sheer exhaustion, leaving the door as fast as they had found it.

"It is of no use to try longer, Sybil, We cannot force it," said Mr. Berners.

"I see that you cannot. The vault keeps its secrets well," she answered solemnly.

And then they returned to their seats near the fire and sat and talked over the projected journey until it was time for Captain Pendleton to go.

When the husband and wife were left alone, they felt themselves tired enough to go to rest, with a prospect of getting a good night's sleep.

"This is the last night that we shall spend in this place, dear Sybil," said Lyon Berners, as he put the smouldering brands together to keep the fire up till morning.

Sybil replied with a deep yawn.

And in a few minutes they laid down to rest, and in a very few more they fell asleep.

How long they had slept Sybil had no means of knowing, when she was awakened by an impression that some cold damp creature had laid down on the front of the mattress close beside her. She opened her eyes and strained them around in a vague dread, but the inside of the chapel was dark as pitch. The fire had gone entirely out; she could not even see the outlines of the Gothic windows; all was black as Tartarus. But still—oh, horror!—she felt the cold damp form pressing close beside her.

A spechless, breathless awe possessed her. She could

not scream, but she cautiously put out her hand to make sure whether she was dreaming, when—horror upon horror!—it touched a clammy face!

Still she did not cry out, for some potent spell seemed to bind her which at once tied her tongue and moved her hand; for that hand passed down over the slender form and straight limbs, and then up again, until it reached the still bosom, when—climax of horror!—it was caught and clasped in the clay-cold hand of the—WHAT?

CHAPTER XXIX.

GHOSTLY AND MYSTERIOUS.

On horror's head
Horrors accumulate.—TENNYSON.

An icy sweat of terror bathed Sybil's form. She tried to cry out, and did utter a low half-stifled scream. But the cold fingers of the ghastly creature closed tightly upon hers, and a thin, hollow voice murmured:

"Hush; don't you make a noise; don't be frightened. I can't hurt you. I'm chilled almost to death. And you were so warm. I crept to your side to tell you something. You are in hiding here, and so— *Ah-h-h!*"

The reed-like murmur ended in a terrific shriek. There was a silent movement, and Sybil felt the clammy form snatched up from her side and borne away in the darkness.

And then the spell that had bound her faculties was unloosed, and she uttered scream after scream as she shook and awakened her husband.

"In the name of Heaven, Sybil, what now?" he exclaimed, as he started up into a sitting posture.

"Oh, Lyon! for the love of mercy, get up! Get a light! I shall go mad in this horrible place!" she cried in a perfect frenzy of terror.

"Calm yourself, Sybil. There is nothing to fear. I am here with you. I will strike a light," answered Lyon Berners quietly, as he got up and groped about in the darkness for the tinder-box.

Striking a light in those days was not the quick and easy matter that it is now. When the tinder-box was at length found, the flint and steel had to be struck together until a spark was elicited to set fire to the tinder. So it was full five minutes from the time Lyon was awakened, to the moment that he lit the candle and looked upon the pale and horror-stricken face of his wife.

"Now then, Sybil, what is it?" he inquired.

"Oh, what is it! This place is full of devils!" she cried, shaking as with an ague fit.

"My dear wife!" he said, in surprise and concern to see her shudder so fearfully, to hear her speak so wildly.

"It *is*, I tell you, full of devils, Lyon!" she repeated with chattering teeth.

There chanced to be a little wine in their stores. He went and poured some into a glass and brought it to her and made her drink it.

"Now then, tell me what has thrown you into this state? What has happened to terrify you so much? another dream, vision, apparition? what?" he inquired, as he took from her hand the empty glass.

"Oh, no, no, no! no dream, no vision, nothing of that sort. It was too dark to see anything, you know; but oh! it was something so ghastly and horrible that I shall never, never get over it!" she exclaimed, while shudder after shudder shook her frame.

"Tell me," he said soothingly.

"Oh, it was a damp girl!" she cried.

"A damp girl!" he echoed in amazement and alarm; for he almost feared his dear wife was going crazy.

"Oh yes, a damp girl! A clay-cold, clammy, corpse-like form of a girl!"

"Where? when? what about her?"

"Oh, I woke up and felt her lying by my side; so close that she chilled and oppressed me! I put out my hand and she caught it in her deathly fingers! I screamed, but she spoke to me! She was about to tell me something, when she was suddenly snatched up and torn away!"

"My dear Sybil, this was nightmare again!"

"Oh, no, no, no! I have had nightmare, and know what it is! It is not like this! All this was real, as real as you and I! This place is full of devils!"

"My darling wife, have you lost your senses?"

"Oh, no; but I shall lose them if I stay in this demon-haunted place a day longer!"

"Thank Heaven! we will not have to stay here a day longer. We leave this coming evening. And see! the morning is dawning, Sybil; and with the coming of the light, all these shadows of darkness and phantoms of fear will flee away," said Lyon with a smile.

"Oh, you don't believe me. You never do believe me. But oh! let me tell you all about this ghastly thing, and then perhaps you will see that it is real," said Sybil.

And still in much agitation of spirits, she told him all the particulars of her strange visitation.

He still believed in his soul that she had been the victim of incubus, but he would not vex her by persisting in saying so. He only repeated that the morning was at hand, when all the terrors of the night would be dispersed; and added that they would not have to pass another night in the "demon-peopled place," as this would be the very last day of their stay.

As soon as it was light enough, they dressed themselves, and set about their simple daily work. He made the fire and brought the water; and she cleared up their housekeeping corner, and prepared the breakfast.

When the sun arose and streamed in at the east windows, lighting up every nook about the interior of the old chapel, they saw that everything remained in the same condition in which they had left it when they had gone to rest on the evening previous.

Lyon Berners felt more than ever convinced that his dear Sybil had been the victim of repeated nightmares; that all the seemingly supernatural phenomena of the Haunted Chapel had been only the creation of her own morbid imagination; that nothing connected with the mystery had been real, with the exception of the appearance of the girl in the red cloak, whom Mr. Berners decided to be an ordinary human habitué of the place.

But the idea of this visitor made him only the more anxious for Sybil's sake, to get away.

This last day of their sojourn in the Haunted Chapel was passed by the refugees in great impatience, but without any event worth recording.

With the night came their untiring friend Captain Pendleton, attended by Joe, who bore upon his broad back a large pack containing the disguises.

After the usual greetings, and while Sybil, with a woman's curiosity, was examining the contents of the pack which Joe opened and displayed before her, Pendleton found an opportunity of whispering to Lyon Berners:

"The false rumor is as rife as false rumors usually are. Every one reports with confidence, and every one else believes with assurance, that you are both in Annapolis, and will certainly be found by the officers within a few days. This is good, as it will lead off all pursuit from your road to Norfolk."

Lyon Berners nodded in reply. And Sybil came up to make some preparations for supper.

"Well, Mrs. Berners," spoke the Captain, gayly, "any more supernatural phenomena?"

"Oh, I wish you had not asked that question!" exclaimed Lyon Berners, while Sybil grew deadly pale, and shivered from head to foot.

"Why, what's the matter now?" demanded the Captain, lifting his eyebrows in surprise.

"Oh, the damp girl!" exclaimed Sybil shuddering.

"The damp girl!" echoed the Captain, in growing wonder.

Lyon Berners shrugged his shoulders, while Sybil, in agitated tones, recounted her strange visitation of the night before.

"As clearly defined a case of incubus as ever I heard in my life," was the prompt decision of Captain Pendleton.

Sybil grew angry.

"I only wish," she sharply answered, "that you would once experience the like, for then you could know that it could not be nightmare."

"Then, my dear Mrs. Berners, if this was not incubus, what do you suppose it to have been?"

"A *real* visitation; but whether a natural or supernatural one, of course I cannot tell," she answered.

Sybil got the supper ready, and they all sat down to partake of that meal together, for the last time in the Haunted Chapel.

After supper the final preparations for their departure were made.

Sybil felt all the reluctance of a beauty to part with her splendid black hair. But on trying the experiment, she found that she could effectually conceal it without cutting it off. She combed it straight back from her forehead, and let it hang down her shoulders under her sack. Then she covered her head and neck with the flowing red locks of Harold's wig.

Lyon cut close his auburn hair, shaved off his moustache, and donned a gray wig and a gray beard, without the slightest remorse.

A very few minutes sufficed to complete their disguise, and they stood forth—Lyon and Sybil transformed into a gray old farmer and a shock-headed country girl.

"And now, about these housekeeping articles that we must leave here? They are of very little value in themselves; but they *may* be found, and if so, may lead to our discovery," suggested Mr. Berners, uneasily.

"Never you mind *them*, Master. I'll undertake to get them away, onbeknowst to anybody, sar," promised Joe.

"And I will see that this is done," added Captain Pendleton in a low voice, for he did not wish to wound poor Joe's sensitive self-love.

"And now, my dear Sybil, are you sure you have got all that you need in your bag?" inquired Mr. Berners.

"All that I shall need until we get to Norfolk, Lyon. There, indeed, we must get a supply of necessary clothing," she answered.

"That of course. And by the way, have you the money and jewels safe?"

"All secure."

"Oh, Lyon! I brought this for you, and I had better give it to you at once, lest I should forget it," put in Captain Pendleton, passing over to Mr. Berners a large roll of gold coins.

"But my dear Pendleton——"

"Oh, nonsense! take them. I can reimburse myself from the revenues of Black Hall. Am I not to have the freedom of that fine estate?"

"Very true," answered Mr. Berners, pocketing the money.

"And now, are we ready?" inquired the Captain.

"Quite," answered Mr. and Mrs. Berners at once.

"Then let us start at once," advised the Captain, setting the example by taking up Sybil's large traveling bag.

Lyon Berners carried his portmanteau on one arm, while he gave his other to his wife.

Joe loaded himself with a great basket filled with provisions for the journey.

And together they all set forth from the Haunted Chapel. It was a clear cold, starlight night. The gravestones in the old churchyard glimmered gray among the brushwood, as the fugitives picked their way through it

When they reached the narrow path leading through the thicket, they had to walk in single file until they emerged from the wood and found themselves upon the old road running along the river bank. Here the wagon with a pair of draught horses was waiting them.

Their luggage was put in on top of bags of potatoes, turnips, etc., with which the back part of the wagon was loaded. Then Captain Pendleton assisted Sybil to mount to a seat made by a low-backed chair with a woolen counterpane thrown over it. Lyon Berners got up into the driver's place. All being now ready for the start, Captain Pendleton and Joe came up to the side of the wagon to bid farewell to the travelers.

"Heaven bless you, Pendleton, for your faithful friendship and zealous labors in our behalf," said Mr. Berners, warmly shaking the Captain's hand.

"Amen, and Amen! We shall never forget, and never cease to thank and bless you, dear friend," added Sybil, with tears in her eyes, as she gave him her hand.

"May the Lord grant you a safe journey and a quick return," said Clement Pendleton, as he pressed the lady's hand and relinquished it.

"And I sez Amen to that! Oh, Marser! Oh, Missus! come back to your poor old Joe soon! His heart will snap into ten thousand flinders, if you don't!" sobbed the poor negro, as he shook hands with his young master and mistress.

Then with a mutual "God be with you," the four friends parted.

Captain Pendleton, sighing, and Joe, weeping, bent their steps up the banks of the river towards the fording place, where they would have to cross to find their horses on the other side.

Lyon Berners cracked his long wagoner's whip, and started on the road leading away from the river towards the east.

It was yet early in the autumn night, and but for the cause of the journey, the young pair would have enjoyed it very much.

"It is a very pleasant evening for the season," said Lyon, cheerfully looking up at the clear, blue-black, star-spangled sky.

"Yes, indeed," answered Sybil briskly.

"Are you quite comfortable, darling?"

"Very! Captain Pendleton, dear Captain Pendleton, arranged my seat so nicely. It is so soft and easy. I could go to sleep here, if I were sleepy."

"You may have to sleep there, dear. We must travel all night, in order to get a good distance from this neighborhood before morning."

"I can bear that very well, as comfortably as I am placed. But you, dear Lyon, you who are driving, you will be tired to death."

"Not at all. My work to-night will not be more than many men frequently undertake for mere amusement."

"And the horses?"

"Strong draught horses like these can work eight or ten hours at a stretch, if they are well fed and rested between times."

"Oh! I'm so glad I have got away from the Haunted Chapel and the ghosts!" suddenly exclaimed Sybil.

"And especially from the 'damp girl,'" laughed Lyon Berners.

"Oh, don't mention her!" shuddered Sybil.

They were now entering one of those frequent mountain passes that diversified their road, and the care of driving required all Lyon's attention.

They traveled all night as nearly in a direct line towards the far distant city as the nature of the ground would permit. At daylight they found themselves in the midst of a deep forest, some twenty miles east of

Blackville. Here, as the road was naturally broad and the trees tall and sparse, and especially as a clear stream of water ran along on one side, the travelers decided to stop and rest, and refresh themselves and their horses until noon.

Lyon Berners got out and, followed by Sybil, went a littie way into the woods, where they found a small opening and a spring of clear water.

Here Lyon gathered brushwood and made a fire, while Sybil returned to the wagon and brought back a basket of provisions. Among them was a bottle of coffee already made, and which she turned into a tin basin and set on the fire to be warmed.

When they had given their horses time enough to rest they resumed their journey, still traveling towards the east.

Lyon consulted his map and his pocket compass, and found that directly in their line lay the small village of Oakville, nestled in an unfrequented pass of the mountains.

"We can reach the place at about ten o'clock this evening, and there we can get a regular supper and good sleep," he said to his wife.

And they traveled all the remainder of that day, and at about half-past nine they arrived at Oakville. The village was off the public road, and consisted only of a sleepy old tavern, to which the neighboring farmers came to drink, smoke, and gossip; a post-office, to which the mail was brought once a week by a boy on horseback; and a blacksmith shop, patronized by the sparse populatain of the immediate neighborhood.

Up before the stable of this old tavern Lyon Berners drove his wagon; and here he alighted, handed out Sybil, and led her over to the house and into the public parlor.

A fat and lazy-looking hostess came to look at them.

"I want accommodations for myself, my girl here, and my horses and wagon, which I left in the stable yard," said Mr. Berners, speaking coarsely, with two lumps of liquorice in his mouth, which he had taken to disguise his voice.

"And what might your name be, farmer?" inquired the landlady.

"My name's Howe," answered Lyon, truly, giving his own patronymic, now his middle name.

"Well, farmer, I reckon we can accommodate you. Going to market?"

"Yes, we're on our way to market."

"You come from far?"

"From the other side of the mountain."

"Well, I reckon we can accommodate you. You must excuse me asking you so many questions; but the truth is you're a perfect stranger to me, and it is very late for you to come here, you know; which I wouldn't think so much of that nyther, only since that horrid murder at Black Hall I have mistrusted every stranger I see."

Sybil's heart gave a bound, and then sank like lead in her bosom, at hearing this allusion. Lyon also felt an increased uneasiness. Luckily they were sitting with their backs to the light, so that the gossiping landlady could not read the expression of their faces, which indeed she was too much absorbed in her subject to attempt to do. So she went straight on without stopping to take breath:

"Not that I mistrust you now, sir, which I see exactly what you are; and which likewise your having of your darter with you is a rickymindation; for men don't go about a taking of their darters with them when they are up to robbery and murder, do they now, sir?"

"I should judge not, though I am not familiar enough with the habits of such gentry to give a decided opinion," said Farmer Howe.

"You'll excuse me, sir; but I'm a lone widow living here, and not used to seeing much of anybody but my old neighbors, which come occasionally to enjoy of themselves; and I do mistrust most strangers—though not you, sir, with your darter, as I said before—but most other strangers, because they *do* say hereabouts that it was a stranger to the place, a red-headed man, as put up at the inn at Blackville that night, and never was seen afterwards, as did that murder at Black Hall."

"Ah! do they say that? I thought they laid it on a lady," observed Farmer Howe.

"La, sir! the idee of a lady doing such a thing! and a rale high-born lady of quality like Mrs. Burns, or whatever her name was, and doing of it to one she had took in for charity too, 'tan't likely, sir."

"But you know, I suppose, that they did accuse a lady?"

"Oh, yes; I know they did, and that the poor lady had to run away and go to Annapolis. But that was that Blackville set, that an't got no sense; but as for us, over this side, *we* believe it was that red-headed stranger as did it."

"There's no doubt of it in the world," said Farmer Howe, recklessly, feeling that he was expected to say something.

And at this moment he looked towards Sybil, and saw that she could not endure the subject of discussion for one moment longer, so he turned to the landlady, and said:

"We have traveled some distance, and feel very tired and hungry. Would you oblige us with supper as soon as possible? We do not need much, only let it be nice and warm."

"Surely, sir, it is late; but we will do the best we can for you," said the landlady, hurrying away.

Mr. Berners stooped to whisper to his wife.

"Sybil, darling, I hail this woman's faith as a good omen. Keep up your courage, and—remain in that shady corner until I come back. I am going out to the stable to see that our horses are properly attended to."

And then Lyon left the room.

By the time he returned a table was set in that parlor, and a good supper spread for the travelers.

When it was over, the landlady showed them to a couple of communicating rooms up-stairs, where they passed a very comfortable night.

At daybreak the next morning they arose and breakfasted, and resumed their journey.

Lyon Berners again consulted his map of the State and his pocket compass, and laid out his road. It lay for all that day up and down, in and out, among the wildest passes of the Alleghany Mountains. At noon they stopped for an hour, to rest and refresh themselves and their horses, and then again went forward. At night they reached another hamlet at the foot of the mountain range. They put up at this hamlet, which was called Dunville, and which boasted one tavern kept by an old Revolutionary pensioner called Purley.

Here also Lyon Berners gave his name as Howe, and here again he and his wife were destined to be told all about the murder.

"You see, sir, a little below us there, on the other side of the mountain, they do say as the murder was done by the woman's husband, as she had run away from; but they are a set of poor ignorant folks out there! Now it stand to reason, sir, it couldn't have been done by him, and it must have been done by some member of that band of burglars that they say is lurking somewhere there-away by Black Hall."

"Band of burglars!" echoed Farmer Howe, in astonishment. And he was almost about to betray himself by saying that there could be no such band there, when he recollected his position, and held his tongue.

Farmer Howe and his daughter spent a refreshing night at old Purley's tavern at Dunville, and at daybreak next morning, after a very early breakfast, they resumed their journey.

And again, as usual, Lyon Berners consulted his map and his compass. He now found that his most direct route lay through a thick forest, between two mountain ridges.

They traveled all the morning, and as usual stopped at noon for rest and food for themselves and their four-footed friends. In the afternoon they set forth again, and traveled until they reached Iceville, a considerable village situated high up on one of the table-lands of the Blue Ridge. In this town there were three taverns. Farmer Howe and his daughter put up at the most humble of the trio. And here too the talk of the hour was the homicide at Black Hall.

"They say about here that it was one of the lady's admirers who killed her in a fit of desperation from love and jealousy; for the lady was well beknown to be a great coquette, said one village authority to another, in the presence of Farmer Howe.

When our travelers found themselves alone that night, in one of the two small adjoining rooms that had been assigned to them, Lyon Berners turned to Sybil, and said:

"You see, my dear Sybil, how it is; 'A prophet hath honor except in his own city.' No one out of the Black Valley thinks of accusing you."

"All the world might accuse me, so that my own old friends and neighbors would justify me," said Sybil, sadly.

They passed another night in peace, and the next morning, at daybreak as usual, they breakfasted, and then set out on their fourth and last day's journey.

Again the map and the pocket compass was called into requisition, and Mr. Berners laid out their route for the day.

Their way lay all that forenoon through the beautifully undulating, heavily wooded, and well-watered country lying east of the Blue Ridge.

As before, they broke their journey by an hour's repose at noon, and then recommenced it. And at twelve, midnight, they arrived safely at Norfolk.

CHAPTER XXX.

FLIGHT AND PURSUIT.

Oh, death were welcome!—COLERRIDGE.

ON reaching Norfolk, Lyon Berners drove at once at an obscure tavern down by the wharves, and near the market. Here he found good stabling for his horses and wagon, and decent accommodation for himself and wife.

"Come to market, I reckon, farmer?" suggested the landlord, taking the stump of an old pipe from his mouth for the purpose.

"Yes," answered Lyon Berners, as "Farmer Howe," taking off his broad-brimmed hat, handing it to Sybil, and then sinking slowly and heavily into a chair, like a very weary old man.

"Your daughter, I reckon, farmer?" continued the landlord, pointing to Sybil with the stem of his pipe.

"My only girl," answered Lyon Berners, evasively.

"And no boys?" inquired the landlord.

"No boys," replied Lyon.

"That's a pity; on a farm too. But you must try to get a good husband for the girl, and that will be all one as a boy of your own! Never had any children but this, farmer, or did you have the misfortune to lose 'em?"

"I never had but this one girl," answered Lyon Berners, still evasively.

"Then you must be very fond of that girl, I reckon."

"She is all the world to me," said Lyon, truly.

"Then he ought to be all the world to you, honey."

"And so I am," said Lyon, answering for Sybil, whom he could not yet trust to act a part; though he saw, the instant he glanced at her, that he might have done so; for Sybil, as soon as she saw attention drawn to herself, began to turn her head down upon one shoulder and simper shyly like an awkward rustic.

"You must excuse *me* for asking so many questions, farmer; but when I see a father and daughter together, like you and your girl, I think of myself, for I have an only daughter of my own. All the rest of my children—and I had a whole passel of boys and girls—are with their dear mother in heaven. So you see, farmer, I am a widower, with one gal like yourself—for I reckon, from what you said you are a widower?"

"My girl's mother has been dead many years," answered Lyon, with a drawl and a sigh.

"Pappy, I'm so hungry and so sleepy I don't know what to do," said Sybil, in a low, fretful tone, frowning and pouting.

"Yes, yes, honey; I reckon you are, sure enough. So landlord, if you have got a couple of little rooms joining onto each other, I wish you'd let us have 'em. And we'd like a bit of supper besides," said Lyon Berners, with a sigh and a grunt.

"To be sure. I'll go and call my girl directly, and she'll walk up to your rooms while I have the supper got ready. Where would you like to have it? down here, or in your room?"

"In your room, Pappy. I hate a place like this a smellin' of liquor and inyuns and things, and men coming in and out," said Sybil, digging her elbow into her "Pappy's" ribs, and turning up her nose at the little tavern sitting-room.

"Well, then, honey, we'll have it up there. Up there, landlord, if it won't be putting of you to too much trouble."

"Oh, not at all, farmer; it's all one to me. Now I'll go and call Rachel."

And the inquisitive and communicative host went out, and soon returned with a young woman of about Sybil's own age.

"This is my daughter, my Rachel, as I was telling you about, farmer. Rachel, honey, you just go, long of the farmer and his daughter and show them where they've got to sleep, that's a good girl. Put 'em in the two little rooms over the bar, you know."

"Yes, father. Come, sir; come, miss," said the landlord's daughter, leading the way from the smoky parlor.

Lyon and Sybil followed her. Lyon walking slowly like a weary old man, and pausing at the head of the stairs, as if to recover his wind.

"Pappy, you look tired to death," said Sybil, in a rough sympathetic voice.

"Ay, ay; it is weary work for an old man to get upstairs," grunted Lyon.

"The stairs are very steep, but here you are," said the landlord's daughter, opening the door leading into two little communicating rooms.

She entered, followed by Sybil and Lyon. She set the candle down on the top of the old chest of drawers, and turned around. And then the travelers noticed, for the first time, how beautiful the daughter of their host was.

Rachel's face was of the purest type of beauty, combining the physical, intellectual, and spiritual. Her form was of medium height and perfect grace; her head was finely shaped, and covered with dark brown hair, parted in the middle and carried over the temples, and arranged in a knot behind; her forehead broad and full; her eyebrows were gently arched, her eyes dark, luminous gray, with drooping lids and long fringes; her nose small and straight, her lips full, small, and plump, and her chin was round and well set. There were some flaws in this otherwise perfect beauty and grace of form and face; for her complexion was very pale, her expression pensive, and her walk slightly limping.

While Sybil was observing her with both admiration and pity, and wondering whether she did not suffer from some hereditary malady that had carried off her mother and all her sisters and brothers, Rachel spoke:

"I think you have everything here that you require; but if you should need anything else, please call, and I will come and attend to your wants."

"Thanks!" answered Sybil, sweetly, forgetting her assumed character, and beginning to speak in her natural voice, for it seemed so difficult to act a part in the presence of this girl.

But Lyon set his coarse boot upon Sybil's foot, and pressed it as a warning, and then answered for both, saying:

"Thank y', honey, but I don't reckon we'll want anything but our supper, and the old man said how he'd send that up here himself."

"Then I will leave you. Good night. I hope you will have a good sleep," answered Rachel, bending her head.

"What a fine face that girl has," said Lyon Berners, as she withdrew.

"Yes; and what a sweet voice!" answered Sybil.

"But she is very pale, and she limps as she walks; did you notice?"

"Yes; I suppose she has ill health—probably the same malady that carried off her mother, and all her sisters and brothers."

"Very likely."

"Consumption?" suggested Sybil.

"Scrofula," sententiously replied Lyon.

"Oh, what a pity!" said Sybil, when their conversation was cut short by the entrance of the landlord, bringing a waiter with the plain supper service and a folded tablecloth, and followed by a young man bearing another waiter piled up with materials for a supper more substantial than delicate.

The little table was quickly set, and the meal arranged, and then the landlord, after asking if anything more was wanted, and being told there was not, left the room, followed by his attendant.

Lyon and Sybil made a good supper, and then, as there were no bells in that primitive house of entertainment, he put his head out of the door and called for some one to come and take away the service.

When the waiter had cleared the table, and the travelers were again left alone, Lyon said to Sybil:

"I must leave you here, dear, while I go down to the water-side and inquire what ships are about to sail for Europe. You will not be afraid to stay here by yourself?"

"Oh, no indeed! this is not the Haunted Chapel, thank Heaven!" answered his wife.

"Nor Rachel, the damp girl," added Lyon.

"No, poor child, but she may very soon become one," sighed Sybil.

And Lyon put on his broad-brimmed hat and went out.

Sybil locked the door, took off her red coarse outer garment, and took from her traveling bag a soft woolen wrapper and a pair of slippers and put them on, and sat down before the fire to make herself comfortable. At first the sense of relief and rest and warmth was enough to satisfy her; but after an hour's waiting in idleness, the time hung heavily on her hands, and she grew homesick and lonesome. She thought of the well-stocked library of Black Hall; of her bright drawing-room, her birds, her flowers, her piano, her easel, her embroidery frame, her Skie terrier, her tortoise shell cat and kittens, her fond and faithful servant, the many grand rooms in the old hall; the negroes' cabins, the ancient trees, the river, the cascade, the mountains—the thousand means of occupation, amusement, and interest, within and around her patrimonial home, the ten thousand ties of association and affection that bound her to her old place, and she realized her exile as she had never done before. Her spirit grew very desolate, and her heart very heavy.

But Sybil really was not a woman to give way to any weakness without an effort. She got up and tried to engage herself by examining the two little rooms that were to be her dwelling-place for a day or a week, as chance might direct.

There was not much to interest her. The furniture was poor and old, but neat and clean, as anything under the care of pale Rachel was sure to be. Then Sybil looked about to try to find some stray pamphlet or book, that

FLIGHT AND PURSUIT.

she might read. But she found nothing but a treatise on tanning and an old almanac until, happening to look behind the glass on the chest of drawers in the inner room, she discovered a small volume which she took to be the New Testament. She drew it from its hiding-place and sat down to read it. But when she opened the book, she found it to be—" Celebrated Criminal Trials."

At once it seemed to have a fearful interest for her, and this interest was terribly augmented when, on further examination, she discovered that a portion of the work was devoted to the " Fatal Errors of Circumstantial Evidence."

To this part of the book she turned at once, and her attention soon became absorbed in its subject. Here she read the cases of Jonathan Bradford, Henry Jennings, and many others tried for murder, convicted under an overwhelming weight of circumstantial evidence, executed, and long afterwards discovered to be entirely innocent of the crimes for which they had been put to death. Sybil read on hour after hour. And as this evening, while sitting in solitude and idleness and thinking of her home and all its charms, she had first realized the bitterness of her exile, so now, in reading these instances of the fatal effects of circumstantial evidence upon guiltless parties, she also first realized the horrors of her own position.

She closed the book and fell upon her knees, and weeping, prayed for pardon of those fierce outbursts of hereditary passion, that had so often tempted her to deeds of violence, and that now subjected her to the dread charge of crime. Yes, she prayed for forgiveness of this sin and deliverance from this sinfulness, even before she ventured to pray for a safe issue out of all her troubles.

Relieved, as every one feels who approaches our Father in simplicity and faith, she arose from her knees, and sat down again before the fire to wait for the return of her husband.

He came at length, looking really tired now, but speaking cheerfully as he entered the room.

"I have been gone from you a long time, dear Sybil, but I could not help it. I had to go to Portsmouth in search of our ship," he said, as he put his hat on the floor, and set down at the fire.

"Then you found a ship?" she inquired, with so much

more than usual anxiety in her expression, that he looked up in painful surprise as he replied to her question.

"Yes, dear; I have found a ship that will suit us. It is the 'Enterprise,' Captain Wright, bound for Liverpool within a few days."

"Oh! I wish it were to-morrow," sighed Sybil.

"Why, love, what is the matter?" tenderly inquired her husband, taking her hand, and looking into her face

"*That* is the matter," replied Sybil, with a shudder, as she took the volume she had been reading from the chimney piece and put it in his hands.

It was a work with which Lyon Berners, as a law student, had been very familiar.

"Why, where did you get this?" he inquired in a tone of annoyance, for he felt at once what its effect upon Sybil's mind must be.

"Oh, I found it behind the looking-glass in the other room."

"Left by some traveler, I suppose. I am sorry, Sybil, that you have chanced upon this work; but you must not let its subject influence you to despondency."

"Oh, Lyon! how can I help it? I was so strong and cheerful in my sense of innocence, I had no idea how guiltless people could be convicted and executed as criminals."

"My darling Sybil, all these cases that you have read were tried in the last century, a period of judicial barbarism. Courts of justice are more enlightened and humane now, in our times. They do not sacrifice sacred life upon slight grounds. Come, take courage! be cheerful! trust in God, and all will be well."

"I do trust in the Lord, and I know all will be well; but oh! I wish it were to-morrow that ship is to sail!" answered Sybil.

"It will sail very soon, dear. And now we had better go to rest, and try to get some sleep. In my character of market farmer, I have to be up very early in the morning to attend to my business, you know," said Lyon with a smile.

Sybil acquiesced, and the fugitive couple retired for the night.

Bodily fatigue so much overcame mental anxiety, that

they slept profoundly, and continued to sleep until near daylight, when they were both aroused by a loud knocking at the door.

"Oh, for Heaven's sake, who is that?" gasped Sybil, starting up in affright, for every knock now, scared her with the thought of sheriff's officers armed with a warrant for her arrest, and excited a whole train of prospective horrors.

"Hush, darling, hush; it is only one of the men about the place waking me up, according to orders, to be in time for the market. We must keep up our assumed characters, my dear Sybil," said Mr. Berners, as the knocking was repeated, accompanied by the calls of,

"Farmer! farmer!"

"Aye, aye! I hear you. You needn't batter down the doors. I'm a-going to get up, though it's very early, and I an't as young as I used to be twenty years ago, nyther," grumbled the "farmer," as with many a grunt and sigh, as of an old and weary man, he got up and began to dress himself.

"Sybil," he whispered to his wife before leaving the room, "I shall have to take my breakfast at a stall in the market-house, and I shall not be back until the market is out, which will be about twelve o'clock. You can have your breakfast brought up here. And mind, my darling, don't forget to put on your wig, and keep up your character."

"I shall be very careful, dear Lyon," she answered, as he kissed and left her.

Lyon Berners went down-stairs, where he found the landlord, who was an "early bird," waiting for him.

"'Morning, farmer. What is it that you've brought to market, anyways?" he said, greeting his guest.

"Mostly garden truck," answered Lyon.

"No poultry, eggs, nor butter?"

"No."

"'Cause, if you had, I might deal with you myself."

"Well, you see, landlord, them kind of produce is ill convenient to bring a long ways in a wagon. And I came from a good ways down the country," explained Lyon, as he took his long leathern whip from the corner where he had left it, and went out to look after his team.

He found it all right, and he mounted the seat and drove to the market space, and took a stand, and began to offer his produce as zealously as any farmer on the ground—taking care, in the mean time, to wear his spectacles and broad-trimmed hat, and to keep up his character in voice and manner; and, as the morning advanced, he began to drive a brisk business.

Meantime Sybil, left alone in her poor room at the little inn, arose and locked the door after Lyon, to prevent intrusion before she should effect her disguise, and when she had thus insured her privacy, she began to dress.

As soon as she had transformed herself, she opened the door and called for Rachel.

The landlord's daughter entered, giving her guest good morning, and kindly inquiring how she had slept.

"I slept like a top! But I'm not well this morning neither. So I'd just like to have my victuals sent up here," answered Sybil.

"Very well; what would you like?"

"Fried fish, and pork-steaks, and bri'led chickings, and grilled bacon, and—let me see! Have you any oysters?"

"Yes, very fine ones."

"Well, then, I'll take some stewed oysters too, and some poached eggs, and preserved quinces, and fried potatoes, and corn pone, and hot rolls, and buckwheat cakes, and cold bread and butter, and some coffee, and buttermilk and sweet milk. And that's all, I believe; for, you see, I an't well, and I haven't come to my stomach yet; but if I can think of anything else, I will let you know.

"Is your father going to eat his breakfast with you?"

"Who? pappy? No; he's gone to market, and will get his victuals at the eating stall. Wouldn't it be good fun to keep a eating stall in a market?"

"I don't think so."

"Well, never mind whether you do, or not. Hurry up with my victuals."

"Yes; but I'm afraid we haven't got all the things you want; but I will bring you up what we have," said the girl, who had opened her eyes widely at the bill of fare ordered by her sickly guest.

FLIGHT AND PURSUIT. 259

"Well, go do it then, and don't stop to talk," said Sybil, shortly.

Rachel went out, and in due time returned with a waiter containing Sybil's breakfast.

"Why, there an't half—no, not a quarter of the things I told you to fetch me," said Sybil, turning up her nose at the waiter that Rachel placed upon the table.

"I have brought you some of everything that we have cooked. I should be glad if I could bring you all you wish," replied Rachel.

"Then I s'pose I must be half-starved in this poor place. And me so weakly, too! I'll tell pappy as soon as ever he comes. I want to go home—I do. We've got as much as ever we can eat at home," grumbled Sybil, doing her best to act her part, and perhaps overdoing it.

But Rachel was not suspicious. She again apologized for not being able to fill her guest's order in its utmost extent, and she remained in the room and waited on Sybil until the breakfast was finished, and then she took away the service, wondering how little her guest had eaten, after having ordered such a vast amount of food.

Again Rachel came back to the room, and made everything tidy in each chamber, and then finally left her guest alone.

Sybil walked about and took up and put down every small object that lay about her humble apartments, and then looked out of each window upon the narrow crowded and noisy street below; and finally, she took the volume of "Celebrated Criminal Trials" that had a terrible attraction for her, in her present circumstances, and she sat down and read until her husband's return.

Lyon Berners drove his empty wagon into the stable yard, at noon. He had sold out all his produce, and pretended to be in great glee at his success. The landlord congratulated him, and some chance loungers in the barroom suggested that, under such circumstances, it would be the right thing for him to treat the company. Lyon thought so too; and in his character of farmer, he ordered pipes and glasses all around. And then he made his escape, and went up-stairs to see Sybil.

"Still moping over that depressing book. Put it away, Sybil, and get on your bonnet, and throw a thick veil over it, and come out with me for a walk; we have to buy something for our voyage, you know," said Lyon, cheerfully.

Sybil with a sigh given to her fears, did as he requested her to do; and the two went downstairs together.

"Going out for a walk, I reckon, farmer?" inquired the landlord, who stood at the bar-room door with a pipe in his mouth.

"Aye, aye. You know these girls—when they find out that their pappies have made a little bit of money, there is no peace till its spent. My girl is taking me out shopping, to buy gimcracks and things! I'll be glad when I get her home again," grumbled Lyon.

"Well, well, she's your onliest one, and you mustn't be hard on her. My Rachel gets all she wants, and deserves it too. Dinner at two o'clock, sharp, farmer."

"Aye, aye! I know. Men o' my age never forget their dinners," said Lyon, as he drew Sybil's arm within his own and led her out into the streets.

They went only into the back streets, and the poor shops, and they bought only what was strictly necessary for their voyage; and having concluded their purchases, they returned to the inn in time for dinner.

Sybil was very much depressed. She could not rally from the effect the reading of that book had had upon her mind She frequently repeated her fervent aspiration:

"Oh! that the ship would sail to-day!"

Lyon encouraged her as much as he possibly could, but he had his own private subject of anxiety. He had not of course told any one of his intention to go abroad. Every one believed that, having sold out his load, he would return home; but he was obliged to stay in the city until the sailing of the ship, and he wanted a fair excuse to do so.

That evening the weather changed, and the sky clouded over. and the next morning it rained, and it continued to rain for three days.

"This here will make them there roads so bad that we shan't be able to travel for a week, even if it does clear up soon," grumbled and growled the self-styled farmer, feeling glad all the while of an excuse to stay until the ship should sail.

FLIGHT AND PURSUIT. 261

"No, that you won't," echoed his friend the landlord, glad to retain a guest with whom he was pleased.

On the third day of the rain, the sky showing signs of clearing, Lyon Berners went over to Portsmouth to hear at what precise time the Enterprise would sail for Liverpool. When he returned he had good news for Sybil.

"The ship will sail on Saturday! That is the day after to-morrow, dear Sybil. And we may go on board tomorrow night."

"Oh! I am so glad!" exclaimed Sybil, clapping her hands for joy. And she began to pack up immediately.

"Moreover, I have sold my wagon and horses to a party at Portsmouth. And so we can put our luggage into it and drive off as if we were going home; but we can go down to the river instead, and take it across in the ferryboat. Then I can have our effects put upon shipboard, and then deliver the team to its purchaser and receive the price," added Lyon.

"Oh, but I am so delighted with the bare fact of our getting away so soon, that all things else seem of no account to me!" joyously exclaimed Sybil, going on with her packing.

The next morning Lyon went out alone to make a few more purchases for their voyage. While he was going around, he also bought all the daily papers that he could get hold of. He returned to Sybil at an early hour of the forenoon. He found her sitting down in idleness.

"Got entirely through packing, my darling?" he inquired cheerfully.

"Oh, yes, and I have nothing on earth to do now. How long this last day will seem! At what hour may we go on board, this evening?"

"At sundown."

"Oh, that it were now sundown! How shall we contrive to pass the time until then?"

"This will help us to pass the day, dear wife," he answered, laying the pile of newspapers on the table between them.

Each took up a paper and began to look over it.

Lyon was deep in a political article, when a cry from Sybil startled him.

"What is the matter?" he inquired, in alarm.

She did not answer. Her face was pale as ashes, and her eyes were strained upon the paper.

"What do you see there?" again inquired her husband

"Oh, Lyon! Lyon! we are lost! we are lost!" she cried in a voice of agony.

In great anxiety he took the paper from her hand, and read the paragraph to which she pointed. It ran thus:

"It is now certain that Sybil Berners accused of the murder of Rosa Blondelle, is not in Annapolis, as was falsely reported; but that she has escaped in disguise, accompanied by her husband, who is also in disguise; and that both are in the city of Norfolk."

Now it was Lyon's turn to grow pallid with fear, not for himself, but for one dearer to him than his own life. Still he tried to control his emotions, or at least to conceal them from her. He compelled himself to answer calmly:

"Take courage, my darling! We are before them. In a few more hours we shall be on board the ship."

Her hands were clasped tightly together; her eyes were fixed steadily upon his face; her own face was white as marble.

"Oh, Lyon! save me! Oh, my husband, save me! You *know* that I am guiltless!" she prayed.

"Dearest wife, I will lay down my life for you, if necessary! Be comforted! See! it is now two o'clock! In two more hours we may be on shipboard!" he said.

"Let us go now! Let us go now!" she prayed, clasping her hands closely, gazing in his eyes beseechingly.

"Very well, we will go at once," he answered; and he took up his hat and hurried down-stairs.

He told the landlord that, as the weather was now good he thought he would risk the roads, and try to make a half-day's journey that afternoon, at least. And then, without waiting to hear the host's expostulations, he just told him to make out the bill, and then he went to the stables to put the horses to the wagon.

In half an hour all was ready for their departure—the bill paid, the wagon at the door, and the luggage piled into it. And Sybil and Lyon took leave of their temporary acquaintances; and Lyon handed Sybil up into her seat, climbed up after her, and started the horses at a brisk trot for the ferry-boat.

They reached Portsmouth in safety. Lyon drove down at once to the wharf, engaged a row-boat, put Sybil and all their effects into it, and rowed her across the water to where the Enterprise lay at anchor.

"Now I'm safe!" exclaimed Sybil, with a sigh of infinite relief, as she stepped upon the deck.

The Captain did not expect his passengers so soon, and he was busy; but he came forward and welcomed them, and showed them into the cabin, apologizing for its unready condition, consequent upon the bustle of their preparations for sailing.

Lyon left his wife in the Captain's care, and went back to the shore to complete the sale of his wagon and horses.

He was gone for nearly two hours, and when he returned he explained his long absence by saying that, after all, the hoped-for purchaser had refused to purchase, and that he had to leave his wagon and horses at a stable in Portsmouth, and to retire to a restaurant and write a letter to Captain Pendleton, and enclose an order for him to receive the property on paying the livery.

Sybil was satisfied—nay, she was delighted. In company with Lyon she walked up and down the deck, looking so joyous that the men about the place could but remark upon it as they gossiped with each other.

The new voyagers took supper in the Captain's cabin and afterwards returned to the deck and remained on it until the sun set and the stars came out.

"Oh, this sense of release from danger! Oh, this delightful sense of freedom! And the heavenly starlit sky, and the beautiful water, and the delicious breeze. Oh, the world is so lovely! Oh, life and liberty is so sweet, so sweet! Oh, dear Lyon, I am so happy! And I love you so much!" she exclaimed, almost delirous with joy at her great deliverance.

It was very late before Lyon could persuade her to leave the deck.

"I am too happy to sleep," she continually answered.

At length, however, he coaxed her to let him lead her to their state-room.

There, in the darkness and silence, she grew more composed, though not less happy. And in a few minutes after she had laid down, she fell asleep.

She slept very soundly until morning, when she was awakened by the cheerful chants of the sailors getting ready to make sail.

She lay a little while enjoying the joyous sounds that spoke to her so happily of liberty, and then she arose and dressed herself, and went up on deck, leaving Lyon still asleep.

The sun was just rising, and the harbor was beautiful She walked about, talking now to the captain, and now to one of the men, and exciting wonder among them all, at her happiness.

At length she was joined by her husband, who had waked up the moment she had left him, and got up immediately, and dressed and followed her.

"Oh, Lyon! is not this a beautiful morning? And the Captain says the wind is fair, and we shall sail in half an hour!" was her greeting.

And Lyon pressed her hand in silence. A great weight of anxiety lay upon his heart; *he* knew, if she did not, that she was not safe, even on shipboard, until the ship should really sail. And now his eyes were fixed upon a large row-boat that was rapidly crossing the water from the shore to the ship.

"Do you expect any more passengers?" he inquired of the Captain.

"Oh, lots!" answered the latter.

"Are those some of your passengers coming in the boat?"

The Captain threw a hasty glance at the approaching object and answered carelessly:

Of course they are! Don't you see they are making right for the ship?"

The boat was very near. It was at the side of the ship. The oars were drawn in. The passengers were climbing up to the deck.

"They look like nice people! I am sure they will make it still pleasanter for us on the voyage," said Sybil, who in her happy mood was inclined to be delighted with every event.

The Captain went to meet the new-comers.

Two gentlemen of the party spoke for a moment with

him, and then advanced towards the spot where the husband and wife were standing.

"They *are* nice people," repeated Sybil, positively; but Lyon said nothing; he was pale as ashes. The two gentlemen came up and stood before Lyon and Sybil The elder of the two took off his hat, and bowing gravely said to Sybil:

"You are Mrs. Sybil Berners of Black Hall?"

Then all at once an agony of terror took possession of her; her heart sank, her brain reeled, her limbs tottered.

"You are Mrs. Sybil Berners of Black Hall?" repeated the stranger, drawing from his pocket a folded paper.

"Yes," faltered Sybil, in a dying voice.

"Then, Madam, I have a most painful duty to perform. Sybil Berners, you are my prisoner," he said, and he laid his hand upon her shoulder.

With an agonizing shriek she sprang from under his hand, and threw herself into the arms of her husband, wildly crying:

"Save me, Lyon! Oh! don't let them force me away! Save me, my husband! Save me!"

CHAPTER XXXI.

THE ARREST.

> Had it pleased Heaven
> To try me with affliction; had He raised
> All kinds of sores and shames on my bare head;
> Steeped me in poverty to the very lips;
> I could have found in some part of my soul
> A drop of patience; but alas, to make me
> A fixed figure for the time of scorn
> To point his slow, unmoving finger at!—SHAKESPEARE.

"SAVE me! Oh, save me!" she continued to cry, clinging wildly to her husband's bosom. "Save me from this deep degradation! This degradation worse than death!"

And it is certain that if the immediate sacrifice of his own life could have saved her, Lyon Berners would have willingly died for Sybil; or even if the drowning of that law officer could have delivered her, he would have incontinently pitched the man overboard; but as neither of these violent means could possibly have served her, he could only clasp her closer to his heart, and consider what was to be done.

At length he looked up at the sheriff's officer, and said:

"I wish to have a word alone with my wife, if you will permit me."

The man hesitated.

"You can do it with perfect safety. We cannot possibly escape from this ship, you know; and besides, you can keep us in sight," he added.

Still the man hesitated, and at length inquired:

"Why do you wish to speak with her alone?"

"To try to soothe her spirits. I know it would be quite useless to tell you how entirely innocent this lady is of the heinous crime imputed to her; for even if you should believe her to be so, you would have to do your duty all the same."

"Yes, certainly; and a most distressing duty," put in the officer.

"This arrest has come upon her so suddenly, and when she is so utterly unprepared to meet it, that it has quite overcome her, as you see; but leave her alone with me for a few minutes, and I will try to calm her mind, and induce her to yield quietly to this necessity," added Lyon.

"Well, sir, I am indeed very willing to do all in my power to make this sad affair as little distressing to the lady as possible," answered the officer as he touched his companion on the shoulder, and they both walked off to some little distance.

As their retreating steps sounded upon the deck, Sybil raised her head from Lyon's breast and looked around with an expression half-frightened, half-relieved, and murmured.

"They are gone! They are gone!"

Then clasping her husband suddenly around the neck, and gazing wildly into his eyes, she exclaimed:

"You can save me, Lyon, you can save me from this deep dishonor that no Berners ever suffered before! There is but one way, Lyon, and there is but one moment. You have a small penknife; but it is enough. Open it, and strike it *here*, Lyon. One blow will be enough, if it is firmly struck! Here—Lyon! here, strike here!" And she placed her hand on her throat, under her ear, and gazed wildly, prayerfully in his face.

"*Oh, Sybil!*" he groaned, in an agony of despairing love.

"Quick! quick! Lyon! We have but this moment! Strike here now—now, this instant! Strike first, and then kiss me! kiss me as I die!"

"Sybil! Sybil, darling, you wring my heart."

"I am not afraid of death, Lyon; I am only afraid of shame. Kill me, to save me, Lyon! Be a Roman husband. Slay your wife, to save her from shame!" she cried, gazing on him with great bright dilated eyes, where the fires of frenzy, if not of insanity, blazed.

"My best beloved! My only beloved! there can be no shame where there is no sin. I will save you, Sybil; I swear it by all my hopes of Heaven! I do not yet see clearly how; but I will do it," he said solemnly, and pressing her again to his heart.

"Do it this way! do it this way!" she wildly entreated, never removing her frenzied eyes from his face.

"No, not that way, Sybil. But listen: there are safe means—sinless means that we may use for your deliverance. The journey back will be a long one, broken up by many stoppages at small hamlets and roadside inns. Escape from these will be comparatively easy. I have also about me, in money and notes, some five thousand dollars. With these I can purchase connivance or assistance. Besides, to further our views, I shall offer our wagon and horses, which luckily were not sold but remain at the livery-stable at Portsmouth—I shall offer them, I say, to the officer for his use and try to persuade him to take us down to Blackville by that conveyance, which will be easier even for him, than by the public stage coach. Take courage, dear Sybil, and take patience; and above all, do not think of using any desperate means to escape this trouble. But trust in Divine Providence. And now, dear Sybil, we must not try the temper of these officers longer, especially as we have got to leave the ship before it sails."

And so saying, Lyon Berners beckoned the bailiffs to approach.

"I hope the lady feels better," said the elder one.

"She is more composed, and will go quietly," answered Mr. Berners.

"Then the captain says we must be in a hurry. So if there is anything you wish to have removed, you had better attend to it at once," said the man.

"I do not wish to leave the side of my wife for an instant; so if you would be so kind as to speak to the captain and ask him to have our luggage removed from our state-room and put upon the boat, I should feel much obliged."

Leaving his companion in charge of the prisoner, the senior officer went forward and gave his message. And the captain, with seaman-like promptness, immediately executed the order.

Then Sybil's hat and cloak were brought her from the cabin, and she put them on and suffered herself to be led by her husband, and helped down to the boat. The Sheriff's officers followed, and when all were seated, the two boatmen laid to their oars, and the boat was rowed swiftly towards shore.

The husband and the wife sat side by side in the stern of the boat. His arm was wound around her waist, and her head was resting on his shoulder. No word was spoken between them in the presence of these strangers; but he was silently giving her all the support in his power, and she was really needing it all, for she was utterly overcome; not by the terrors of imprisonment or death, but by something infinitely worse, the horror of degradation.

All this time too Lyon Berners was maturing in his own mind a plan for her deliverance, which he was determined to begin to carry out as soon as they should reach the shore.

In a few minutes more the boat touched the wharf, and the party landed.

I must trouble you to take my arm, Mrs. Berners," said the sheriff's officer, drawing Sybil's hand under his elbow.

She would have shrunk back, but Lyon looked at her significantly, and she submitted

"Where do you mean to take us first?" inquired Mr. Berners, in a low tone.

"I wish to make this matter as little painful to this lady as the circumstances will permit. So I shall take her for the present to a hotel, where she must of course be carefully guarded. To-night we shall start by the night coach for Staunton, en route for Blackville," answered the elder officer, as with Sybil on his arm he led the way into the town. Mr. Berners walked on the other side of his wife, and the second officer followed close behind.

"We thank you for your consideration Mr.—Mr.——" began Lyon.

"Purley," continued the elder officer. "My name is Purley."

"I do not remember you among the officers of the Sheriff's staff, however."

"No; I am a new appointment. I must tell you, sir, that so strong was the feeling of sympathy for this lady, that not one of the bailiffs could be induced to serve the warrant; they resigned one after another."

"They all knew Sybil from her childhood up. I thank them, and will take care that they shall lose nothing in resigning their positions for her sake," said Lyon Berners with much warmth, while Sybil's heavy heart swelled with gratitude.

"And to tell the whole truth, had I known this lady, I should have felt the same reluctance to serving this warrant that was experienced by my predecessors in office."

"I can well believe you," answered Mr. Berners, gravely.

"Now, however, having undertaken the painful duty, I must discharge it faithfully," added the officer.

"Yes, Mr. Purley, but gently and considerately, I know; You will inflict as little of unmerited mortification as may be consistent with your duty."

"Heaven knows I will."

"Then I have a plan to propose, and a favor to ask of you."

"If I can gratify you with safety to the custody of my charge, I will do so; but here we are at the hotel now, and you had better wait until we get into a private sitting-room. The people of the place need not know that we are officers in charge of an accused party; but may be left to suppose that we are ordinary travelers."

"Oh, I thank you for that!" exclaimed Mr. Berners, warmly.

"They entered the hotel, a second-class house in a cross street, where the elder officer asked for a private sitting-room, to which they were immediately shown.

As soon as the four were seated, Mr. Berners turned to the elder officer and broached his plan.

"You spoke of taking the night coach for Staunton. Now, if another conveyance could be found—a private conveyance that would be more comfortable for all parties, and would also be entirely under your own control—would you not be willing that we should travel by it?"

"Oh! if you are able and willing to furnish a private conveyance for the journey, and place it as you say at my own exclusive orders, I shall be happy to take the lady down that way, rather than expose her in a public stage coach."

"Thanks. I have a wagon and horses here at livery. They can be put to use at a few minutes' notice. So, if you prefer, you can start at once upon this journey, and make some twenty-five or thirty miles before night."

"Let us see the team first, and then we shall be able to judge," said the officer.

And after a few minutes' conversation it was arranged that Sybil should be left in charge of the second officer, and that Mr. Purley should go with Mr. Berners to the livery stable to look at the horses and wagon. These two went out together, and Purley took the precaution to lock the door and put the key in his pocket.

"Why have you done that?" inquired Lyon, reproachfully.

"Because women are irrational and impulsive. I have always found them so! She might suddenly cut and run; and although it wouldn't be a bit of use, you know, because she would be sure to be retaken in an hour or less time yet, you see, it would cause a fuss, and be very unpleasant to me and you and her and everybody."

"I see," said Mr. Berners, with a sigh, acknowledging the truth of the position.

THE ARREST.

Meanwhile Sybil sat, absorbed in despair, and guarded by the second officer. Suddenly she heard her name softly murmured, and she looked up. The young bailiff stood before her. He was a sturdy looking young fellow, swarthy skinned, black haired, and black bearded.

"Miss Sybil, don't you know me? I beg your pardon! Mrs. Berners, don't you know me?" he inquired in a low tone, as if fearful of being heard.

Sybil looked at him in surprise, and answered hesitatingly:

"N-no."

"You forget people that you have been good to; but they don't forget you. Try to recollect me, Miss Sybil—Mrs. Berners."

"Your face seems familiar; but——"

"But you don't recollect it? Well, may be you may remember names better than faces. Have you any memory of a poor boy you used to help, named Bob Munson?"

"Bob Munson—oh, is it you? I know you now. But it has been so long since I saw you!" eagerly exclaimed Sybil.

"Eight years, Mrs. Berners; and I have been fighting the Indians on the frontier all that time. But I got my discharge and came back with Captain Pendleton. You know it was him as I went out with, when he was a third lieutenant in the infantry. I 'listed out of liking for him, and we was together from one fort to another all these years, until Captain Pendleton got a long leave, and come home. I couldn't get leave, but the Captain got my discharge. And when he goes back to his regiment, I mean to enlist again and go with him."

"But how came you to be a sheriff's officer? and oh, above all how *could* you come to take *me?*" reproachfully inquired Sybil.

"Oh, Miss—I mean, Madam,—can't you guess in your heart? When all the bailiffs throwed up their places rather than serve a warrant on you, and Mr. Purley, who was a stranger, got an appointment and kept it, they wanted another man. And then my Captain said to me, 'Munson, apply for the place; I will back you. And then if you get it, you will have an opportunity of serving, and perhaps freeing Mrs. Berners.' And a great deal more he said, to the same purpose, Ma'am; and so I did apply for the situation, and got it. And now, Madam, I am here to help you with my life, if necessary," added the young man, ardently.

"Give me your hand. God bless you, Bob! Help me all you can. I ought to be helped, for I am innocent," said Sybil, earnestly.

"Don't I know it? Don't everybody with any sense know it? Don't even old Purley know it, ever since he first clapped eyes on your face?"

"Heaven grant that all may soon!" prayed Sybil.

"They will be sure to, Miss—I mean Madam."

"Bob, tell me: how was it that we were found out?"

"Well, you see, Miss—Ma'am—when you were at Dunville, where you was said to have stayed all night, there was a fellow there who had a habit for which he ought to be hung—of looking through the key-holes and watching ladies when they thought themselves unseen. And this fellow saw you take off your red wig."

"And so discovered and denounced me?"

"No, he didn't, Ma'am; he didn't even suspect who you was. He took you for a circus woman. And as for reporting what he had seen to anybody in that house, it would have been as much as his life was worth. Old Colonel Purley—he's a uncle of our bailiff—old Colonel Purley would have peeled the skin offen his body, if he had a-known he had done such a mean thing in his tavern."

"Then how——"

"I'll tell you, Ma'am. It was this way. That fellow, which his name was Batkin, was on his way to Blackville. And all along the road he kept telling the yarn about the beautiful black-haired young lady he had seen, and who had disfigured herself by wearing a red wig; and of course he raised suspicions there. And when he was questioned farther, he described the wagon and horses, and the man and the woman, so accurately that the authorities thought it worth while to take the description down; and old Purley has it in his pocket along with the warrant. And then, as I told you, the bailiffs all resigned rather than go after you; and old Purley had

THE ARREST.

to be appointed. And I applied, and got appointed too, only to help you!"

"Heaven reward you for this kind thought! But, Bob, there were some of the old set found who were willing to take me; for they went to Annapolis after me, armed with warrant for my arrest."

"Yes; them two: Smith and Jones! Sink 'em! I've swore oath to thrash 'em both within an inch of their lives the first time I set eyes on them! Well, they didn't find you, Satan burn 'em! that's one comfort."

"How was it that you found us?"

"Oh, Miss Sybil—Mrs. Berners, I should say—we did it easy when we once had got the clue. We went first to Dunville to inquire after the gray-bearded man and his red-headed daughter, and we learned the road you had taken, and followed you from stage to stage until we got to Norfolk. There we inquired in the neighborhood of the market, and found where you had put up. There, at the 'Farmers' Hotel,' we were told, you had left for home that afternoon. Of course we knew *that* was a ruse. We knew that if you had left, it was for the deck of some outward bound ship. So we inquired, and found out that the Enterprise was to sail in the morning. And we stayed at this house all night, and boarded the ship this morning as you saw."

"Oh, Bob! if you could have delayed for a half hour, the ship would have sailed, and I should have been free!" sighed Sybil.

"I did all I could to make a delay. I put laudanum in his coffee last night. I was afraid to put in too much for fear of killing him, so I suppose I didn't put in enough, for he laid wide awake all night."

"Ah, yes! that would be the effect of an under-dose of laudanum."

"Well, then, Ma'am, I put back our watches a whole hour. But, bless you, he didn't go by the watches, he went by the sun; and as soon as it was light he was up, and he sent me down to order an early breakfast. And then I got a chance to put laudanum in his coffee again, and this time I overdid it and put in too much, for he tasted something wrong, and he said it was vile stuff, and he wouldn't drink it! No, Miss—Ma'am, I didn't neglect no means to let you get clean off. But you see it was no go this time; and I had to help old Purley to arrest you. I'm glad you didn't know me, hows'ever. And I would advise you not to know me at all whenever old Purley is about. Keep dark, Miss Sybil, and I'll find a way to get you off. I haven't been hiding and seeking and hunting among the red-skins these eight years for nothing. Hish-sh! Here they come," whispered Bob Munson, creeping away to the other end of the room, and putting himself on guard.

The elder officer unlocked the door, and entered, followed by Mr. Berners. He announced that the wagon was at the door, and that they were ready to start on the return journey. And then Purley gave his arm to Sybil, and led her to the wagon, and placed her on the back seat, while Mr. Berners and Bob Munson lingered behind, the former to gather up Sybil's little personal effects, and the latter to settle the hotel bill. But there was no opportunity, among the crowd of guests and servants, for Munson to make his friendly intentions known to Mr. Berners by any other means than a significant look and a pressure of the hand, which Lyon Berners could not more than half understand. He felt, however, that in this younger officer he and his unhappy wife had a friend. They went out together, followed closely by the hostler, who wanted his own fee; but both Mr. Berners and Bob Munson were too much annoyed by his presence to feel like rewarding his attendance.

Lyon Berners mounted to the seat beside his wife, and Bob Munson to that beside Purley, who held the reins. And in this manner they set out on their return journey.

They crossed the ferry without attracting particular attention.

CHAPTER XXXII.

A DESPERATE VENTURE.

I have set my life upon a cast,
And I will stand the hazard of the die.—SHAKESPEARE.

It was yet so early in the morning that they drove ten miles out to a small village on the road before they thought of breakfast. There Mr. Berners reminded the officer in charge that Sybil had not yet broken her fast. Whereupon Purley drew up before the one little tavern of the place, alighted, and assisted his charge to alight, and then keeping fast hold of her arm, led her into the house, and ordered breakfast.

While the meal was being got ready he kept his party of four well together in the sitting-room where they waited. And as soon as breakfast was over, they all re-entered the wagon and resumed their journey. They traveled twenty miles before stopping to dine at a lonely road-side tavern, where again Purley watched his charge with such vigilance that she had no opportunity to speak privately either to her husband or their friend. Still she hoped this opportunity would be afforded when they should stop for the night. After an hour's rest they went on again, traveling with moderate haste all the afternoon. They made fifteen more miles before sunset, and then, having driven forty-five miles that day, and finding their horses very tired, they determined to put up for the night at a small hamlet, whose comfortable little hotel promised rest and refreshment.

Still Purley kept close to his charge. They all had supper in a private sitting-room. And when that meal was over and the hour for retirement arrived, Purley himself accompanied Mr. and Mrs. Berners to their bedroom to see that it was secure. It was a front chamber, on the upper floor, with two front windows overlooking the village street, and but one door, which opened upon the passage.

"That is all safe," said Purley, casting a glance around. "So I may leave you two alone here together, where no doubt, you are glad enough to be. But I'm sorry to say I must turn the key on you; not that I have any right to lock you up, sir, without your consent; but of course you *will* consent to that, for the sake of staying with your wife."

"Of course I will; and thank you for the privilege," answered Mr. Berners.

"All right then. Good-night to you both," said Purley, closing and locking the door, and withdrawing the key.

And then he took a farther precaution for the security of his charge, by ordering a mattress to be brought and laid down before that chamber door. And there he and his companion stretched themselves to rest like a pair of watch dogs.

As soon as Sybil found herself alone with her husband, she beckoned him to that end of the room which was farthest from the door, and when he was close beside her she whispered in the lowest tone:

"Did you observe anything peculiar in the manner of that younger bailiff?"

"I observed that he tried to attract my particular attention whenever we happened to be unnoticed for a moment. But as we were so very closely watched I had no opportunity of asking, or he of telling, what he meant," said Lyon Berners.

"Then I will tell you all about it. When Mr. Purley went away with you, and left that young man guarding me, the first thing he did was to make himself known to me, and to place himself at my service even to the death!"

"Who was he?"

"Robert Munson; a boy that I was so fortunate as to be kind to in his childhood and mine. Afterwards he was a private soldier in Captain Pendleton's company, and served under him for eight years, fighting the Indians on the frontier. At Captain Pendleton's suggestion, and with his own hearty free will, he volunteered for this service of pursuing me, only that he might more effectually try to free me"

"Sybil, what are you saying? Have we a friend in one of our captors?" exclaimed Lyon, in astonishment.

"Yes; a friend who will serve us to the death! Listen, dear Lyon, and I will tell you all about it," answered Sybil.

And she commenced, and related all the circumstances of her acquaintance with Robert Munson; of his motives for entering upon his present avocation, and of his discovery of himself to her in the hotel at Portsmouth.

"Now may heaven grant that some day I may have an opportunity of rewarding that good fellow for his willing service, whether it ever avail us or not," said Lyon Berners, earnestly.

"But, dear Lyon, we must be very careful not to betray by any word or look that we have any acquaintance, much less understanding, with Munson, for to do so would be to ruin our only chance of escape," said Sybil.

"Of course! of course! I understand that perfectly well!"

"But watch your opportunity, and when you feel it to be perfectly safe, communicate with Robert Munson."

"I understand, dear Sybil, and I shall be very prudent and very vigilant," answered Mr. Berners.

And then they retired to rest.

"Very early the next morning they were aroused by their keeper who never left his post at their door until he saw them come out of their room. And then he drew Mrs. Berner's arm within his own and led her down to breakfast.

After breakfast they resumed their journey.

This first day and night on the road was a type of all that followed. The bailiff Purley never lost sight of his charge except at night, and then he first assured himself that her room was a secure prison, from which it would be impossible for her to escape; and then, to make assurance doubly sure, he always locked the door on the outside, put the key into his pocket, and stretched himself on a mattress across the threshold.

There was no opportunity afforded to Sybil, Lyon and their new friend to speak together in private; and as day followed day and night succeeded night in this hopeless manner, their spirits fell from despondency even to despair.

But as it is said to be darkest just before dawn, and that when things are at their worst they are sure to mend, so it proved in their case.

On the evening of the fourth day of their tedious journey, they stopped to sup and sleep at a lonely farmhouse, where for "a consideration," the poor farmer consented, whenever he got the chance, to entertain travelers.

Here their wagon and horses were comfortably stabled, and themselves were lodged and feasted.

Here, as usual after supper, Mr. Purley accompanied his charge to her bedroom, which, to his perplexity, he found to have two doors; the one opening upon the upper hall, and the other communicating with an adjoining vacant chamber.

After some consideration, he solved the difficulty of guarding his prisoner by saying to his assistant:

"Well, Munson, all that can be done is this: one of us will have to sleep across one door, and the other across the other. And as I haven't slept in a room for three nights, I reckon I'll take the vacant room, and you may take the hall. But mind, don't forget to draw the key out of the door when you lock it, and put it into your pocket. And mind also, to be sure to pull your mattress quite up to the door and lay directly across it, so that if the lock should be picked, no one can pass without going right over your own body; and, last of all, mind to sleep only with one eye open, or all the other precautions will be of no use at all."

"I will be very careful, sir," answered young Bailiff Munson, touching his hat to his superior officer in military style.

"And now, as your legs are younger than mine, I wish you would run downstairs and ask the farmer to send me up a mug of that home-brewed bitter beer he was talking about."

"Yes, sir," answered the young bailiff, starting off with alacrity, while the elder remained on guard at the door of his charge.

In five minutes or less time, Munson returned with a

quart measure of the "home-brewed," which he handed to Purley.

"Souls and bodies! but it is bitter, sure enough! I have heard of bitter beer, but this beats all for bitterness that ever I tasted! However, the bitterer the better, I suppose; and this is really refreshing," said Purley, as he drained the mug, and handed it empty to a negro boy, who had just brought in and laid down the mattress upon which Munson was to sleep.

Munson smiled to himself.

Then Purley reiterated all his cautions for the careful guarding of his charge, and at length bade his comrade good-night, and retired to the vacant chamber, to guard the door on that side.

Munson drew his mattress across the hall-door as he had been directed to do, and laid himself down in all his clothes—not to sleep, but to listen and watch until the house should grow quiet; for on this night he was resolved to effect the deliverance of Sybil, or perish in the attempt."

Meanwhile Mr. and Mrs. Berners had retired to their chamber—not to rest, but to wait for events; for on this night a sure presentiment informed them that Robert Munson, on guard there at their outer door, would be sure to use his opportunities for attempting a rescue. So they quietly coöperated with what they divined to be his intentions.

First Sybil went and hung a towel over the knob of the lock, so as to darken the key-hole of the door guarded by Purley. Then she slipped the bolt, saying:

"He may guard us if he must, but he shall neither look in upon us, nor intrude upon us, if I can help it."

And then, instead of undressing for bed, they did the opposite thing, and quietly dressed for an escape. And lastly, they concealed their money and jewels about their persons, and threw a few of the most necessary articles for their journey into one traveling bag, and then sat down to listen and watch on the inside, as their friend was listening and watching on the outside.

Then they heard Purley arranging and re-arranging his bed against his door, and tumbling down upon it, like a man utterly overcome by fatigue and drowsiness; after which all was silent, until the stertorous breathing of the bailiff assured them of the depth of his sleep. After that, not a sound was heard in the house. Lyon looked at his watch. It was but nine o'clock, though the whole house was at rest. In these remote country places, people go to roost with the fowls, or very soon after.

Still for another hour of silent, breathless suspense they waited; and then they heard a faint tapping on the door that was guarded by Munson.

Mr. Berners wen tup, and tapped gently in response.

"Hist!" breathed the voice from without, through the key-hole.

"Well!" murmured Lyon, through the same channel.

"Take some of the melted tallow on the top of your candle, and grease the key-hole as well as you can, and then I will come in and talk to you, if you will let me."

"Thanks; yes."

And Mr. Berners did as he was requested to do, and Munson slipped his key into the lubricated key-hole, and silently unlocked the door.

"Oh, our deliverer!" fervently exclaimed Sybil, as he softly entered the room and closed the door behind him, holding up his finger in warning to them to be silent.

"And now sit close for a few minutes, while I tell you what I have done and am going to do," said Munson, drawing a stool and seating himself upon it, before Mr. and Mrs. Berners.

"Go on," muttered Lyon, fervently pressing the hand of his friend.

"Oh, yes, go on, dear Bob!" eagerly whispered Sybil.

"First I put nearly half an ounce of laudanum in old Purley's bitter beer, which made him think it so uncommon prime and bitter, that he drank the whole quart."

"Good heaven! Munson, you have killed the man!" said Lyon, in dismay.

"No, I have only doubled the dose I gave him before, which took no effect on him, so this will only put him to sleep for twelve hours or so. Lord, listen how he snores! A thunder-storm wouldn't wake him."

"Well?"

"Next, as soon as he was asleep, I went into his room in my stocking-feet, and closed all the solid wooden shutters, to make him believe it is still night when he does awake and feel drowsy, as he will be sure to feel, so that he shall go to sleep again, and sleep until evening, and that will give you nearly twenty-four hours start on him."

"Right! Quite right," said Mr. Berners.

"Well, well; but go on, dear Bob," impatiently murmured Sybil.

"I locked his door on the outside, and took away the key, to make the farmer or any of the family, if they should go into his room to see why he slept so long, think that he had locked himself in. For the rest I shall stay here and pretend to sleep very late myself. In fact I shall sleep until they wake me up, and then I shall be very angry, and tell them they had better not play that game on Mr. Purley, as he would be in a fury if his rest should be broken. And so I will guard these two rooms from intrusion, and your escape from being discovered, as long as I possibly can."

"But when it shall be discovered, my poor fellow, will you not get yourself into trouble?" inquired Lyon.

"Even if I should, what will my trouble be to this lady's? But at worst I shall only be cussed by old Purley, and turned out of my place by the sheriff; and as I'm used to being cussed, and don't like my place, it don't matter."

"And in any case, you shall be well rewarded, dear Bob. Not that such a service as you are about to render us *can* ever be adequately rewarded; but as far as——"

"Oh, dear Madam, don't speak of reward! I owe you a debt of gratitude, which I am glad to pay. I have told you what I *have* done, and what I shall do, to relieve you of anxiety; and now we had better quietly leave the house. Are you ready?" inquired Munson.

"We have been quite ready for these two hours, in anticipation of your help."

"Come, then; but come very silently, though there is not the slightest danger, either, of our being heard. The farmer is a beer swiller, and sleeps heavily, and his women folks all sleep up in the garret. I saw them all go up myself; they passed with their candle, as I lay on the pallet," whispered Munson, as he quietly led the way out into the hall and softly closed and locked the door, and withdrew the key.

"It is just as well to do this, to guard against the chance of any one opening the door while I am gone," he added, as he softly preceded the party down the stairs.

He silently opened the front door, and they passed out into the free air.

A watch-dog that lay upon the mat outside got up and wagged his tail, and laid down again, as if to express his willingness that any inmate might leave the house who wished to do so, though no stranger should enter it except over his dead body.

"Sensible dog!" said Munson, as with more precaution he closed and locked the outer door, and took that key also with him.

"You must not attempt to escape with your wagon; but must ride your horses, which will be much more efficacious both for swiftness and for their ability to go through places where you could not take a wagon," said Munson, as they walked across the farm-yard.

But when they drew near the stable, they were set upon by a couple of watch-dogs, who, barking furiously, barred their farther progress.

"There is no other way!" exclaimed Munson, and drawing a double barreled pistol from his pocket, he shot one dog dead, while the other ran howling away.

Then with some difficulty they forced the door, and while Lyon remained on the outside with Sybil, young Munson entered the stable and led out their two horses.

"Here are several bridles, and here is one side-saddle, which will suit Mrs. Berners, if you have no scruple about borrowing them," suggested Munson.

"I should have no scruple about borrowing anything from anybody to aid my wife's escape. Besides, there is my wagon more than double the value of the things that we require; I will leave that in pledge," said Mr. Berners.

"Just so," assented Munson.

And all this time he had been arranging the side-saddle and bridle upon Sybil's horse. As soon as it was ready Mr. Berners came around to lift his wife into her seat

"One moment, dear Lyon," said Sybil, pausing to adjust her dress.

While she did so, Munson again spoke to Mr. Berners.

"You have your pocket compass?"

"Yes."

"Then I advise you to use it as soon as it is light, to direct your course. And do not go toward the east, for old Purley will pursue you in that direction, under the impression that you will try to reach another seaport town, and get off in a ship. But make for the interior, for the West, and get away as fast and as far as you can. Be careful to keep as much as possible in the woods, even though your progress should be slower through them than it would be in the open country. And now excuse my presuming to give you so much counsel; but you know I have been upon the war-path, out among the red-skins, and am up to hunting and flying."

"I thank you—we both thank you from the depths of our souls. And we pray that the day may come when we shall be able to prove our gratitude," said Lyon, earnestly.

"Never mind that! But put madam into her seat. She is ready now; and, indeed, the sooner you are off the better," answered Munson.

Mr. Berners advanced towards Sybil, when the whole party was stopped by a terrible event.

"No you don't, you infernal villain! I have caught you, have I? STAND!" exclaimed a voice of thunder, and the stout farmer stood before them, at the head of all his negroes, and with a loaded musket in his hand!

Like lightning young Munson threw himself before Sybil, drew a pistol from his breast, and leveled it straight at the heart of their opponent, exclaiming:

"Out of the way, you devil! and let her pass. Out of the way this instant, or, by my life, I will kill you! I will! I will kill you, and hang for her sake!"

The man raised his musket, and aimed it at the head of him whose hand pointed the pistol to his own heart. And thus, like two duelists, they stood fatally eyeing each other.

CHAPTER XXXIII.

A FATAL CRISIS.

Each at the life
Leveled his deadly aim ; their fatal hands
No second stroke intended.—MILTON.

"HOLD! on your lives!" exclaimed Lyon Berners, rushing between the opponents, and with swift hands striking up the pistol of Robert Munson, and turning aside the musket of Farmer Nye. "Would you shed each other's blood so recklessly? Here is some mistake. Farmer, whom did you take us for?"

"Who did I take you for, is it? For that cornsarned band of robbers as have been mislesting the country for miles round this month past."

"Robbers?"

"Yes, robbers! as has been tarryfying the whole country side ever since Hollow Eve!"

"I never heard of them."

"May be you didn't, but I took you for them all the same."

"And aimed your musket at that lady! And might have shot her dead, had not this brave man thrown himself before her, with a loaded pistol in his hand, leveled at your heart."

"How did I know it was a lady! How could I see in this dim light? I took her for one of you, and I took you all for robbers," said the farmer, sulkily.

"Well, you see who we are now?"

"Yes; I see as you are my new lodgers. Though why you should be out here at the stables after your beasts at this hour of the night, and wake me up with a row; or should take my darter's side-saddle, and kill my watch-dog, blame you, I *don't* see!" growled the farmer.

"Come, walk aside with me for a few minutes, and I will show you why," said Mr. Berners, soothingly, laying his hand on the farmer's shoulder.

"Hands off, if you please! No! I don't think as I *will* walk aside with you. You might do me a mischief."

"Bosh! you are armed, and I am unarmed. How can I harm you? Come, and I will tell you something to your advantage," coaxed Mr. Berners.

Partly urged by curiosity and partly by interest, Farmer Nye reluctantly consented to follow where Mr. Berners led him. When they had passed out of hearing of the negroes, Mr. Berners stopped, and turned to his host, and said:

"You know who we are?"

"I know you are my new lodgers—that's all I know about you."

"Yet you must have observed something you of the common about our party?"

"Yes; I took notice as you and your wife must have been dreadful 'fraid of being robbed and murdered on your journey, when you kept two men to travel with you, and guard you all day long, and sleep outside of your doors like watch-dogs all night long. Which me and my darter made it out between us as you must have lots of money with you to make you so cautious. And which, if we had known you was going to be so mistrustful of *us*, we'd have seen you farther before we'd have took you in."

"And so that is the way in which *you* accounted for matters and things that you couldn't understand?"

"To be sure it was; and very natural too."

"Shall I tell him the whole truth?" inquired Lyon Berners of himself. "I will sound him first," he concluded. Then speaking up, he said:

"Well, you cannot blame people for being cautious, after that horrible murder at Black Hall."

"That's so too," admitted the farmer.

"And yet," added Mr. Berners, "they *do* say that it was no robber that did that murder, but the lady of the house who did it."

"The lady of the house!" indignantly echoed the farmer, to Lyon's great astonishment. "Don't you go to say that; for if you do, devil burn me if I don't knock you down with the butt end of my gun!"

"I do not say it. I only tell you what other people say."

"They lie! the hounds! And I wish I could meet any of them venomous backbiters face to face. Satan fly away with me if I wouldn't tear their false tongues out of their throats, and throw them to the dogs! *You* don't mean to say you believe she did it?" fiercely demanded Sybil's rough champion.

"No; Heaven knows I do not! I believe her to be as guiltless as an angel."

"I'm glad to hear you say that! I don't want to pitch into an unarmed man, but I should a' been strongly tempted to a' done it if you'd said anything else."

"You know this injured lady, then?"

"Yes; I have knowed her ever since she was a little gal. Not as ever I met her face to face in my life, but I know her as every poor man and poor child and poor brute in the whole country knows her: as the kindest, gentlest, tenderest-hearted lady in the whole world—she who has been known to take the fur cloak off her own back, and lay it over the form of a sick beggar, while she went home in the cold to send her warm blankets. Yes, and known to have done scores of deeds as good and self-sacrificing as that. *She* do the thing they accuse her of! Why, sir, she no more did it than I, or you, or your own sweet wife did it! And Satan burn *me!* when I hear of any man accusing her of it, if I don't feel just like knocking his dull brains out, and taking the consequences— that I do!" swore the farmer.

"I will trust him," said Lyon Berners to himself.

—"And to think that men who call themselves law officers, not to say Christians, should hunt that lovely lady through the country as if she was some wild beast or highway robber! I wish one of them hunters was to come my way. I'm blowed to flinders if I wouldn't set my whole pack of dogs on 'em till they would be torn to pieces. I'd give 'em hunting! But excuse *me*, Mr.—Mr. —What's your name; I've gone away from the pint, which I always do fly off at a tangent and lose my bearings whenever I hear that lady accused. Now, sir, what had you to tell me to my advantage?" inquired the farmer, drawing a handkerchief from his pocket and wiping his heated face.

"I will tell him all," said Lyon Berners to himself; and then he spoke up:

"First, good friend, let me assure you that you have not wandered a hair's breadth from the point at issue between as."

"Oh yes, I have; for I have been raving about Mrs. Berners; but I couldn't help it."

"Mrs. Berners is the lady who is with me," said Mr. Berners.

Farmer Nye jumped three feet from the ground and came down again like a man that was shot, and then stood with open mouth and eyes staring at the speaker.

"I am her husband, and the men who are guarding us are the officers who have her in custody."

"WHAT? Say that again!" uttered the farmer, panting for breath.

Mr. Berners repeated all that he had said, adding:

"I had got her away from this neighborhood, and on shipboard. And she was rejoicing in her supposed safety and freedom, for the ship was within a half hour of sailing, when these officers came on board with a warrant and arrested her."

"THEY DID! Wait till I get my niggers together. The boys will want no better fun than to tar and feather them devils, and set them afire and turn 'em loose. And blame me if I don't give the best feather-bed in my house to the service. Come along," exclaimed the farmer, starting off to commence the work.

"Stop!" said Lyon Berners, laying his hand soothingly upon the shoulder of the excited man. Above all, you wish to serve my unhappy wife, do you not?"

"Yes, with my 'life, and fortune, and sacred honor,' as the Declaration of Independence says."

Then you cannot serve her by any violence done to the officers, who are only doing their duty."

"Doing their duty! Duty! That's a matter of opinion! I consider I should be doing of *my* duty if I was to order my niggers to take 'em out and tar and feather 'em. Yes, and set 'em afire afterwards—burn 'em!"

"Yes; but that would be doing a great injustice to them, and also a great injury to Mrs. Berners. If you really wish to serve my dear wife, you can do so by helping her to escape."

"I'll help her to escape, with all my heart and soul! And with all my heart and soul I'll shoot down anybody that dares to start from here in pursuit of her!" emphatically declared the farmer.

"That is not necessary. You can cover our retreat by more peaceable means. And now I must advise you that both these officers have used us with the greatest kindness and consideration, concealing our identity and shielding us from the curiosity and intrusion of strangers, whenever they could do so, as is proved by your own experience, for you had no suspicion as to who we might be."

"No, that I hadn't! And a good thing I hadn't too! for if I'd a known that lady had a been kept a prisoner here in my house, I'd a pitched her jailers neck and heels out o' the windows, and then set the dogs on 'em!"

"But that would have been very unjust to them, and injurious to the lady you wish to befriend. And especially it would have been the very greatest injustice to the younger officer, who has been our partisan from the first."

"Eh! what? One of them jailers your partisan?"

"Yes; let me explain," said Mr. Berners. And he commenced and detailed all the circumstances of their acquaintance and relations with Robert Munson.

"And so, out of gratitude for the kindness this lady showed him in his childhood, he got himself put on this service o' purpose to watch his opportunity of reskying her."

"Just so."

"Well, he's an honest fellow, that he is!" said the farmer, approvingly.

"Now, Mr. Nye, all you have to do, if you wish to help us, is just to let us go free. When we are gone, keep the house quiet, and let the elder officer sleep as long as possible, for the longer he sleeps the farther we shall get away from pursuit."

"I'll lock him up and keep him prisoner for a month, if necessary."

"But it is not necessary. A day's start is all that we shall need, and that, I think, you can secure to us, by simply letting the man sleep as long as he will. And furthermore, I may ask you to be cautious and not to betray our friend Robert Munson's agency in our escape."

"I'll protect Robert Munson with my life."

"A thousand thanks! And now, as we understand each other, let us go on to my wife, who is anxiously waiting the issue of this interview," said Lyon Berners, turning and leading the way towards the stables.

"Now, squire, you may rely upon me, and rest easy in your mind. You sha'n't be followed in less than twenty-four hours," said the farmer, as they went along.

"Again I thank you from my heart. And now I have something else to say to you," began Lyon Berners.

Then he paused, as finding a real difficulty in saying what he wished; for the truth is, that when Mr. Berners had called Mr. Nye aside for a private interview, he had intended to offer him a heavy bribe to connive at the escape of Sybil.

Now, however, he found the farmer not exactly the sort of man to affront with the proffer of a bribe, or even scarcely of a reward; and yet he was a poor man who evidently needed money, and would probably always need it; for Farmer Nye, as has been shown in his championship of Sybil, was a man of impetuous emotions, hasty judgments, and reckless actions, and was always sure to be in troubles, social, domestic, and pecuniary.

So Mr. Berners, while wishing to reward his services, felt a difficulty as to the manner of doing so.

At length, however, he continued:

"Mr. Nye, I said at the beginning of our talk, that I could tell you something to your advantage."

"Well, and, bless my soul alive, haven't you done it? I wonder if I could hear of anything more to my advantage than the chance of helping to resky that lady as I have felt for so much?" warmly inquired the farmer.

"You have a generous and noble nature to look upon it in that light."

"No, I haven't; but I'm a man, I reckon, and not a beast nor a devil, and that's all about it."

"Well, farmer, I confess that when I first spoke to you, I thought of offering you a heavy bribe to allow us to go free, and that was what I meant when I said I had something to propose to your advantage."

"Then I'm glad you didn't do it—that's all."

"I am glad too, for now I know your magnanimous heart would have led you to serve us without reward, and even at great loss."

"Yes, that it would, naively," assented the farmer.

"And even so we accept and shall ever be grateful for your services," added Lyon Berners, gravely. And all the while he was slily examining the contents of his pocket-book. At length he drew a five hundred dollar note from the compartment in which he knew he kept notes of that denomination, and he slipped it into a blank envelope, and held it ready in his hand.

In another moment they were at the stable door, before which Sybil stood, leaning on the bowed neck of her own horse, while Robert Munson held the other horse.

Before Lyon Berners could speak, Farmer Nye impetuously pushed past him, and rushed up to Sybil, pulled off his hat and put out his hand, exclaiming:

"Give me your hand, lady. I beg your pardon ten thousand times over for all I said and did to affront you, not knowing who you was. But now, lady, here is a man who don't *believe* you to be innocent, because he *knows* that you are so, and who will fight for you as long as he has got a whole bone left in his body, and shed his blood for you as long as he has got a drop left in his veins."

Overcome by this ardent testimonial to her innocence, Sybil burst into tears, and took the rough hand that had been held out to her, and wept over it, and pressed it warmly to her lips, and then to her heart.

"Yes, that I will. I'll die before a hair of your head shall be hurt," exclaimed the farmer, utterly overwhelmed and blubbering.

Meanwhile Lyon Berners was explaining to Robert Munson that they had found a friend and helper in Farmer Nye; but advising Munson to try to infuse enough of discretion into the impetuous mind of Nye to modify his reckless actions.

"And now, dear boy," added Mr. Berners, "I will not speak to you of reward for this great service; but this I *will* say, that henceforth you shall be to me as a younger brother, and I shall take charge of your future fortune even as though you were the son of my mother."

"You are too generous, sir; and indeed I want no recompense whatever, answered Robert Munson, sincerely.

Then Mr. Berners went over to his wife and lifted her into her saddle; and when he had settled her comfortably in her seat, he mounted his own horse, and once more called Robert Munson to him.

"Good-bye, and God bless you, Robert," he said, warmly shaking hands with the young man.

"And you too, sir! and you too, sir!" feelingly responded Munson.

And then Sybil called him.

"Good-bye, dear Bob. I will remember you and love you as long as I live for this," she said.

"And so will I you, ma'am," he answered, and turned away to hide his tears.

Lastly Lyon Berners rode up to where Farmer Nye stood apart.

"Farewell, Farmer Nye! And may you indeed fare as well as your great heart deserves all your life," said Lyon.

"The same to you and your dear wife, sir, with all my soul in the prayer!" responded the farmer.

"And here, Mr. Nye, is a testimonial—I mean a memorandum—that is to say, something I wish you to take for my sake."

"A keepsake, sir?"

"If you choose to consider it so, yes."

"What might it be sir?" inquired the farmer, receiving from Mr. Berners the small envelope containing the large note.

"It *might* be a lock of my wife's hair, or it might be my miniature; but whatever it is, hold it tight, and do not look at it until you get back to the house."

"All right, sir; but you have raised my curiosity," replied the farmer, as he carefully deposited his unsuspected little fortune into the pocket of his waistcoat.

"Now direct me as to how I shall find the best and most private road westward," said Lyon, gathering the reins in his hands.

"You are facing east now. Ride straight on for about

a hundred yards, till you come to the cross-roads, then take the road to your left, and follow it for about an eighth of a mile until you come to another road still on your left; take that and follow it as far as you please, for it leads straight west."

"Thank you again and again! We shall do very well now. Good-bye, all; and God bless you forever!" exclaimed Lyon Berners, waving his hat in adieux to the friends he was leaving behind.

Then the husband and wife rode forth in the night together.

Before we follow them, we will see how it fared with the faithful friends who had risked so much in their service.

CHAPTER XXXIV.

THE PURSUIT.

Horse! horse! * * * * and chase!—MARMION.

FARMER NYE and Robert Munson remained standing with their heads uncovered, looking after the fugitives until the sound of their horses' hoofs died away in the distance, and then they turned towards each other and impulsively grasped each the other's hand and shook hands as comrades.

Next Farmer Nye turned to the negroes who were squatting about the stable-yard, wondering, no doubt, at all they had seen and heard; and he told them to disperse to their quarters, and keep still tongues in their heads, if they wished to keep their heads on their shoulders.

"And now we'll go back to the house and get a drop of home-brewed, and go to bed," said the farmer, starting off at a brisk trot, and beckoning his young companion to follow him.

"I mean to manage so as old Purley shall be made to believe as the prisoner escaped through *his* door," said Munson, as he came along.

"That'll be bully!" said the farmer.

THE PURSUIT. 293

They went back to the house, consulted the tall old-fashioned clock in the corner of the hall, found it was just eleven, and they took their drop of "home-brewed," and went to rest.

Robert Munson, with design, threw himself down upon the mattress outside the carefully locked door of the chamber, from which he had helped his prisoners to escape. And being very much fatigued, he fell asleep, and slept long and late.

The first persons up in the house were the farmer's daughter Kitty, and her old maiden aunt Molly.

They came down from their attic chambers and walked on tiptoes past the sleeping Munson, so as not to wake him. They went down-stairs and had breakfast got ready, but had to wait very long before either the farmer or the young man appeared. When they did come down, however, and apologized for their tardiness, the women inquired for the other guests, and were told that they must not be disturbed.

The day passed slowly.

It was late in the afternoon before old Purley awoke; and finding the room quite dark, and feeling himself still very drowsy, he merely turned over and went to sleep again. And still overpowered by the combined action of the laudanum and the beer-opium and hops, he slept on until a very late hour of the night, when at length he awoke; but perceiving that all was quite dark and still, he lay quietly in bed thinking this was about the longest night he had ever spent in his life. At last he got up, and opened the blinds to see if it were near day. And perceiving by a faint light streak along the horizon that the morning was at hand, he opened the other blinds, and began to dress himself as well as he could in the semi-darkness.

By the time he had got on all his clothes, the day was a little lighter, and he went into the passage to see after the safety of his prisoner.

He found young Munson stretched upon the mattress immediately before the door.

"Quite correct," he thought; but he resolved to go up to the door to make a closer examination. First he saw that the key had been taken out of the lock.

"All right," he said to himself. "Munson has obeyed orders, and put the key in his pocket."

And then still farther to assure himself of the safety of his charge, he bent over the sleeping form of Munson and tried the lock, and found it fast.

"Quite correct! Nothing has been neglected. He is a careful officer, and shall be well reported at head-quarters," he muttered, with much satisfaction.

But to reach the lock at all, he had been obliged to bend so far over the sleeping body, that now, in trying to recover his perpendicular, he lost his balance, and fell heavily, nearly crushing and quite waking Munson, who, in struggling to throw off the burden, recognized old Purley, but pretending to mistake him for Mr. Berners, grappled him by the throat, exclaiming :

"No you don't, you villain! You don't get her out of this room except over my dead body!" And he shook him furiously.

"It's me—me—me, Bob! Do-do-don't choke me to death!" gasped old Purley, as he struggled and freed his throat for an instant from the grasp of Robert's hands.

But Munson throttled and shook him more furiously than before, singing out :

"Help! murder! arson. Here's this man reskying of my prisoner!" And he shook him until his teeth rattled in his head.

"Oh, my good Lord! I shall be strangled with the best of intention," sputtered the terrified and half-suffocated victim, as for an another instant he freed his throat from his assailant's clasp, and breathed again.

"Help! murder! fire!" yelled Munson, renewing the attack.

"Bob! Bob! It's me, I tell you!—Purley! Wake up and look at me! You're asleep yet! And oh, my Lord! the man will murder me by mistake before I can make him know," panted the poor wretch, desperately striving to keep off the strangling hands of his assailant, and growing weak in the struggle.

And meanwhile the household, aroused by the outcry, had hurried on their clothes, and now came pouring into the passage—the women down the garret stairs, and the men up the lower back stairs.

"Now I've got you!" exclaimed Munson, triumphantly as he knocked the feet from under Purley, and threw him down upon the floor. Then stooping to gaze at the fallen foe, he condescended at length to recognize him.

"Oh! is it you, Mr. Purley? I really thought it was Mr. Berner, reskying of his wife!" said Munson, with provoking coolness.

"Then I wish you would make surer another time, you stupid donkey! You've all but killed me!" panted the victim, wiping the perspiration from his face.

"What is the matter?"

"What's all this?"

"Is anybody hurt?"

Such were the hasty questions put by old Farmer Nye and his family, as they gathered around the scene of action.

"Yes! I'm choked and shaken nearly to death!" gasped old Purley, in a fury.

"It was done for the best," said Munson, soothingly.

"Oh, for the best, indeed! Set fire to you! would you murder an innocent man out of kindness?" fiercely demanded Purley.

"You see, he fell upon me, and woke me up. It was so dark here, with the window shutters closed, that I could not see well, so I mistook him for Mr. Berners broke loose and trying to carry off his wife," explained Robert Munson.

"Oh! well, I reckon you're not hurt much; only startled and shaken a bit! Come and take a glass of morning bitters. That will set you up again, and give you an appetite for your breakfast besides," said the farmer, kindly.

"Thank you. I'll take the bitters, if you will send them up here! I mustn't leave this floor until I see my charge out. And it's time for them to get up too!" replied Purley, rising and knocking loudly at the chamber door.

Of course there was no response.

He knocked again and again, more loudly than before, and he called to them in a high tone.

But still there was no answer.

"Good Lord, how sound they sleep! I will go around to the other door and rap there. It is near the head of their bed, and they will be sure to hear me."

And so saying, old Purley went to the adjoining chamber, where he had slept, dragged his mattress away from the door, and drew the key from his pocket, when, to his astonishment and terror, he found the door unlocked!

Without waiting an instant, from any scruples of politeness, he rushed into the room.

To his horror and amazement, he found it empty!

"They've gone! they've fled!" frantically exclaimed Purley, rushing back into the passage, where he found the other bailiff still on guard before the fast door, and the farmer waiting with the glass of bitters in his hand.

"Fled!" echoed Munson. "How can that be? This door as fast as it is?"

"Blast 'em! they've had the impudence to escape right through my door! and right over my body!" panted Purley.

"Then you can't blame *me!*" naively put in Munson.

"Who says I can? ' angrily demanded Purley. "I can't blame anybody! And how the demon they managed to pick the lock and open the door, and climb over me, *I* don't know! Nor have we time to inquire!"

"Take your bitters, Mr. Purley," said the host, offering the glass.

The bailiff quaffed the offered restorative at a draught, and then said;

"Farmer, saddle a couple of horses for us, directly! We must pursue them without loss of time! They cannot have got very far ahead of us in these few hours!" he added, being totally unconscious of the length of time he had slept, and the whole day he had lost.

"My—my horses will be busy all day hauling wood," replied the farmer.

"Don't care! I order you in the name of the Commonwealth of Virginia, to saddle those horses, and place them at our disposal to pursue our prisoner," said Purley, in a peremptory tone

The farmer was quite uncertain whether or not that was an order he was bound to obey; and besides, he was very unwilling that his horses should be taken off their work at all, and especially for the purpose of pursuing Sybil Berners. But still he felt that it would be safer for her, if not for himself, if he should yield to the demand of the sheriff's officer; he could put him on the wrong track, by counseling him to ride towards the east, while he knew that Sybil was far on her route to the west.

So without further demur, he went out to execute the order.

"And, farmer, when you have seen to that matter, I want you to gather all your men and maids into the breakfast room, that I may question them while I eat my breakfast, so as not now to lose a moment," he called after his retreating host.

All this was done as he directed. And when the family and the house servants were assembled in the breakfast room, and Purley examined and cross-examined them as to whether they had seen or heard anything of the prisoner or her husband during the night, they could all answer with perfect truth, that they had not. So old Purley got no satisfaction from them.

The bailiff hastily dispatched his breakfast, and the horses being ready, he called to his young assistant to follow him, and he went out and got into his saddle.

"Where the deuce am I to go after them, when there are so many roads to choose from?" groaned old Purley, in sore perplexity of spirit.

"Would they not be likely to make straight for the east and a seaport?" inquired farmer Nye suggestively.

"To be sure they would," exclaimed Mr. Purley. "So now, Munson, we will go right back upon the road we came last night, " he added, being still in ignorance as to the lost day.

"And as the stable boy told me, they had taken the wagon horses to ride, and those horses were then fairly knocked up with fatigue, while ours are now quite fresh, we may very soon overtake them," put in Munson, artfully.

And waving their hats in adieux to the farmer and his family, they rode off at full speed in pursuit of the fugitives. But they had not ridden more than a hundred yards, and had but just reached the four cross-roads, when they were both startled by a shrill—

"Whist!"

They drew their reins, and looked around just as the head of a negro boy emerged from the bushes, exclaiming

"Hallo, Marster!"

"Who are you? What do you want?" demanded Purley.

"I'm Bill, and I don't want nothing. But I know what *you* want!"

"What do I want?"

"To know which way the run-a-way lady and gemplan went."

"I do know, they went this way," said Purley, pointing straight before him.

"No, they didn't neyther! they was too sharp for that, they said how you would be sure to search for 'em on that road, just as you are a doing of now; so they would take another road."

"That was likely too! Boy, do you know which road they took?"

"Yes, sirree."

"Then tell me."

"I will if you'll give me a quarter," were the moderate conditions of this treaty.

"Here, take it!" exclaimed Mr. Purley, pitching the boy the silver coin in question.

"Thanky, Marster," grinned the lad, picking up the treasure.

"Now tell me."

"Well, Marster, they went along that left han' road till they got to the next turning, and then they turned to the left ag'in and kept on that tact towards that gap in the mountain where you see the sun set in the arternoon."

"How did you know all this boy?"

"I was out coon-hunting when I heerd them talking, and I listened and heerd all about it. And as I couldn't find any coons, I follyed arter them; and their horses was *tired*, as they kept on complainin' to each other. And so they went slow and I could keep up long of 'em."

"How far did you follow them?"

"Well, Marster! I could n't help it! I follyed of 'em all night."

"And they never discovered you?"

"No, sar, they never did. I was barefooted and did n't make no noise, and keeped nigh the bushes on the road side, and so they never found me out."

"And where did you part from them?"

"Well, Marster, I didn't part from 'em till I seed whar they stopped. And if you'll take me up behind you, I'll show you the way to the place where they are hiding. It an't fur from here, not so very fur I mean."

"Oh! no! that is good! So, so, my run-a-ways! I shall nab you, shall I?" exclaimed Purley in triumph, as he beckoned the negro imp to jump up behind him.

"But stop!" said Robert Munson, in an agony of terror for the safety of Sybil Berners. "Stop! What are you about to do? You are about to abduct Farmer Nye's slave!"

"Do you belong to Farmer Nye, boy? Though it don't matter a bit who you belong to. I'll take anybody I can lay hold of to guide me to the hiding-place of my prisoner—in the name of the Commonwealth of Virginia," said this new bailiff, who seemed to think that formula of words, like an absolute monarch's signet ring, was warranty for every sort of proceeding.

"But I don't belong to nobody. I's fee, and so's mammy. We an't got no master, and I an't got no daddy to lord it over me!" put in the boy.

"That's right jump up behind," said the elder bailiff. And as soon as little Bill was safely perched up in the rear of his patron, the latter put spurs to his horse and gallopped off at full speed.

They went down the left hand, or south fork of the cross roads, and galloped on until they reached the branch road leading west. They turned into that road and pursued it mile after mile, through field and forest, mountain pass and valley plain, until, late in the afternoon, they reached another mountain range, and heard the roaring of a great torrent. They entered the black gap, and slowly and cautiously made their way through it. By the time they had emerged from the pass, the night was pitch dark.

"How shall we ever find our way?" inquired Purley who, fatigued and half famished, was ready to sink with exhaustion.

"Do you see that there gabble ind stickin' up through the trees?" inquired the boy.

"Yes, I see it!"

"Well, him and her is in there?"

"Are you sure?" inquired Purley, anxiously.

"Here I is, Marster! If him and her ar'n't in there, here I is in your power, and you may skin me alive!"

"All right!" exclaimed Purley, and dismounting from his horse, he advanced toward the thicket, followed by Munson and the negro boy.

CHAPTER XXXV.

THE FUGITIVES.

> They may not set a foot within their fields,
> They may not pull a sapling from their hills,
> They may not enter their fair mansion house.—HEWITT.

Lyon and Sybil had ridden on through the darkness, over that wild country road. Their horses had had a very hard day's work in the wagon harness, and had not recovered from their fatigue. They were still very tired, and all unaccustomed to the saddle. The road was also very rough, and the night very dark. Their progress was therefore difficult and slow.

Unconscious of being followed and overheard, they talked freely of their plans. Their prospects of final escape were not now nearly so hopeful as they had been on their two former attempts. They were now undisguised, and unprovided for the journey, except with money and a change of clothing. For necessary food they would have to stop at houses, and thus incur some degree of danger. All this they discussed as their horses slowly toiled along the rugged road up hill and down, through woods and fields, until they came near the mountain pass that they had been dimly seeing before them all night long, and that looked like a gray cleft in a black wall.

"It must be near morning now. But I have not a very clear idea where we are. I shall be glad when it is light if it is only to consult my map and compass," said Lyon, uneasily.

"I never was on this side of the mountain before, but it does seem to me that that must be a spur of the Black Ridge which we see before us," suggested Sybil.

"I was thinking of the very same thing," added Lyon. "But if that is so, we must have wandered far out of our way."

"And hush! Don't you hear something?" inquired Sybil, when they had ridden a little farther on.

"No, what is it?"

"Listen! I want to know if you recognize it," she said.

"I hear a faint, distant roaring, as of a water-fall," he answered, stopping his horse to hear the better.

"It is our Black Torrent!" exclaimed Sybil.

"Good Heaven! Then we have wandered out of our way with a vengeance. However, there is no help for it now. We must go on, or stop here until it is light enough to consult the compass."

"And at any rate, Lyon, no one will think of looking for us so near home," she added.

"That is true," he admitted.

And they rode on slowly, looking about as well as they could through the darkness, for a convenient place on which to dismount from the jaded steeds.

Their path now lay through that deep mountain pass. Steep precipices arose on either side. They picked their way slowly and carefully through it, until they entered a crooked path leading down the side of a thickly wooded hill. Here they rode on, a little more at their ease, until they reached the bottom of the hill and the edge of the wood, and came out upon an old forsaken road, running along the shores of a deep and rapid river, with another mountain range behind.

"Well, Heaven bless us! here we are!" exclaimed Lyon Berners, reining up his horse and looking around himself in a ludicrous state of mind, made up of surprise, dismay, and resignation.

"Yes; on the shores of the Black River, at the head of our own Black Valley," chimed in Sybil, in a tone of voice in which there was more of satisfaction than of disappointment. Poor Sybil was sentimental and illogical, like all her sex.

"But at a point at which, I may venture to say, that even you, it's owner, never reached before," added Lyon, as he touched up his horse and led the way up the road, still looking about as well as he could through the darkness, for a place in which to stop and rest their horses.

Suddenly, as they rode slowly onward, they heard approaching them from the opposite direction the sound of a wagon and horse, accompanied by a human voice singing:

> "Brothers and sisters there will meet,
> Brothers and sisters there will meet,
> Brothers and sisters there will meet—
> Will meet, to part no more!"

"Yes, bress de Lord! so dey will. And all departed friends will meet, and meet to part no more! GLORY!" rang out the voice of the singer, who seemed to be working himself up into enthusiasm.

"It is only some negro with his team," said Lyon Berners, to soothe the spirits of Sybil, which always took the alarm at the approach of any stranger.

"Yes; but what an hour for a negro, or for any one else but fugitives like ourselves, to be out," said Sybil, doubtingly.

"Oh, he is making an early start for market perhaps. It *must* be near morning."

> "Oh, there will be glory—
> Glory! glory! glory!—
> Oh, there will be glory
> Around the throne of God!"

sang the unseen singer, making the mountain caves and glens ring with his melody.

"Yes; bress Marster! there WILL be Glories and Hallelujahs all through heaven," he added; "for—

> "Saints and angels there will meet,
> Saints and angels there will meet,
> Saints and angels there will meet—
> Will meet to part no more."

"And me and my young missis there will meet! And meet to part no more! GLORY!" added the singer, with a sudden shout.

"Lyon, that's our Joe!" exclaimed Sybil, in joyful surprise.

The cart and horses now loomed dimly through the darkness, being almost upon them.

"Joe!" called out Sybil, in a gleeful voice—"Joe!"

"Who dar?" answered the man, in affright.

"It is I! Sybil, Joe!"

"Oh, my good gracious Lord in heaven! it's her spirit as is calling me, and she must be dead!" gasped the man, in a quavering voice.

By this time the two horses were beside the cart, upon the seat of which the driver sat in an extremity of terror.

"Joe, don't be alarmed! It is Mrs. Berners herself who speaks to you, and I am with her," said Mr. Berners, soothingly.

"Oh, Marse Lyon! Is it ralely and truly her herself and you yourself?" inquired the man, very doubtingly.

"Really and truly Sybil and myself, Joe."

"Oh! Lord! how you did scare me!"

"Compose yourself, Joe, and tell me what you are doing here at this time of the morning."

"Oh, Marse Lyon, sir, I came arter the housekeeping truck as you left here, which I couldn't get a chance to fetch it befere, 'cause I was afraid o' 'citing 'spicion."

"And have you the things in that cart?"

"Yes, Marse,"

"Then hold on for a moment, and spread the mattress on the bottom of the cart for your young mistress to lie down upon and rest, while you and I have a little talk."

Joe promptly obeyed this order; and when the rude bed was ready, Lyon lifted Sybil from her seat and laid her upon it. The tired horses were then relieved from their saddles and turned loose for a while. And then Mr. Berners and Joe sat down by the roadside to consult.

"And first I want you to tell me, Joe, whether our sojourn at the Haunted Chapel ever was found out," said Mr. Berners.

"Lor', no, sir! it never were even suspicioned! quite contrary wise, indeed."

"How so?"

"Why, it was ported 'round as you was bofe at Marster Capping Pendulum's all the time, which when himself was taxed with it, he never let on as you wasn't there; quite contrary wise, as I said afore."

"But how now?"

"Well, he up and 'fied 'em all, and said his house was his cassil, which he would shelter any one he pleased, and specially a noble and injured lady."

"High heart! I thank him!" exclaimed Mr. Berners.

"Which 'fiance you see, sir, confarmed everybody in the faith that you was bofe hid in his house, so artfully as even the sarch-warranters as went there couldn't find you. And so, sir, nobody, from first to last, has once said 'Haunted Chapel.'"

"Joe, how far are we from the Haunted Chapel?"

"Not more'n a mile, sir, from the little path that leads up to it."

"Well, I think we had better go there again and rest to-day, and resume our journey to-night. There can be no safer place."

"Now har' in all the world, sir."

"Then we will go at once. Throw the saddles into the cart, at your mistress' feet, so as not to crowd her. I will then drive the cart, and you may lead the two riding horses after us," said Mr. Berners, going at once to the side of the rude vehicle where Sybil lay in so deep a sleep that she did not wake, even when he mounted the seat and started the springless cart jolting along the rough road.

Joe led the saddle horses close behind, and so they went on.

"Joe," said Mr. Berners, "I hope that all things go on well at home."

"As well as can be, sir, marser and missus being away. Capping Pendulum, he shows his powerfnl 'torney, and tends to the 'state. And Missus Winterose and her darters minds the house. Only they's in constant terrors all along o' that band o' bugglers."

"Band of burglers, Joe?"

"Yes, sir, and highway robbers as well."

"Indeed! Joe, I have twice lately heard this band spoken of. Does such a one really exist?"

"Well, sir, it *do*. The neighborhood never was so mislested with robbers since a neighborhood it has been. Why, sir, Mr. Morgan's new store, at Blackville, was broke open and robbed of about twelve hundred dollars' worth of goods in one night."

" And none of it recovered ! "

" No, sir. And, sir, Capping Pendulum's own house was entered and robbed of jewelry and plate to the tune of about two thousand dollars."

" I am very sorry for that ! And no clue to the robbers ? "

" No the leastest in the world, sir ! And no later'n last night, Judge Beresford was riding home from the village, where he had been at the tavern, playing cards with a lot of gentlemen, and had won a deal of money, which he had about him, when, in the middle of the long woods below his own house, he was stopped by two men; one who seized his bridle, and one who pinted a pistol at his head, and gave him his choice of his money or his life. The Judge he choose his life, and handed over his winnins."

" I'm not sorry for him ! A man who gains money in that way deserves to lose it. But I *am* astounded at all that you have told me."

" Yes, sir ! and the old ladies in charge of Black Hall is more 'stounded than you are, sir ; being 'stounded to that degree that they sleep with the dogs in the room, long of 'em."

" This should be seen to. There should be a vigilance committee. But here we are at the path, Joe, and my wife is still in a deep sleep; and I do not wish to wake her; nor can we drive the cart through the thicket. Hold ! I'll tell you what we can do. We can take the mattress by its four corners, and carry her on it to the chapel. If we are careful, we need not even wake her," said Mr. Berners, as he stopped the cart and got down from his seat.

Joe tied the two saddle horses to one of the trees, and came around to the cart to help his master.

Between them they cautiously lifted the mattress, and bore it along towards the opening of the path.

On first being moved, Sybil sighed once and turned over and then she fell into a still deeper sleep, from which she did not again awake even when they bore her into the dreadful Haunted Chapel, and laid her down, still on the mattress, in the old place, to the right of the altar.

"Poor child! She was so tired, so worn out in body and mind, that she could scarcely sit her horse. Yet she never once complained, nor should I have even surmised the extent of her prostration, were it not for this coma-like sleep. She will not wake now. We may safely leave her alone while we go back and bring our saddle horses here, for we must bring them in order to hide them to-day and use them to-night. And you, Joe, after you have helped me to bring the horses through the thicket, must go to Blackville and buy food and bring it to us to-night before we resume our journey."

"Yes, sir; and meantimes, there is some crackers and cheese and sweetmeats, and likewise a bottle of port wine, in the cart, as you left in the chapel when you went away."

"Oh, indeed! that will be a godsend, Joe! We must bring that back to the chapel with us when we come," said Mr. Berners, as with his servant he bent his steps back to the thicket path.

Sybil, left alone in the interior of the haunted chapel, slept on soundly for some little time. She had not really been quite unconscious of her removal thither. She had half waked on being taken from the cart, but had immediately fallen asleep again; though she was still vaguely conscious of being borne along to some place of safety and repose, and that her devoted husband and her faithful servant were her bearers—vaguely conscious also of being laid down upon some level place of perfect rest, with a roof above her head; but beyond this she knew nothing, cared nothing, being too utterly prostrated in mind and body to rouse herself to any utterances, or even to save herself from sinking to sleep.

How long she had slept she never could tell, when at length she was suddenly and fearfully aroused—aroused to a degree of wakefulness that neither the noisy jolting over the rocky road, nor the painful dragging through the thorny thicket had been able to effect.

And yet it was but by a touch—the touch of an ice-cold little hand passing lightly over her face.

She started up in a panic and glared around. All seemed black as pitch, and at first she could see nothing; but as she strained her eyes, she dimly discerned the shapes of the gothic windows, with the dark night sky and the ghostly trees beyond; and she recognized the Haunted Chapel!

They had brought her here while she was sleeping; and now, "in the dead waste and middle of the night," she had waked up, alone in this demon-peopled place.

She tried to cry out in her fear; but her voice died in her throat, and she sank back upon her mattress and closed her eyes, lest some shape of horror should blast them.

Then again she felt hands at work about her person. They were creeping under her shoulders and under her limbs; they were lifting her from her mattress. Her eyes flared open in wild affright, and she saw two black shrouded forms, the one at her head the other at her feet.

She tried to cry out in her agony of terror but again her voice died away in her bosom, and all her powers seemed palsied. They raised her up and bore her on—great heaven! whither?

To the open door of the vault, from whose haunted depths a spectral light gleamed!

They bore her down the dreadful steps, and laid her on the deadly floor!

The iron door clanged loudly to, resounding through the dismal arches.

"We have her now!" muttered a hoarse voice. A hollow laugh responded.

And Sybil swooned with horror!

Sybil's further adventures will be related in the sequel to this work, to be immediately published, under the title of "Tried For Her Life."

THE END.

BOY AVIATORS' SERIES

BY CAPTAIN WILBUR LAWTON

Absolutely Modern Stories for Boys

Cloth Bound   Price 50c per volume

The Boy Aviators in Africa
Or, An Aerial Ivory Trail

In this absorbing book we meet, on a Continent made famous by the American explorer Stanley, and ex-President Roosevelt, our old friends, the Chester Boys and their stalwart chums. In Africa—the Dark Continent—the author follows in exciting detail his young heroes, their voyage in the first aeroplane to fly above the mysterious forests and unexplored ranges of the mystic land. In this book, too, for the first time, we entertain Luther Barr, the old New York millionaire, who proved later such an implacable enemy of the boys. The story of his defeated schemes, of the astonishing things the boys discovered in the Mountains of the Moon, of the pathetic fate of George Desmond, the emulator of Stanley, the adventure of the Flying Men and the discovery of the Arabian Ivory cache,—this is not the place to speak. It would be spoiling the zest of an exciting tale to reveal the outcome of all these episodes here. It may be said, however, without "giving away" any of the thrilling chapters of this narrative, that Captain Wilbur Lawton, the author, is in it in his best vein, and from his personal experiences in Africa has been able to supply a striking background for the adventures of his young heroes. As one newspaper says of this book: "Here is adventure in good measure, pressed down and running over."

Sold by Booksellers Everywhere

HURST & CO.   Publishers   **NEW YORK**

BOY AVIATORS' SERIES

By Captain Wilbur Lawton

Absolutely Modern Stories for Boys

Cloth Bound   **Price, 50c per volume**

The Boy Aviators in Nicaragua
Or, Leagued With Insurgents

The launching of this Twentieth Century series marks the inauguration of a new era in boys' books—the "wonders of modern science" epoch. Frank and Harry Chester, the BOY AVIATORS, are the heroes of this exciting, red-blooded tale of adventure by air and land in the turbulent Central American republic. The two brothers with their $10,000 prize aeroplane, the GOLDEN EAGLE, rescue a chum from death in the clutches of the Nicaraguans, discover a lost treasure valley of the ancient Toltec race, and in so doing almost lose their own lives in the Abyss of the White Serpents, and have many other exciting experiences, including being blown far out to sea in their air-skimmer in a tropical storm. It would be unfair to divulge the part that wireless plays in rescuing them from their predicament. In a brand new field of fiction for boys the Chester brothers and their aeroplane seem destined to fill a top-notch place. These books are technically correct, wholesomely thrilling and geared up to third speed.

Sold by Booksellers Everywhere

HURST & CO.   **Publishers**   **NEW YORK**

BOY AVIATORS' SERIES

By Captain Wilbur Lawton

Absolutely Modern Stories for Boys

Cloth Bound   **Price, 50c per volume**

The Boy Aviators on Secret Service
Or, Working With Wireless

In this live-wire narrative of peril and adventure, laid in the Everglades of Florida, the spunky Chester Boys and their interesting chums, including Ben Stubbs, the maroon, encounter exciting experiences on Uncle Sam's service in a novel field. One must read this vivid, enthralling story of incident, hardship and pluck to get an idea of the almost limitless possibilities of the two greatest inventions of modern times—the aeroplane and wireless telegraphy. While gripping and holding the reader's breathless attention from the opening words to the finish, this swift-moving story is at the same time instructive and uplifting. As those readers who have already made friends with Frank and Harry Chester and their "bunch" know, there are few difficulties, no matter how insurmountable they may seem at first blush, that these up-to-date gritty youths cannot overcome with flying colors. A clean-cut, real boys' book of high voltage.

Sold by Booksellers Everywhere

HURST & CO.   **Publishers**   **NEW YORK**

BOY AVIATORS' SERIES

BY CAPTAIN WILBUR LAWTON

Absolutely Modern Stories for Boys

Cloth Bound   Price 50c per volume

The Boy Aviators Treasure Quest
Or, The Golden Galleon

Everybody is a boy once more when it comes to the question of hidden treasure. In this book, Captain Lawton has set forth a hunt for gold that is concealed neither under the sea nor beneath the earth, but is well hidden for all that. A garrulous old sailor, who holds the key to the mystery of the Golden Galleon, plays a large part in the development of the plot of this fascinating narrative of treasure hunting in the region of the Gulf Stream and the Sagasso Sea. An aeroplane fitted with efficient pontoons—enabling her to skim the water successfully—has long been a dream of aviators. The Chester Boys seem to have solved the problem. The Sagasso, that strange drifting ocean within an ocean, holding ships of a dozen nations and a score of ages, in its relentless grip, has been the subject of many books of adventure and mystery, but in none has the secret of the ever shifting mass of treacherous currents been penetrated as it has in the BOY AVIOTORS TREASURE QUEST. Luther Barr, whom it seemed the boys had shaken off, is still on their trail, in this absorbing book and with a dirigible balloon, essays to beat them out in their search for the Golden Galleon. Every boy, every man—and woman and girl—who has ever felt the stirring summons of adventure in their souls, had better get hold of this book. Once obtained, it will be read and re-read till it falls to rags.

Sold by Booksellers Everywhere

HURST & CO.   Publishers   **NEW YORK**

BOY AVIATORS' SERIES

BY CAPTAIN WILBUR LAWTON

Absolutely Modern Stories for Boys

Cloth Bound   Price 50c per volume

The Boy Aviators Polar Dash
Or, Facing Death in the Antarctic

If you were to hear that two boys, accompanying a South Polar expedition in charge of the aeronautic department, were to penetrate the Antarctic regions—hitherto only attained by a few daring explorers—you would feel interested, wouldn't you? Well, in Captain Lawton's latest book, concerning his Boy Aviators, you can not only read absorbing adventure in the regions south of the eightieth parallel, but absorb much useful information as well. Captain Lawton introduces—besides the original characters of the heroes—a new creation in the person of Professor Simeon Sandburr, a patient seeker for polar insects. The professor's adventures in his quest are the cause of much merriment, and lead once or twice to serious predicaments. In a volume so packed with incident and peril from cover to cover—relieved with laughable mishaps to the professor—it is difficult to single out any one feature; still, a recent reader of it wrote the publishers an enthusiastic letter the other day, saying: "The episodes above the Great Barrier are thrilling, the attack of the condors in Patagonia made me hold my breath, the—but what's the use? The Polar Dash, to my mind, is an even more entrancing book than Captain Lawton's previous efforts, and that's saying a good deal. The aviation features and their technical correctness are by no means the least attractive features of this up-to-date creditable volume."

Sold by Booksellers Everywhere

HURST & CO.   **Publishers**   **NEW YORK**

BOY AVIATORS' SERIES

BY CAPTAIN WILBUR LAWTON

Absolutely Modern Stories for Boys

Cloth Bound   Price 50c per volume

The Boy Aviators in Record Flight

Or, The Rival Aeroplane

The Chester Boys in new field of endeavor—an attempt to capture a newspaper prize for a trans-continental flight. By the time these lines are read, exactly such an offer will have been spread broadcast by one of the foremost newspapers of the country. In the Golden Eagle, the boys, accompanied by a trail-blazing party in an automobile, make the dash. But they are not alone in their aspirations. Their rivals for the rich prize at stake try in every way that they can to circumvent the lads and gain the valuable trophy and monetary award. In this they stop short at nothing, and it takes all the wits and resources of the Boy Aviators to defeat their devices. Among the adventures encountered in their cross-country flight, the boys fall in with a band of rollicking cow-boys —who momentarily threaten serious trouble—are attacked by Indians, strike the most remarkable town of the desert—the "dry" town of "Gow Wells," encounter a sandstorm which blows them into strange lands far to the south of their course, and meet with several amusing mishaps beside. A thoroughly readable book. The sort to take out behind the barn on the sunny side of the haystack, and, with a pocketful of juicy apples and your heels kicking the air, pass happy hours with Captain Lawton's young heroes.

Sold by Booksellers Everywhere

HURST & CO.   **Publishers**   **NEW YORK**

OAKDALE ACADEMY SERIES
Stories of Modern School Sports
By MORGAN SCOTT.

Cloth Bound. Illustrated. Price, 60c. per vol., postpaid

BEN STONE AT OAKDALE.
Under peculiarly trying circumstances Ben Stone wins his way at Oakdale Academy, and at the same time enlists our sympathy, interest and respect. Through the enmity of Bern Hayden, the loyalty of Roger Eliot and the clever work of the "Sleuth," Ben is falsely accused, championed and vindicated.

BOYS OF OAKDALE ACADEMY.
"One thing I will claim, and that is that all Grants fight open and square and there never was a sneak among them." It was Rodney Grant, of Texas, who made the claim to his friend, Ben Stone, and this story shows how he proved the truth of this statement in the face of apparent evidence to the contrary.

RIVAL PITCHERS OF OAKDALE.
Baseball is the main theme of this interesting narrative, and that means not only clear and clever descriptions of thrilling games, but an intimate acquaintance with the members of the teams who played them. The Oakdale Boys were ambitious and loyal, and some were even disgruntled and jealous, but earnest, persistent work won out.

OAKDALE BOYS IN CAMP.
The typical vacation is the one that means much freedom, little restriction, and immediate contact with "all outdoors." These conditions prevailed in the summer camp of the Oakdale Boys and made it a scene of lively interest.

THE GREAT OAKDALE MYSTERY.
The "Sleuth" scents a mystery! He "follows his nose." The plot thickens! He makes deductions. There are surprises for the reader—and for the "Sleuth," as well.

NEW BOYS AT OAKDALE.
A new element creeps into Oakdale with another year's registration of students. The old and the new standards of conduct in and out of school meet, battle, and cause sweeping changes in the lives of several of the boys.

Any volume sent postpaid upon receipt of price.

HURST & COMPANY - Publishers - NEW YORK

FRANK ARMSTRONG SERIES

Twentieth Century Athletic Stories

By MATHEW M. COLTON.

Cloth Bound. Illustrated. Price, 60c. per vol., postpaid

FRANK ARMSTRONG'S VACATION.

How Frank's summer experience with his boy friends make him into a sturdy young athlete through swimming, boating, and baseball contests, and a tramp through the Everglades, is the subject of this splendid story.

FRANK ARMSTRONG AT QUEENS.

We find among the jolly boys at Queen's School, Frank, the student-athlete, Jimmy, the baseball enthusiast, and Lewis, the unconsciously-funny youth who furnishes comedy for every page that bears his name. Fall and winter sports between intensely rival school teams are expertly described.

FRANK ARMSTRONG'S SECOND TERM.

The gymnasium, the track and the field make the background for the stirring events of this volume, in which David, Jimmy, Lewis, the "Wee One" and the "Codfish" figure, while Frank "saves the day."

FRANK ARMSTRONG, DROP KICKER.

With the same persistent determination that won him success in swimming, running and baseball playing, Frank Armstrong acquired the art of "drop kicking," and the Queen's football team profits thereby.

Any volume sent postpaid upon receipt of price.

HURST & COMPANY - Publishers - NEW YORK

MOTOR RANGERS SERIES
HIGH SPEED MOTOR STORIES
By MARVIN WEST.

Cloth Bound. Illustrated. Price, 50c. per vol., postpaid

THE MOTOR RANGERS' LOST MINE.

This is an absorbing story of the continuous adventures of a motor car in the hands of Nat Trevor and his friends. It does seemingly impossible "stunts," and yet everything happens "in the nick of time."

THE MOTOR RANGERS THROUGH THE SIERRAS.

Enemies in ambush, the peril of fire, and the guarding of treasure make exciting times for the Motor Rangers—yet there is a strong flavor of fun and freedom, with a typical Western mountaineer for spice.

THE MOTOR RANGERS ON BLUE WATER; or, The Secret of the Derelict.

The strange adventures of the sturdy craft "Nomad" and the stranger experiences of the Rangers themselves with Morello's schooner and a mysterious derelict form the basis of this well-spun yarn of the sea.

THE MOTOR RANGERS' CLOUD CRUISER.

From the "Nomad" to the "Discoverer," from the sea to the sky, the scene changes in which the Motor Rangers figure. They have experiences "that never were on land or sea," in heat and cold and storm, over mountain peak and lost city, with savages and reptiles; their ship of the air is attacked by huge birds of the air; they survive explosion and earthquake; they even live to tell the tale!

Any volume sent postpaid upon receipt of price.

HURST & COMPANY - Publishers - NEW YORK

DREADNOUGHT BOYS SERIES
Tales of the New Navy
By CAPT. WILBUR LAWTON
Author of "BOY AVIATORS SERIES."

Cloth Bound. Illustrated. Price, 50c. per vol., postpaid

THE DREADNOUGHT BOYS ON BATTLE PRACTICE.

Especially interesting and timely is this book which introduces the reader with its heroes, Ned and Herc, to the great ships of modern warfare and to the intimate life and surprising adventures of Uncle Sam's sailors.

THE DREADNOUGHT BOYS ABOARD A DESTROYER.

In this story real dangers threaten and the boys' patriotism is tested in a peculiar international tangle. The scene is laid on the South American coast.

THE DREADNOUGHT BOYS ON A SUBMARINE.

To the inventive genius—trade-school boy or mechanic—this story has special charm, perhaps, but to every reader its mystery and clever action are fascinating.

THE DREADNOUGHT BOYS ON AERO SERVICE.

Among the volunteers accepted for Areo Service are Ned and Herc. Their perilous adventures are not confined to the air, however, although they make daring and notable flights in the name of the Government; nor are they always able to fly beyond the reach of their old "enemies," who are also airmen.

Any volume sent postpaid upon receipt of price.

HURST & COMPANY - Publishers - NEW YORK

BUNGALOW BOYS SERIES
LIVE STORIES OF OUTDOOR LIFE
By DEXTER J. FORRESTER.

Cloth Bound. Illustrated. Price, 50c. per vol., postpaid

THE BUNGALOW BOYS.

How the Bungalow Boys received their title and how they retained the right to it in spite of much opposition makes a lively narrative for lively boys.

THE BUNGALOW BOYS MAROONED IN THE TROPICS.

A real treasure hunt of the most thrilling kind, with a sunken Spanish galleon as its object, makes a subject of intense interest at any time, but add to that a band of desperate men, a dark plot and a devil fish, and you have the combination that brings strange adventures into the lives of the Bungalow Boys.

THE BUNGALOW BOYS IN THE GREAT NORTH WEST.

The clever assistance of a young detective saves the boys from the clutches of Chinese smugglers, of whose nefarious trade they know too much. How the Professor's invention relieves a critical situation is also an exciting incident of this book.

THE BUNGALOW BOYS ON THE GREAT LAKES.

The Bungalow Boys start out for a quiet cruise on the Great Lakes and a visit to an island. A storm and a band of wreckers interfere with the serenity of their trip, and a submarine adds zest and adventure to it.

Any volume sent postpaid upon receipt of price.

HURST & COMPANY ▪ Publishers ▪ NEW YORK

BORDER BOYS SERIES

Mexican and Canadian Frontier Series

By FREMONT B. DEERING.

Cloth Bound. Illustrated. Price, 50c. per vol., postpaid

THE BORDER BOYS ON THE TRAIL.

What it meant to make an enemy of Black Ramon De Barios—that is the problem that Jack Merrill and his friends, including Coyote Pete, face in this exciting tale.

THE BORDER BOYS ACROSS THE FRONTIER.

Read of the Haunted Mesa and its mysteries, of the Subterranean River and its strange uses, of the value of gasolene and steam "in running the gauntlet," and you will feel that not even the ancient splendors of the Old World can furnish a better setting for romantic action than the Border of the New.

THE BORDER BOYS WITH THE MEXICAN RANGERS.

As every day is making history—faster, it is said, than ever before—so books that keep pace with the changes are full of rapid action and accurate facts. This book deals with lively times on the Mexican border.

THE BORDER BOYS WITH THE TEXAS RANGERS.

The Border Boys have already had much excitement and adventure in their lives, but all this has served to prepare them for the experiences related in this volume. They are stronger, braver and more resourceful than ever, and the exigencies of their life in connection with the Texas Rangers demand all their trained ability.

Any volume sent postpaid upon receipt of price.

HURST & COMPANY - Publishers - NEW YORK